Art from Africa
Long Steps Never Broke a Back

Art from Africa

Long Steps Never Broke a Back

Pamela McClusky

With a contribution by Robert Farris Thompson

Seattle Art Museum

Princeton University Press

This book has been published in conjunction with an exhibition on view at the
Seattle Art Museum from February 7 through May 19, 2002.
Operating funds from the Institute of Museum and Library Services, a federal agency,
are being used to support this project; publication of the book was made possible
in part by a research and planning grant awarded by the National Endowment for the Arts.

The exhibition, organized by the Seattle Art Museum, has been generously supported by

Presenting Sponsor

Washington Mutual

Additional Support

Seattle Post-Intelligencer
Seattle Arts Commission
PONCHO
(Patrons of Northwest Civic, Cultural and Charitable Organizations)
American Express
The Allen Foundation for the Arts
Contributors to the Annual Fund

Deepening the Dialogue, an initiative funded by the Wallace-Reader's Digest Funds, is a key component
of this exhibition, strengthening SAM's programming and community partnerships.

Published by the Seattle Art Museum in association
with Princeton University Press.

© 2002 by the Seattle Art Museum
All rights reserved.

Seattle Art Museum
100 University Street
Seattle, Washington 98101
    www.seattleartmuseum.org

Princeton University Press
41 William Street
Princeton, New Jersey 08540
    www.pup.princeton.edu

Project manager: Zora Hutlova Foy
Editor: Patricia Draher Kiyono
Proofreader: Jennifer Harris
Indexer: Laura Ogar
Designed by Ed Marquand with assistance by Elsa Varela
Typeset by Jennifer Sugden
Primary photography by Paul Macapia
Color separations by iocolor, Seattle
Produced by Marquand Books, Inc., Seattle
    www.marquand.com
Printed and bound by C & C Offset Printing Co., Ltd.,
Hong Kong

Library of Congress Cataloging-in-Publication Data
McClusky, Pamela.
    Art from Africa : long steps never broke a back /
Pamela McClusky ; with a contribution by Robert Farris
Thompson.
        p. cm.
    Published in conjunction with an exhibition held at
the Seattle Art Museum, Feb. 7–May 19, 2002.
    Includes bibliographical references and index.
    ISBN: 0-691-09275-3 (Princeton Univ. Press : alk.
paper)—ISBN: 0-691-09295-8 (Princeton Univ. Press :
pbk. alk. paper)—ISBN: 0-85331-848-8 (cloth : Lund
Humphries : alk. paper)
    1. Art, African—Exhibitions. 2. Art, Black—Africa,
Sub-Saharan—Exhibitions. 3. Masks—Africa, Sub-
Saharan—Exhibitions. 4. Ethnology—Africa, Sub-
Saharan—Exhibitions. 5. Art—Washington (State)
—Seattle—Exhibitions. 6. Seattle Art Museum—
Exhibitions. I. Thompson, Robert Farris. II. Seattle
Art Museum. III. Title.
N7391.65 .M28 2002
709'.67'074797772—dc21   2001049735

Frontispiece: pl. 98, Seydou Keita, *Untitled (Family with Car
no. 266),* 1951–1952

Contents

Preface

African art was a source of inspiration for the art of Europe and America in the twentieth century. Once artists in Paris turned attention toward its restless and inventive formal qualities, modernism was forever altered. Not long into the century, this awareness spread to New York and led to waves of influence in gallery circles. In other neighborhoods, African aesthetics had long ago infused American icons, actions, music, and movement with compelling expressive force. By the end of the twentieth century, art from the African continent was admired not only for its striking forms but also for its meaningful impact on many other levels. Whereas African art's calling card of sculptural brilliance has been widely recognized, inquiry into the complex role it enacts in African lives is still growing.

Art from Africa: Long Steps Never Broke a Back catches up with that inquiry. Not a comprehensive survey of many objects, this publication instead pursues a small selection in depth and relies on a curator's individual voice to begin the exploration. Inside museums, curators pose questions about collections and construct domes of reference to contextualize objects. How curators trace the multiple histories of an object, its passage through different hands, its changing status and significance, is often secreted within museums, not explained to a public audience. This text renders more transparent the insider view of collecting, a complex and changing process. The book features a wide range of primary African sources—music, film, novels, and personal interviews—to reflect the fact that this art comes from settings immersed in many media. The publication and exhibition seek to recapture the joy, emotion, and meaning integral to the creation and use of these objects.

Long Steps is an invitation to learn more about collecting not just the objects but the meanings, stories, and ideas attached to them. A landmark scholar of African and African American art history long associated with the museum's collection, Robert Farris Thompson, was asked to revise a fundamental text. His contribution from *African Art in Motion* looks carefully at the basic stance a figural sculpture takes—standing, sitting, balancing, kneeling, or riding—in an interpretation guided by his broad sweep of experiential scholarship. After Professor Thompson's overview, Pamela McClusky adeptly guides the reader, providing the insight of a curator. She hands viewers tools to enhance their enjoyment of the art, finding them in treasure houses, palaces, shrine complexes, performances, and community settings, and in the mix of voices of the leaders, priests, scholars, and artists whose words animate each chapter.

The Seattle Art Museum has been a major repository for African art since the 1980s. Before then, Dr. Richard Fuller, the museum's founder, had purchased only a small sampling of African objects from a few dealers. Gifts to the museum were rare but occasionally distinguished, such as the selection of miniatures offered in 1968 by Nasli and Alice Heeramaneck. In this quiet arena of acquisition an explosion was set off when the collector Katherine White offered the museum her holdings of nearly two thousand objects for a token purchase price. The Boeing Company made an unprecedented gift in 1981 that enabled Seattle to become home to a vast and distinguished gathering of art from Africa.

Katherine White was renowned for her exceptional dedication to buying what she considered the highest quality and the least recognized forms of art; she made her purchases from dealers and on trips to Africa throughout the 1960s and 1970s. Her death in 1980 at the age of fifty-one unveiled a new chapter in her legacy. When the downtown building of the Seattle Art Museum opened in 1991, the Katherine White collection formed the backbone of three major permanent-collection galleries. Following in the footsteps of White's two decades of rapid purchases, the collecting of the 1990s has been more selective and still relies on significant gifts. A new layer of contemporary art is moving into place, as is a fresh definition of the collecting process, seen in the final chapters of this book.

The Seattle Art Museum's strength in, and celebration of, African art is the work of curator Pam McClusky. She deserves accolades for the brilliance of this project, and for Seattle's acquisition of the Katherine White collection some twenty years ago. Pam and Katherine White shared a single passion; Pam's close relationship with Katherine White convinced the collector that SAM would be the most appropriate home for her art. In both the exhibition and this book, Pam, with characteristic modesty and unassuming demeanor, steps aside, bringing to the fore primary voices, African voices. She, however, is the leader, orchestrating the voices, writing the majority of this publication, and ensuring rigorous intellectual context and an imaginative approach.

This project, exhibition, and publication could not have taken place without the generous support of institutions and individuals. Vital corporate sponsorship for the exhibition was provided by Washington Mutual, whose community giving emphasizes education and reinforces the Seattle Art Museum's strong commitment to schools and teachers in the region. Additional support for the exhibition has come from *Seattle Post-Intelligencer*, the Seattle Arts Commission, PONCHO (Patrons of Northwest Civic, Cultural and Charitable Organizations), American Express, The Allen Foundation for the Arts, and the Wallace-Reader's Digest Funds, strengthening the museum's programming and community partnerships. New photography of the collection and the initial stages of the book were made possible by a research and planning grant awarded by the National Endowment for the Arts. The project was also supported by operating funds from the Institute of Museum and Library Services.

African art still beckons for admiration. Its geometric features, twisting planes, and vast formal vocabulary issue continual surprises for the eyes. Now, the swift surprise may expand into a sustained exchange with the artists, scholars, and original owners of this art. Our eyes no longer work in isolation, but are learning to take the long looks that activate appreciation.

Mimi Gardner Gates
Illsley Ball Nordstrom Director
Seattle Art Museum

Acknowledgments

The Artists
We are all indebted to those whose work is interpreted herein.

The Collaborators
Many thanks to Daniel "Koo Nimo" Amponsah for refining written phrases, and for calling Kumasi for second opinions. Fu Kiau Bunseki gave lessons in cosmograms, medicines, and careful translations. Kakuta Hamisi offered challenging discussions about museums. Gilbert Mbeng coordinated research in the Kom kingdom. Won Ldy Paye must be thanked for years of keeping Liberian creativity alive in the Northwest. And we all benefit from Robert Farris Thompson's intensity that never lets up.

The Collectors
Katherine White gave Seattle her life's work, saying Virginia and Bagley Wright enticed her to do so. John Hauberg kindly set up a fund that supported research. Oliver and Pamela Cobb, Mark Groudine, and Cynthia Putnam now reign as generous patrons of African art, offering many friendly arguments about collecting.

The Scholars
Notes of appreciation go to David Conrad for clarifying elements of hunters' behavior, Donald Cosentino for allowing the use of his collected stories, Manthia Diawara for inspired writing, Perkins Foss for maintaining current information about Urhobo research, Babatunde Lawal for narrating Gelede performances, Cynthia Schmidt for locating Mende women to consult, Evan Schneider for constant access to his outstanding photographic archives, and the late Gilbert Schneider for answering questions.

The Photographer
The photographer of the collection was Paul Macapia, whose attention to visual details is always evident.

The Book Producers

Zora Hutlova Foy, Manager of Exhibitions and Publications, cajoled and consoled, often in the same conversation. Patricia Draher Kiyono, editor, monitored how much unorthodox was too much, and guarded the entire configuration with diligence. Susan Bartlett, Exhibitions and Collections Coordinator, was a study in grace—supremely calm despite constant twists. The whole was delivered to Ed Marquand, designer, and his assistant, Elsa Varela, whose artistry stepped it up to another level of distinction. Marie Weiler managed the details for all of us.

The Staff

Many people at the Seattle Art Museum went far beyond the call of duty; I thank everyone who did so, but can mention only a few pivotal individuals: I will never forget Erika Lindsay, Public Relations Associate, who on a doubtful day told me she and her fiancé were together reading the draft of each chapter. Or Helen Abbott, former Publications Manager, who insisted I write more than labels. Or Mike McCafferty, Exhibition Designer, who often seems to have better taste in African art than I do.

I owe a large debt to a sequence of Deputy Directors: Patterson Sims and Trevor Fairbrother were supportive, but Chiyo Ishikawa was the constructive catalyst who made a three-month leave possible for the final writing. Two assistants endured the endless debates sparked by not following a formula: Leasa Fortune kept pace during a year of changes and wrote "The Trouble with Tarzan," an essay that reviews the creation of African clichés in the American film industry and the ways in which African films are overcoming them. Carol Hermer never faltered in any dimension of research, from videotaping interviews to tracking down source material.

Some museum work is best when invisible. High points of perfection in mount making were reached by a group of artists working in the museum's basement. There could be no better gathering of talent to work with than Chris Manojlovic, Jack Mackey, Gordon Lambert, Paul Martinez, Ken Leback, and Scott Hartley. Care and handling of the art was overseen by Gail Joice, Deputy Director of Museum Services, whose exacting standards and sympathetic solutions set a tone for a large division in which Lauren Tucker, Marta Pinto-Llorca, and Julie Creahan have been especially attentive.

The waves of grants and fundraising efforts that sustained all the affiliated museum projects were deftly managed by Maryann Jordan, Deputy Director for External Affairs. Among her staff, Carol Mabbott, Laura Hopkins, and Laura Bales finessed innumerable documents and meetings with government and corporate donors.

The Allies

Charlotte Beall, Marita Dingus, Teresa Domka, Kathy Fowells, P. Raaze Garrison, Evelyn Reingold, Kay Tarapolsi, and Victoria Moreland continue to be the best African art docents imaginable. Our finest era of training was enhanced by Beverly Harding, Educator, and is continually sustained by the assistance of Elizabeth deFato, Librarian.

The Originators of Quotations

Thanks to all of the following individuals whose words have added a wealth of perspectives to this text: Roland Abiodun, Obo Addy, Emma Agu, T. J. Alldridge, Daniel "Koo Nimo" Amponsah, Jina Bo II, Yaw Boaten, Fu Kiau Bunseki, Kwame Butuakwa, Seydou Camara, Maryse Conde, Camille Coquilhat, Donald Cosentino, Manthia Diawara, George Ellis, Ralph Waldo Emerson, William Fagg, M. J. Field, Eberhard Fischer, Perkins Foss, Paul Gebauer, Colonel Hall, David Hammons, G. W. F. Hegel, Hans Himmelheber, Obaro Ikime, Nsemi Isaki, Pa Joe, Cheick Mahamadou Cherif Keita, Salif Keita, Seydou Keita, Babatunde Lawal, Kenneth Little, Wyatt MacGaffey, John Mack, Patrick McNaughton, Susan Minot, Paul Nchoji Nkwi, Linda Nochlin, Mvemba Nzinga, Bruce Onobrakpeya, Won Ldy Paye, Chano Pazo, Ruth Phillips, John Picton, Prempeh I, Kane Quaye, Darrell Reeck, Theodore Roosevelt, William Rubin, Malcolm Ruel, André Salmon, Thierry Secretan, Banzumana Sissoko, William Smith, Renée Stout, P. Amaury Talbot, François-Xavier Tchoungui, Jean Marie Teno, Joseph Thomson, Issa Traore, Leon Underwood, and John H. Weeks.

My Teachers

This writing draws from Dorothy Cooper's stories, Wanda Corn's art history, Charlie Grebo's visits upcountry, the late Jacques Hymans's history, Michael McColly's truthful writing, and Fred Wilson's curatorial prowess.

My Family

Kris McClusky introduced Duncan and me to it all. I hope GK and I can do the same for Aldo Jan. We count on help from Toyin Ajayi, Andy Frankel, Gene, and Lolade.

Pamela McClusky
Curator of African and Oceanic Art
Seattle Art Museum

Introduction

Long steps never broke a person's back.
Irin nla ko kan eyin ri.   —Yoruba saying

A Parisian describes long steps taken to ragtime music in 1902: "The dancer thrusts the torso forward and throws the shoulders backward, bending as much as possible; the arms are extended horizontally, then folded, while counting two beats to the measure. In this position, in which balance is rather unstable, it is a question of advancing while raising the knee just as high as it will go with each step."[1] This image of the cakewalk comes to mind when I pick up an African mask in museum storage and prepare it for display. While holding it carefully and walking with a measured pace, my mind begins taking the mental leaps that connect the object with its origins on another continent. One foot remains grounded in the present, but the other dangles in midair, attempting to span great distances.

A bit of irony hovers in the air while one holds this pose. The cakewalk was originally intended to satirize the pompous manners of white plantation owners, just as museum-handling procedures can seem overly precious. Wearing gloves to place a mask in a velvet-lined storage cart, and pushing it through the hushed repository, is in extreme opposition to the dynamics of a masquerade. As the caretaker for the ideas and associations that once surrounded the mask, I envision taking steps away from the sterile enclosure and back into the messy vitality of the mask's home environment.

The first step on the imaginary return of this object from the museum to its original home is Los Angeles, where it once joined a dense crowd of African faces, figures, jewelry, and furniture that had overtaken every room in the house of an American woman named Katherine White. In 1961, at the age of thirty-one, she began buying art and never stopped until her death at fifty-one. In an intense effort over twenty years, she compiled her collection, which came to the Seattle Art Museum in 1981. Conscious that she was enacting a private quest for what would someday become public property, White kept a journal of her journeys to galleries and museums in Europe and America, and of her experiences in African markets, palaces, and ceremonies.

Katherine White's records open the door to the process of collecting, revealing some of its complexities and concealing others. At times, she documents all the details of an acquisition, including her own doubts about how to recognize excellence in objects from other cultures. But in many situations, she simply states a dealer as the source and goes no further. By the 1960s, silence surrounds the removal of many African objects from their original owners. "Runners," or African agents, supplied dealers in Europe and America with art obtained from sources that are rarely recorded. Several exceptions to these undocumented sales are featured in this publication: gifts from palace treasuries given by Cameroonian kings to American friends, an Ejagham costume in which a certain professor was initiated, and a recent collaboration with the Maasai that closed out the century.

A scholar renowned for his long steps was asked to revise an essay instructing viewers in how to read the stances, postures, and gestures of a range of African figural sculpture. Robert Farris Thompson's prose doesn't just step; it cartwheels and propels readers to think in complexes of sound and motion. Thompson equates his interpretive method with crossing a stream on stepping stones, but he also updates the cakewalk with the lunge of a *capoeira bencao*.[2]

The remaining texts, twelve case histories, I devised to encourage an American audience to collapse the juju fetish witch doctor in the savage spaces of the mind. This space is occupied by stereotypes that may unexpectedly swing into place. Author Wole Soyinka refers to the Neo-Tarzanism phenomenon, the tendency for Western-ers to peg Africa as the place of animal, jungle, and discord requiring a white savior (preferably from an aristocratic family). However outdated, an excerpt from Edgar Rice Burroughs's *Tarzan and the Leopard Men* of 1935 depicts a crude cliché of an African "gallery and curator" that prevails:

> The wavering torchlight played upon carved and painted idols; it glanced from naked human skulls, from gaudy shields and grotesque masks hung upon the huge pillars that supported the roof of the building. It lighted, more bril-liantly than elsewhere, a raised dais at the end of the chamber, where stood the high priest.... Below and around him were grouped a number of lesser priests; while chained to a heavy post near him was a huge leopard, bristling and growling at the massed humanity before him, a devil-faced leopard that seemed to the imagination of the white man to personify the savage bestiality of the cult it symbolized.[3]

Replacing this torchlight bestiality, the case histories offer a chance to visit many real galleries and curators. In Ghana, one enters a royal sitting room where skilled linguists preside. In Cameroon, within a remote mountaintop palace, a king's council-lor is preparing a display of thrones. In Sierra Leone, a forest sanctuary conceals the place where female teachers are putting on full costumes. In Nigeria, a marketplace theater hosts a masquerader who sings all night about the problems of men and women. The case histories introduce the African equivalents of highly trained cura-tors and the storage rooms or galleries they have worked in. They present biographies of objects usually displayed in the galleries with minimal texts. This museum limits labels to seventy-five words, mandatory terse shorthand notes. While the literature on African art has greatly expanded in the last three decades, it is often not adapted for typical museum visitors who want to know specific things about particular objects: "Who collected this and why?" "Is this a fetish?" "Why is this on display in a museum?" "Is this significant or ordinary, rare or common?" "Are these kingdoms still in existence?" "Do people still perform this masquerade?" Such questions are often asked but require more thorough answers than labels can provide. In response, these texts offer an involved look at a select few rather than a hurried survey of hundreds.

Extreme restraint kept the number of case histories small, pushing aside thousands of objects that could have been chosen. Receiving attention here are a few objects known to have unique stories of collection and documentation. Their sequence is guided not by region, geography, or importance, but by the evolution of the collecting process from 1969 to 1999. The first discussion, of hunters' shirts, reveals how museum doors were opened to their range of provocative media. During the 1970s, the notion of securing complexes or multiples inspired Katherine White to acquire assemblies of art, largely from West Africa. From the 1980s to the end of the century, collecting became more experimental, as seen in the gift of a coffin, the purchase of photography, and an exchange enacted with a community in Kenya. The momentum for collaboration led to an exhibition of the same name. Numerous individuals whose work is cited in this text visited Seattle to add new facets to this documentation.

In essence, the case histories are an extension of the exercise I perform as I cakewalk with an African mask. If long steps could catapult me across the Atlantic, where would I meet the person who was closely connected to this object and what might we talk about? What has been said that needs to be corrected? The case histories unveil multiple paths of interpretation and the many voices that contribute to the exploration. Primary sources, from proverbs to epics, songs to films, guide the texts. Misreadings and conflicting views about the same art are not avoided, but are put forward to show how words and realizations evolved through history. Individuals who loom large in African history but whose names remain largely unknown to an American audience are introduced—Afonso, Prempeh, Sundiata, and Yu. And no accounts leave readers in the past, but instead follow the steps an object takes into the present.

Long steps carry an African mask from America to its home and back again. To this purpose, Robert Farris Thompson sets out the framework of a "democratic opera without divas," and the notion of seeing art moving in places far beyond museum walls. I add the specifics of following that mask through performances, both in Africa and in America. For it is right in front of us that we find African creativity camouflaged in American yards, music, dance, and altars. In and out of the museum, we witness how a spiritual buoyancy keeps the back from breaking.

Notes

1. Jody Blake, *Le Tumulte Noir: Modernist Art and Popular Entertainment in Jazz-Age Paris, 1900–1930* (University Park, Penn.: Pennsylvania State University Press, 1999), 21.

2. *Capoeira* is an Afro-Brazilian martial art that combines elements of tumbling, dance, self-defense, and percussion. *Bencao* is a straight kick.

3. Edgar Rice Burroughs, *Tarzan and the Leopard Men* (Tarzana, Calif.: Edgar Rice Burroughs, Inc., 1935), 148–49.

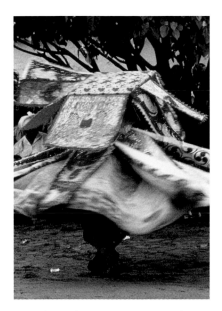

African Art in Motion

The body as metaphor is an all-important concept in the art south of the Sahara. Combine that metaphor with metaphors of motion and, in the words of an African American rap group of the 1980s, one "steps into the cipher." We enter, in other words, a code, a stylized form of consciousness, involving all in deep and primary vitality.

Tropical Africa has elaborated a different art history, a history of danced art, art danced by multimetric sound and multipart motion. Danced art completes things, returns them to themselves by immersion in stylized motion. It was in the village of Oshielle, not far from the Egba metropolis of Abeokuta in southwestern Nigeria, in the winter of 1962, that I began to notice how African statuary, not only masks, could be involved in motion, how icons called for corresponding actions. For as the women gathered their twin images, they cradled them in their arms and danced them, singing, to a special mat and placed them there to be photographed. And then they danced them back to their shrine, tenderly nestled them in special cloths, and closed the door.

Years before, intellectual ancestors, Fernando Ortiz working in Cuba and Frances and Melville J. Herskovits working in Trinidad, had noted the same phenomenon—that dance in black Atlantic contexts moved objects beyond the more obvious extensions, like headdresses for a sacred dance, or knitted costumes, or other forms of straightforwardly choreographic paraphernalia.

For the Herskovitses witnessed an Afro-Trinidadian, overcome by the spirit, swinging his body on his knees, "dancing" in his hands a candle and a glass filled with flowers before an altar. Ortiz, similarly, saw objects that one would not ordinarily associate with the dance turned into special emblems for higher service and sacred meaning when taken in hand or hoist upon the body. The tradition leads, in the black Americas, to the dancing of paintings: Haitians once celebrated the completion of an important commission by dancing the canvas through the streets of Port-au-Prince. In these instances, African and African American dance overcomes material, re-creates it, extending the aliveness that an object must embody to function as a work of art.

Pl. 13 (detail)

Fig. 1. *The Old Plantation,* 1800, watercolor, H. 45.7 cm (18 in.). Courtesy of the Abby Aldrich Rockefeller Folk Art Museum, Williamsburg, Virginia.

The semantic range of the concept "dance" appears therefore broader in Africa and African-influenced regions than within the West. As to the last point, compare the *Concise Oxford Dictionary:*

> *dance* 1. Move with rhythmic steps, glides, leaps, revolutions, gestures, etc. usua. to music, alone or with a partner or set (~ to one's tune or pipe, follow his lead); jump about, skip, move in a lively way (of heart, blood, etc.) (~ upon nothing, be hanged); perform (minuet, waltz, etc.) ... cause to dance

However full these definitions—built around the core concept of enacting rhythmic motions, patterns, gestures to music—they nevertheless do not include sharing the motion with objects. Yet "causing to dance" is an English idiom that prepares the way for grasping the African phenomenon. For if Westerners "dance" an infant with affection, then an equation for understanding danced sculpture stands before us. We have only to fill in, or insert, the following—[objects, cloths, and other things activated by love, ecstasy, and respect for higher force]—to move within the wider, inherently spiritual, sub-Saharan domain of meaning. An immediate example of danced art: among the Tiv of Nigeria the verb *vine* means to dance. But one can also dance a top, imparting a spin to the object, or dance a cutlass, twirling the metal, causing the blade to glitter as it bites into the wood.

Without my realizing it, black Puerto Rican mambo dancers culturally prepared me for African dancing of cloth, to impart special motion to an object, as early as 1955, six years before I went south of the Sahara. In the early spring of 1955, in the southwest corner of the Palladium ballroom on Broadway at Fifty-third Street in New York, connoisseurs tacitly reserved space for the hottest and most inventive black and Puerto Rican mambo dancers. Enter Anibal Vasquez, star *mamboista.* He danced part of his clothing as he moved in ways I had never seen before, let alone imagined. He tugged on his jacket with thumb and forefinger, causing the cloth to fan in and out, mirroring the mambo eighth notes, sounding on the offbeat all around us. Vasquez was not only dancing as Westerners would understand it, making his body move to the beat; he was simultaneously breaking up a part of his dress into rhythmic fragments, alive pulsations, pattern on pattern, beat on beat, as if he were personally reinventing cubism right then and there. I stared, taken and compelled. Then I looked at the band. Men on saxophones and trumpets were swaying from side to side while playing mambo. They were dancing their instruments.

Centuries earlier a painter in South Carolina documented a woman of African ancestry "dancing" a strip of cloth held before her body (fig. 1). I was to see this very action many times in Yorubaland in the 1960s and 1970s: women dancing, swinging suddenly close to the earth, showing off youth and flexibility, dancing a strip of cloth held before their bodies as a final fillip of design. They were dancing a cloth while dancing the dance. They were, in the terms of Zora Neale Hurston, decorating the decoration.

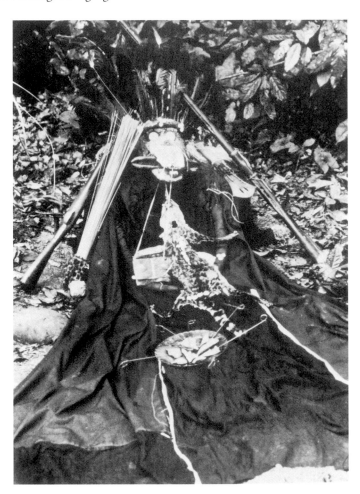

If love of an infant makes you want to rock the tender body, love of the spirit, caught in an object, makes you want to give spirit back its motion. Here is part of the rationale for dancing a coffin to its grave in numerous African civilizations. This over-laps a portion of the New Orleans black jazz funeral, pallbearers "dip-stepping" and followers "second-lining" on the casket's way to glory. If dance includes the ritual twirling of a sword in Edo, or the transformation of hammer on anvil into a sonic means of salutation among the blacksmiths of Efon-Alaiye, among the Ekiti-Yoruba it reminds us that objects can, con-versely, embody an aliveness and vitality of their own.

The fact that Basinjom, the famous witch-finding gowned figure among the Ejagham and Ejagham-influenced civilizations, must be spiritually moored with two crossed rifles when at rest (fig. 2) is a measure of its believed visual aliveness. In Kongo, ritual experts are famously skilled for making and elaborating "medicines of God" (*minkisi*), the aliveness of which is enhanced by all sorts of astonishing touches of feathers, earths, buttons, and beads. Some spirits dwelling in such spectacularly capari-soned objects must be specially arrested or controlled. The image is, accordingly, bound up with ties of string or cord or cloth. Handling superalive images by binding is a tradition that carries over directly into the myriad tied charms and figures on the Petwo, or largely Kongoizing side, of Hai-tian vodun worship in the West Indies as well as among the Fon of Benin and the Fon-influenced Rada side of vodun. I shall never forget a life-size human figure shrouded in red literally chained to a wall in a Petwo shrine near Gressier in the spring of 1970.

Jackson Pollock's concentration on bodily gesture daringly oscillographed upon the canvas (fig. 3) and Duane Hanson's unsettlingly alive image of his own son as doctor (fig. 4) remind us that modern art, as well as African, in its own powerful

Fig. 2. Basinjom costume displayed in grove, Cameroon, 1973.

ways builds the riddle, How do we distinguish art from life? Or, as Yeats voiced the matter in a celebrated line, "How can we know the dancer from the dance?"

All art that is truly physical, as David Anfam argues, has an organic life beyond words. What, then, is the difference between modernist vitality in painting and sculpture and the active potentiality of the sculptural image south of the Sahara? Provisionally, I would suggest: contexts of ancestoristic reverence and spiritual reembodiment. Pollock and Hanson were operating as free spirits, avatars of self-expression in a world outside religious patterns of belief. Their art went into strange, agnostic temples, often characterized by white walls, polished floors, and indirect lighting. True, there is such a thing as mixed-media installation art in the West, but it is a far cry from the famed unity of the arts in African performance, a democratic opera without divas, a people's orchestra without conductor, all graced with lickety-split cameo leaps into the dancing ring, enabling anyone, anyone with confidence and courage, to share the limelight for a moment.

What all this leads to, in understanding African danced art, is not to empha-size motion over sculpture, or painting at the expense of music. Sculpture is not the central art south of the Sahara, but neither is the dance. For both depend on words and music, and even dreams and divination, sources indicating the very sanction of the other world. Music, dance, and visual objects are all important, separate or together, and if motion gives body to music or special zest to art, sculpture deepens the understanding of time and motion by freezing aspectual unfoldment into a single text for comprehension. This strong interrelationship—sound, motion, vision—obviously stems from a combined aesthetic. Shared norms of quality structure the media. Shared organizing principles, in turn, underlie the confidence and quality in African act and icon.

Fig. 5. Dan Gle Gbee stilt masquerade, Liberia, 1967.

Fig. 6. Oloko (Lord of the Farm) masquerade, Epa festival, Otun, Ekiti, Nigeria, 1977.

We study icons and we look at attitudes, defined as positions of the body. Ritual reenactments of important attitudes, it is said, restore ancient modes of self-presentation to modern contexts. A Yoruba priest of Egungun from Ouidah in the Republic of Benin told me in the summer of 1972 that a person who stands well is born with that power. He said this apropos of a photograph of a Montol image of a standing woman, knees and arms richly inflected with readiness for the dance (pl. 1). Africans in other places have similarly observed that commanding attitude and commanding presence are gifts of the spirit. In fact, Bernard de Grunne has shown how ancient Malian images set in different postures of reverence and worship are placed on altars expressly to show the supplicant the way to move and gesture within his worship. Taking on the attitudes of the ancestors and the gods turns the person into sculpture, in ultimate relation to the goddesses and the gods.

Sculptural icons in African art therefore take their radiance in part from important attitudes of the body. These, in turn, appear in groupings that suggest a grand equation of spiritual stability and response. Thus icons of command (standing, being enthroned, riding on horseback) correspond to icons of service or submission (kneeling, supporting objects with both hands, and balancing loads upon the head).

There are many things to learn, but one seems paramount: if spirits can challenge gravity by moving on stilts twelve feet in the air (fig. 5) to stirring slit-gong percussion and hocketed singing in the forest villages of the Dan of northeastern Liberia; if athletes in northeastern Yorubaland can shoulder nearly a hundred pounds of carved wood sculpture for a quarter of an hour while dancing before their king (fig. 6); if initiates honoring the collective moral dead can spin and spin and spin and spin and spin

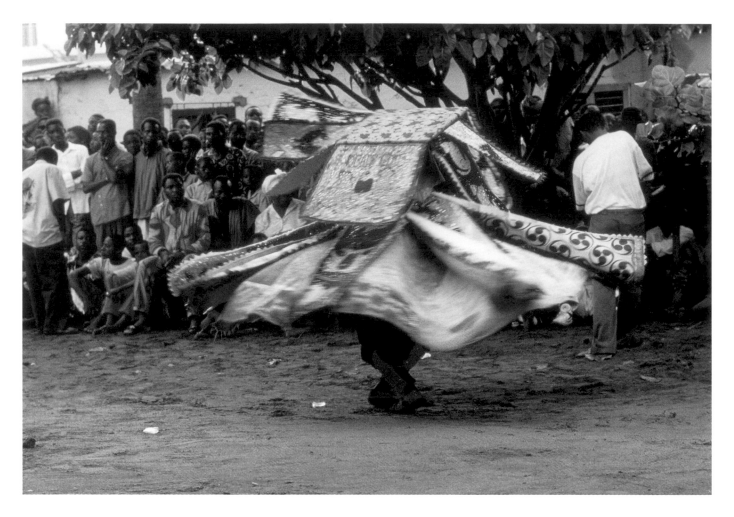

Fig. 7. Yoruba Egungun performance, 1994.

(fig. 7) until the very concept of human dizziness begins to lose its meaning—then anything is possible.

Ideally, the reader of such phenomena will emerge with respect for what happens when hard work combines with discipline and the spirit in traditionalist villages and barrios of modern Africa. African danced art, in all its spiritual complexity, invokes an ideal future. Women dance cloths held before their bodies, honoring themselves, honoring their guests, honoring God, teaching us to live, strongly and well.

Icon and Attitude

> There is in the African a latent lyricism which tends to
> express itself in movement, so that every gesture, every
> attitude of the body takes on a special significance which
> belongs to a language of which I caught only a few words.
>
> —Richard Wright, 1954[1]

Traditionalist Yoruba believe that the founders of their civilization created the styles of proper bodily address and dance.[2] To adopt them, in the deepest spiritual outlook or belief, is to align oneself with the best of the past, with the Great Time of the ancestors. Elsewhere in Africa traditionalists similarly believe that when they perform ritual dances, or strike an honorific pose, they are standing or moving in the image of their ancestors.[3] Ritual forms of flexibility and communal strength therefore take on an aura of reincarnation.

Ancestorism, the belief that the highest experience reflects the closest harmony with the ancient way, shapes stance, attitude, and gesture in the art of Africa. "Stance" refers to standing. "Attitude" refers to stylized positions of the body or self-carriage, indicative of mood and status. "Gesture" refers to motions of the body and the limbs, communicating thought or emphasis.[4] The stylized positions of the body considered in this text are strongly present in known collections—standing, sitting, riding, kneeling, supporting, and balancing. The close relation between art and the dance in African aesthetics causes us to reread Marcel Griaule with a pointed interest:

> The dance only repeats essential gestures. It is accompanied by a staccato
> rhythm and a few words alluding to the events which determined the creation
> of the personage in question. [This] simplification should teach us to study
> every detail.[5]

Griaule's point, intensification of the icon through simplification of its formal means, is important. Listen to traditionalist Africans hinting of such matters when remarking just the single attitude of standing:

> Yoruba in Benin: "One who is standing like that is born with that stance."
> Banyang (Cameroon): "He stands like a person," that is, in a principled
> manner.
> Suku (Democratic Republic of the Congo): "I have seen that pose. It reminds
> me of what I was told: long ago at the feast for our ancestors, they calcu-
> lated, 'what was the image of our grandfather' . . . and they remembered their
> grandfather when he was standing. [And then] they began to make standing
> images of the ancestors."[6]

Tradition selects. Bodily positions defining lordliness and command come to predominate: standing, being enthroned, riding on a horse. Tradition also underscores postures set at levels of respect: kneeling, supporting, and balancing things upon the head without the use of hands. Service confirms command and vice versa. Reading the details of the icon at rest, we sometimes discern split-second freezing

Pl. 1
Standing figure
Montol, Nigeria
19th–20th century
Wood
H. 32 cm (12⅝ in.)
Gift of Katherine White and the Boeing Company,
81.17.541

Pl. 2
Mother and child
Osei Bonsu (1900–1977)
Asante, Ghana
1930s
Wood, gold leaf, silver
H. 45 cm (17¾ in.)
Gift of Katherine White and the Boeing Company,
81.17.323

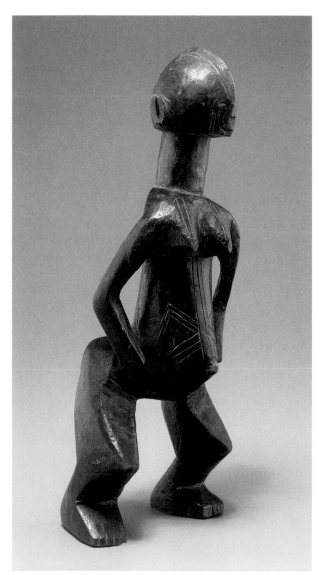

of a complex of actions. Implied condensation of vital enactments makes it seem almost inevitable that statuettes and icons and even monolithic sculptures like the *aguru epa* headdresses of the Ekiti-Yoruba area would be danced, would be pulled into motion. Part of the marvel has to do with what one distinguished ethnomusicologist calls "polycentrality" in the dance of Africa and another calls "the two-part body system": the torso divides both icon and dancer into two related parts. A twist at the waist, in dance, often underscores the division. Upper and lower portions of the body engage in different motions and directions, not only in African hip-swinging dances but even in some forms of work.

Such icons blur into the Yeatsian vision, confounding dancer with the dance. This is splendidly true with respect to the Montol figure of a standing woman (see pl. 1). Unheard dance music divides her body at the waist into two different axes of expression. Head, spool-like neck, and upper torso align in shared, assertive verticality. But precisely at the waist, already emphasized by concentric cicatrization about the navel, she surges forward with a countervailing, forward accent. This thrust, in turn, is simultaneously mirrored by a surging backward of the hips. The line of the torso thus zigs back to the buttocks, then forward and down, legs flashing facets. Her body turns into lightning. The Montol figure does more than stand. With arms akimbo, she challenges the world. In the ballet of African iconography, head erect, lips back, feet flat upon the ground, she performs on her own terms the first position.

Being seated is also outwardly simple but inwardly rich. It can conceal the spiritual electricity of several ideal actions coming together as one. This was made clear to me by a young Mu-Suku named Piluka Ladi, in the city of Kinshasa, Democratic Republic of the Congo, March 1973. I showed him a photograph of a sculpture attributed to a master carver of Kumasi, Ghana, Osei Bonsu (pl. 2), and asked him to comment. What he said was extraordinary:

> She is purely there. She gives milk to the child. She secures his body with the other hand. She is sitting well, like a person of character.

He caught three verbs in sculptural allusion—sitting, giving, securing. And since her position blends generosity, the highest form of morality in many of the religions of the black Atlantic world, with the inherent dignity of the enthroned position, she emerges, as Piluka Ladi says, being purely there. That purity of presence becomes the subject matter of this book.

Pl. 3
Standing figures
Kulango, Ghana
19th–20th century
Wood, chalk, metal
Left: H. H. 81.9 cm (32¼ in.); right: H. 96.5 cm (38 in.)
Gift of Katherine White and the Boeing Company,
81.17.225.1+.2

Pl. 4
Twin statuette *(flanitokole)*
Bamana, Mali
19th–20th century
Wood
H. 48.3 cm (19 in.)
Gift of Katherine White and the Boeing Company,
81.17.27

Standing

The perpendicular is an opposition.   —Bruce Glaser, 1964[7]

Standing is a task. The remorseless pull of gravity makes it so. To stand against magnetic earth is to intervene in a decisive way, keeping vertical and maintaining balance. Engaging the whole of the person, standing is a complex of energy and strength as distinguished from a simple species of immobilization, like fixing an iron bar within the earth. A person, unlike an object, stands with affect and expression. The way a person stands ultimately communicates lived relation with the world. Standing embodies vitalized persistence and becomes an icon of ideal righteous being.

Begin with the Akan of Ghana, who see the twelve hours of the day, dominated by the light of heaven, as that time when women and men are "standing up alive."[8] Standing up thus corresponds to light and life. It is the stance of daytime, the time of morality. So we assume two standing figures, attributed to the Akan-related Kulango civilization of Ghana, were meant to have their touches of spiritualized white clay (*hyire*) gleam with implications of purity and the light of day (pl. 3). These images are definitely standing up alive. The positive associations of their stance are deepened by the quality of their gesture. Both place their hands near the heart. Their purity of presence is already secured by application of the sacred white porcelain clay. But hands extend that purity by pointing out the heart:

> If he wants to refer to the person's goodness … the Adjukur [an ethnic group in southern Côte d'Ivoire affiliated culturally with the Akan] will localize it within two central organs of the body: the stomach and the heart. The heart is a source of life, in that it is the literal headquarters of respiration or breath, thought, sentiments [and] will.… Goodness comes from the heart and stomach and is an internal realization.[9]

The Kulango figures embody assertion in their verticality. But, with their hands, they also indicate mind and internal goodness.

A Bamana twin statuette (*flanitokole*, literally, "the double who remains") evidences another form of ideal standing (pl. 4). Elaborate coiffure alludes to life lived well, for such a crest could be made only through the cooperation of others, sympathetic sisters or co-wives. There is great subtlety to the gentle bending of her knees, creating the slightest modulation to the uprightness of her noble posture. Against that axis, buttocks and breasts form strong assertions of vitality. She lends, in turn, an ordering, vital posture to the world.

The famous twin statuettes of the Yoruba (*awon ere ibeji*) present a fascinating instance of nuanced iconic standing (pls. 5, 6). First of all, twins are traditionally described as "standing straight and tall" (*aduro gangan*). According to Araba Eko of Lagos, "their position, hands at the sides, arms parallel to the body, is a sign of alertness, being ready to do everything. They do not relax. They are standing, either to hear a prayer or to act."[10] God himself stands this way, as envisioned in the Yoruba saying, "Great God almighty, standing upright behind the power to make things happen truly" (*olodumare aduro gangan lehin ashe otito*).[11]

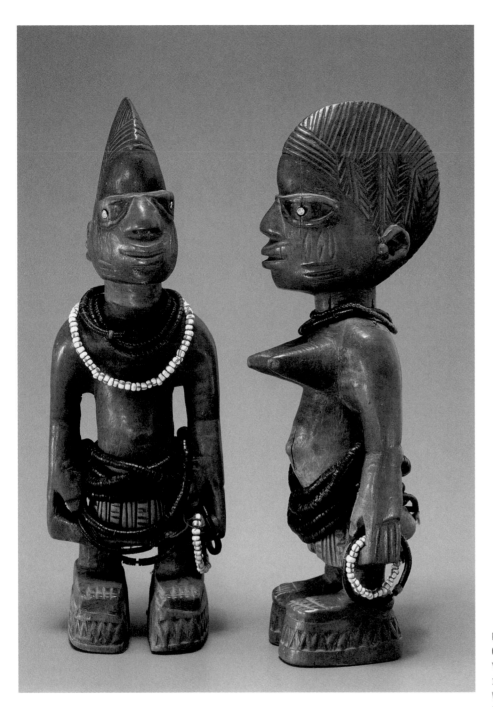

Pl. 5
Commemorative twin figures *(awon ere ibeji)*
Yoruba, Nigeria
19th–20th century
Wood, pigment, beads, encrustations
Left: H. 32.4 cm (12¾ in.); right: H. 34.9 cm (13¾ in.)
Gift of Katherine White and the Boeing Company,
81.17.610.1+.2

Pl. 6
Commemorative twin figures *(awon ere ibeji)*
Yoruba, Nigeria
19th–20th century
Wood, beads, nails
Each: H. 24.5 cm (9⅝ in.)
Gift of Katherine White and the Boeing Company,
81.17.611.1+.2

In his study of human motion, F. J. J. Buytendijk argues that "however the final phase or the initial moment of a movement are characterized, the standing position is always the first phase of a new activity."[12] That power, to initiate or begin things standing, becomes a setting for further strengths. The exorbitant eyes hint that the images take power from above, the power to make things happen, even as the eyes of an actual devotee of the Yoruba gods in Brazil, when taken and compelled by the force of a god, faces the world with a laserlike stare that sees across worlds. The constant placing of the arms of the twin statuettes by the sides is more than a sign of spiritual alertness. Dejo Afolayan, the distinguished Yoruba linguist, in the process of translating a long string of praise epithets for the twins, shows how the very presence of these beings attests a life well lived, for God gives twin children specially to the generous and the upright:

Let she who fantasizes having twins adopt a gentle character
Let him remain transparently honest.[13]

Blessings become truth. The advent of twins magnetizes the luck of heaven to the family of the double child. That gift from above is written into their stance—that is, holding their arms tightly parallel to their sides:

Stand, o twins, with anus straight and parallel
That earth might touch the sky.[14]

From the Yoruba we come now to the Guro of Côte d'Ivoire. We contemplate a standing image of a woman, possibly carved for a Dan patron to the west (pl. 7). She projects a handsome verticality. Her eyes narrow down. This wreaks erotic havoc on the young men of the Dan, who border on Guro country. The image fulfills another Dan canon of fine standing: "It is not good for a beautiful person to be stiff in body when standing" (*me sa ba do kpei da sy ka sa*).[15] Relaxed arms and relaxed legs fulfill this demand. And the outstretched arms are seen as positive, "as if to embrace [a person]."

A woman standing naked with her breasts exposed communicates, in Africa, far more than is dreamt of in the philosophy of Freud or other theorists. She stands thus to give life to the righteous—or death to the evil. Among the western Dan, a mother swears on her breasts, or upon life itself, when sealing a vow. But when confronted with an enemy, she can squeeze, in righteous anger, a droplet of milk from her left breast and slap her thigh. This unleashes a curse of unfathomable dimension. By standing naked, and using the breasts as instruments of grace or punishment— far removed from ordinary contexts of lactation or sexual arousal—women are exalted. They empower themselves, they empower their family, in the depths of their femininity. This is the case with the famous Dan *wunkirmian,* or "feast-making spoon," a "spoon woman" object, bringing together handsome legs (or a handsome head) with a symbolically generous ladle (pl. 8). Dan carve such spoons for Wunkirle (Feast-Making Woman), the most hospitable woman of the village. The spoon is her badge of honor, symbolizing her acts of generosity. Only Wunkirle can carry *wunkirmian.* She and her kin are by definition enterprising cultivators. They have plenty of rice.

Pl. 7
Standing figure
Guro, Côte d'Ivoire
19th–20th century
Wood
H. 42 cm (16⅝ in.)
Gift of Katherine White and the Boeing Company, 81.17.257

They share it. On feast days Wunkirle swings and dances the spoon-emblem before her, in the midst of a chorus of hocketing women. They back their sister with call-and-response. Other women follow, carrying bowls brimming with rice. When all have arrived at the village square, Wunkirle dips into the bowls and begins a distribution, dancing out ideal largesse.

The spoon compacts the ceremony. Beautifully inflected legs allude to a lovely woman and her readiness to dance. The ladle is generosity. The lizard on its back alludes to prayer: reptiles move on the earth, where the dead are hidden, indicating the place where calls for children ultimately are heard. The extraordinary fusion of object and person in the making of the *wunkirmian* matches the marvel of the dress of Wunkirle. Blasting away ordinary differences of gender, Wunkirle appears at her feast wearing a flowing male robe and a striking male helmet.

Further examples of heraldic standing grace the collection. For brevity I now incorporate them, lawyer-like, by reference (pls. 9, 10). All illustrate the insight of Guido von Kaschnitz-Weinberg, namely, that the standing position represents a world that is intelligible and clear. Mind and body, in expression of strength, align with the vertical axis. Women and men standing in life, standing as sculpture, standing as dancers, contest the laws of gravity. In so doing, they memorably establish a principle of assertion.

Pl. 8
Feast-making spoon *(wunkirmian)*
Dan, Côte d'Ivoire
20th century
Wood, iron
H. 61.4 cm (24¼ in.)
Gift of Katherine White and the Boeing Company, 81.17.204

Pl. 9
Figure of Akua's child *(akua-ba)*
Asante, Ghana
20th century
Wood, beads, polychrome
H. 25.1 cm (9⅞ in.)
Gift of Katherine White and the Boeing Company,
81.17.329

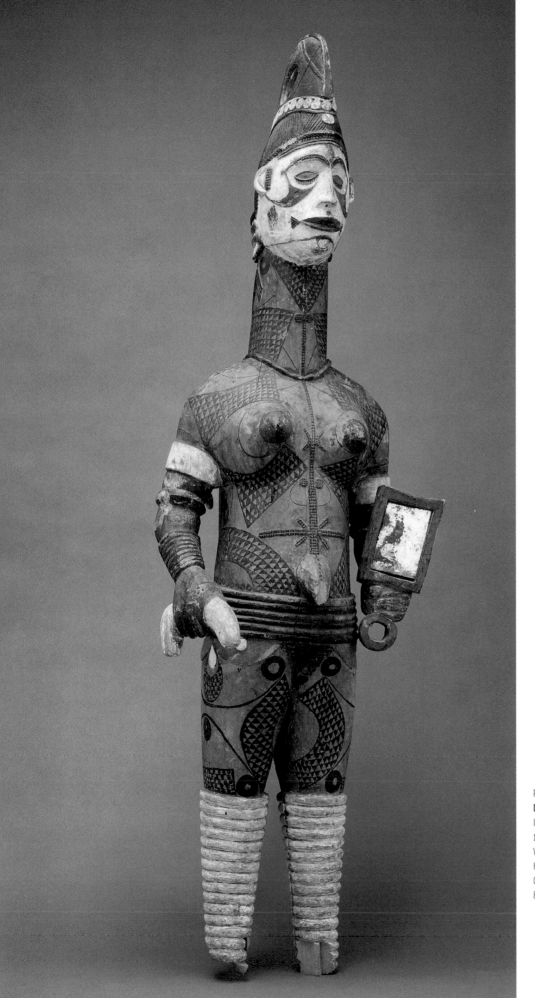

Pl. 10
Display figure *(ugonachomma)*
Igbo, Nigeria
19th–20th century
Wood, pigment, mirror
H. 127 cm (50 in.)
Gift of Katherine White and the Boeing Company,
81.17.525

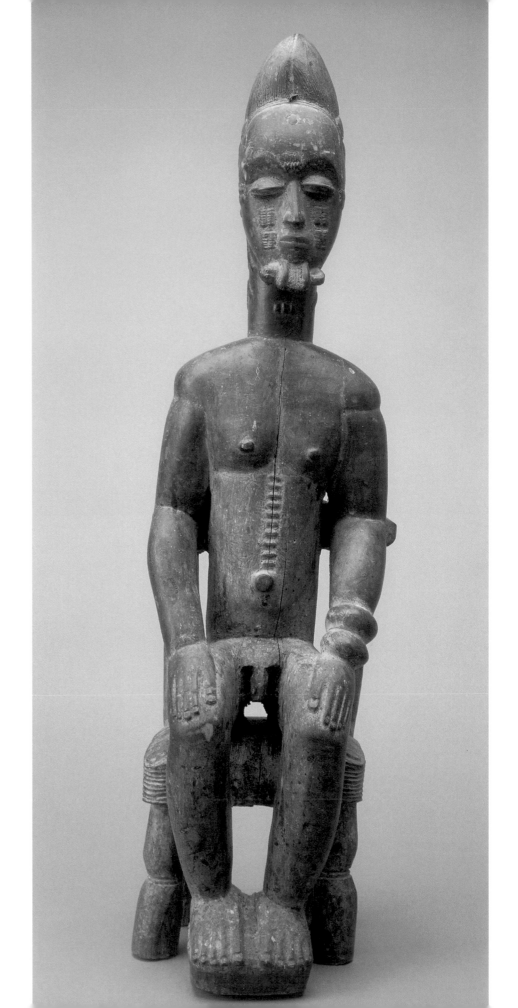

Sitting

When an actual ruler dies, the incident is referred to as
"the stool has fallen" [*akonnwa ato*].   —Peter Sarpong, 1971[16]

The enthroned position in African art communicates a complex aura of cultural permanence and fineness of character. Calm emerges in the easing of standing; the privilege of enthronement provides a frame for concentration upon important matters. Permanence or important residence are idiomatic meanings embedded in African verbs of being seated. Thus in Yoruba the phrase for place of enthronement also means place of residence. Restlessness (*aijoko*) literally means lacking a place where one can sit down. The Efik of eastern Nigeria have an expression of permanence cognate with the Yoruba. They say "that town is seated by the river," as opposed to temporary settlements of farmers in the forest.[17] In faraway Suriname, among members of African-descended Saamaka civilization, the phrase *sidon muyee*, literally "a sit-down woman," honors a woman a man can trust. In tropical Africa, the seated person, conscious of the privilege of her position, must show awareness of herself as an object of perception. The seated dignitary, in other words, must present a fitting image to the world. One instructs by enthroned composure.

This ideal lights up Akan seated statuary. Their order of seating honors the old. It begins with the eldest person present and ends with the youngest. The Akan ideally sits on a chair or stool. Failing that, he sits on animal skins or mats. Failing that, he crouches. But he must never, ever sit on the ground, as if he were an animal.[18] In this civilization sitting completes the presentation of the self. The rules that govern this bodily position are strict. A person should not cross his legs.[19] Head and torso remain erect. The gaze is frontal. Looking down communicates sadness, evil, or heavy unwillingness. The person enthroned becomes an ideal frontal pattern of perfection, symmetrically disposed and focused. He embodies, ideally, the power of the throne to counter chaos and disorder. We sense all that, and more, in a noble image of a seated Baule male dignitary (pl. 11). His flesh is hard and muscular, denoting virility and strength. His luminous body exudes an ideal: "a state of well-being, bathed, shining with pomade."[20] Hands evenly rest on either thigh, fingers strictly parallel, in self-conscious precision. When we study this image in the flesh, we see how carefully the sculptor fused his royal subject with an upright axis. There is an incredible rightness to the way the center line of the coiffure is picked up by the beard, then continued by the line of cicatrization leading to the navel, then to the membrum, seal of manhood, and then straight on down to the earth. The canon of enthronement here unfolds in complexity and richness. With pursed lips and lidded eyes, the figure seems conscious of his impact on the people, of the imperative of communicating order, down to the smallest nuance of the fingers and the styling of his narrow beard.

Consider also a terracotta depicting an Akan queen mother with a child seated on either knee (pl. 12). This image, first of all, extends the idea of the main duties of

Pl. 12
Seated figure with children
Akan, Ghana
19th–20th century
Terracotta
H. 46.4 cm (18¼ in.)
Gift of Katherine White and the Boeing Company,
81.17.442

Pl. 13
Mother and child figure for Sango
Yoruba, Oshogbo, Nigeria
19th century
Wood, glass beads
H. 43 cm (17 in.)
Gift of Katherine White and the Boeing Company,
81.17.594

the queen mother: giving life, to clan or state, as its foundation and maintaining this vitality. Here queen mother and two children, wonderfully heraldic, transform being seated into a shorthand disclosure of character and continuity. Her spiritualized calm, magnified by enthronement, involves the children in a superior influence. Queen mother supports her children with consummate impartiality. More than that, she positions them on either thigh so that they must face one another, preparing the way for dialogue and acceptance. This is appropriate to a real life role as judge and counsel. In cases of minor offenses, women may rush into her presence, crying out, "Mother save me!"[21]

Very exciting, as an example of just how far the Yoruba master carver can take the theme of enthronement, is a mother-and-child ensemble for the thunder god, Sango Alado (pl. 13). A priestess sits upon a modified object, possibly a mudfish, alluding to the famed high voltage of that creature, which restates the presence of the lightning of Sango. A child sits upon the priestess. And, most dramatically, Sango's thunderstone is seated upon her head. All this rewards devotion—as instanced in the presentation of a bowl for sacrifice. And so she receives the ultimate seating, the descent of the lord in the form of his flaming meteorites, alighting upon her head. Fire, life, and continuity seal themselves within her bodily position. This complex presentation of truth and miracle intimates what happens when a person undergoes initiation into the service of the gods (*isin orisa*). When the postulant, like this carved woman, receives such protection, initiators paint upon her head powerful patterns, including the spots of the leopard, king of the forest, thereby exalting her by allusion to nobility. Seated on a throne, the initiate, as Drewal and Abiodun show, is "painted with substances, colors, and patterns to attract and direct the spirits that will be important in the life of the person."[22]

Finally, there is another beginning stated in this sitting—enthronement at the moment of initiation, as in the creolized Yoruba worship in Afro-Cuban New York and New Jersey. This gives rise to structures that rebuild a place for the descent of the spirit: cloth-emblazoned thrones, which express an ancient idea in a different way.

We turn now to the world of Bantu, starting with the Fang of Gabon. The *eyema bieri*, or reliquary guardian figure, sits to block passage to the place where the bones of the ancestors are gathered in honor (pl. 14). This is being seated to keep away the unauthorized. But the body of the guardian is so vertically poised and brilliantly muscled it is hard to perceive that he is sitting instead of standing. His face is a cryptic skull, his musculature reflects, it is said, not merely a healthy vitality and athleticism but a mysterious mirroring of the fatty passages on the body of an infant.[23] Skull, athlete, infant—a mysterious continuum is seated here to block the way to the ancestors and their resting place. The gist of the *eyema bieri* is therefore vigilant enthronement.

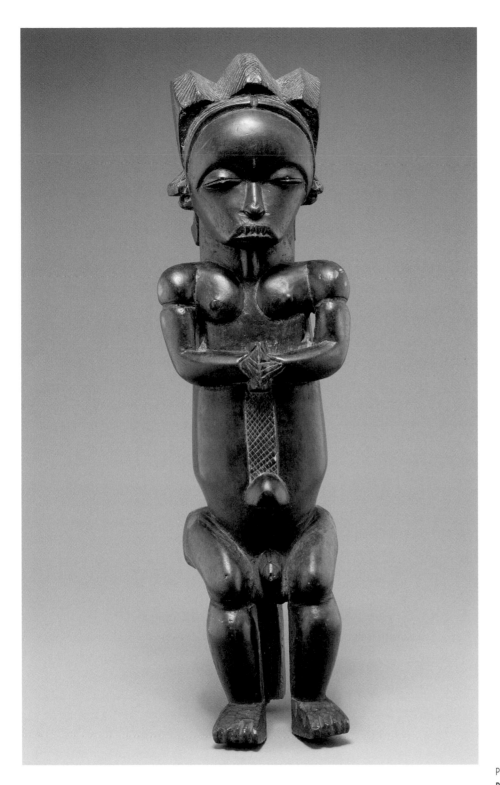

Pl. 14
Reliquary guardian figure *(eyema bieri)*
Fang, Gabon, Equatorial Guinea and Cameroon
Late 19th–early 20th century
Wood
H. 51.1 cm (20⅛ in.)
Gift of Katherine White and the Boeing Company,
81.17.783

Pl. 15
Horse and rider
Yoruba, Nigeria
19th century
Wood
H. 66.6 cm (26¼ in.)
Gift of Katherine White and the Boeing Company,
81.17.606

Pl. 16
Horse and rider
Senufo, Mali
19th–20th century
Wood
H. 28.5 cm (11¼ in.)
Gift of Katherine White and the Boeing Company,
81.17.267

Riding

> In front of the great dais the Keke-Tigui, or war chiefs, made their
> horses perform dance steps under the eyes of the Mansa. The horses
> whinnied and reared, then, overmastered by the spurs, knelt, got up
> and cut little capers, or else scraped the ground with their hooves.
>
> —Djibril T. Niane, 1965[24]

Riding embodies arrogant enthronement. Speed, motion, and elevation combine when one is seated on a horse. "You see [a rider]," a traditional leader once told me in western Cameroon, "you think—war!"[25] In the West the image of the horseman similarly invoked a martial order, "so much so [that] in Rome during the reign of Marcus Aurelius equestrian figures were the prerogative of the emperor."[26] The mounted person in Africa acquires special power and resonance because the horse is rare, expensively imported, and in some instances mystically associated with the rider. The horse is not indigenous to Africa. It was not until the Hyksos invasion of Egypt, circa mid-second millennium B.C., that the species was introduced to the continent. Thereafter horses and horsemanship spread to the west of black Africa, fully developed there by the rise of the Mali Empire in the Middle Ages. Yet the cultivation of horsemanship remains problematic in tropical Africa. The climate, areas of dense rainforest, and the bite of the tsetse fly are deadly to horses. Nevertheless, horsemen in Africa have exerted power and supremacy all out of proportion to their numbers. It is said that certain states arose in West Africa on the backs of horses and their intrepid riders: Mali, Bornu, Songhai, Hausa, Bariba, Gurman, Gonja, Mossi-Dagomba.[27]

Africans south of the Sahara never used the horse for agricultural labor, but reserved the animal for the transport of important persons. In addition, horsemanship was sometimes charged with mystical beliefs. Viewing a photograph of an equestrian figure (pl. 15) triggered an immediate response from a priest of Egungun near Ouidah: "That rider sits with force [*joko pelu agbara*], the force of the horse [*agbara esin*]. He has the speed and the power of the horse within his body."[28] Some riders are thus believed to absorb the physicality of their mount.

Reviewing other horse and rider figures, we sometimes note a blurring together of animal and human, unlike the straightforward realism of the equestrian theme within the West. Our first rider comes from the northern Senufo in southern Mali (pl. 16). Frontally viewed, the horseman seems anchored in the flesh and muscle of his mount. The legs of the beast are carved to resemble a metal apron protecting the horseman's legs. Seen from the side, the highly stylized body of the rider is countered by an enormous spear, as big as his body, held in his right hand. The vertical warrior is brilliantly countered by the horizontal massing of the horse. The legs of the animal, made human by reduction to two columns, complete the body of the rider as well as the body of the mount. Strong and streamlined, this virtuoso piece of sculpture brings alive its subject by interplay of diagonal and curve.

Still in the Sudan, we consider a Dogon horseman from Mali (pl. 17). The relaxed legs of the rider reveal how lightly seated on his horse he is. It is as if the animal were

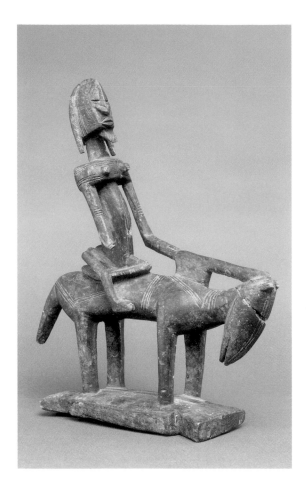

Pl. 17
Horse and rider
Dogon, Mali
19th–20th century
Wood
H. 36.5 cm (14⅜ in.)
Gift of Katherine White and the Boeing Company,
81.17.46

Pl. 18
Epa mask
Alaga of Odo-Owa (ca. 1895–1978)
Yoruba, Nigeria
19th–20th century
Wood, pigment
H. 124 cm (48⅞ in.)
Gift of Katherine White and the Boeing Company,
81.17.579

a figurated piece of furniture, a bench with head and tail both pointed down. The nonchalance of the position might mean that the rider cannot fall because his journey is mystically imbued. Griaule and Dieterlen argue that mounted figures in Dogon art symbolize the god Amma, and that in such cases the animal symbolizes one of the original eight genies of the Dogon, extraordinary water spirits.[29] The same scholars assert that the horse in Dogon lore associates with descent from the sky. Perhaps this is why the horseman's visage seems somnambulistic, eyes half-shut. The aura is quiet rather than alert. The gentle zigzag traversing the body of the animal could suggest the descent of the Dogon ark of creation, but this is far from certain.

Riding has been a theme in Nigerian art history since the Igbo-Ukwu culture, dated to around the ninth century. The image of the mounted warrior, god, or ruler is important in the world of Yoruba sculpture. Carved wooden figures of horsemen abound and usually honor, according to Robert Smith, an actual warrior.[30] Such images were kept in the house of a commander of the veteran warriors, or in the house of other military leaders in the last century. The commander kept them with his divination tray, thus linking past to future. In visual exposition, the mounted lord often becomes a master and entourage, as in a work attributed to the Alaga of Odo-Owa (pl. 18), the formal title by which the artist wished to be remembered (other art historians perversely persist in calling him by his prechiefly name of Bamgboye). Here, balance between man and beast is richly established. The leader is amazing. His towering headgear with frontal sash combines indications of knowledge of the Western helmet with the world of the square-sided phylacteries (*tira*) of Islam. He suavely pulls together sword and spear in his right hand while (again in Yoruba fashion) taking the reins in his left, but combining that gesture with the grasping, too, of a rifle. He calls with mastery of weapons and motions; his entourage responds with the sounding of flute and pressure drumming and, given other Muslim touches, perhaps even that ultimate Islamism in the field of sound—rifle music, the firing of a weapon for prestige and effect. Below the circular platform over which all this action unfolds there appears another level of drama and response. We witness the enormous eyes and exaggerated open mouth of an ancestor, so heightened as to remind us that in the earliest days the gods, the founding fathers, walked the earth as giants.

The richness of phrasing of the horseman theme can be sensed even in this modest survey. Riding is an activity that demands gestural asymmetry, sharply angled positionings of the arms and hands, as functions of an essential arrogance of action. Senufo and Yoruba riders take firm seats and maintain verticality, whereas the Dogon image rides with an air of dreamy detachment. This surely reflects a special expression of Dogon religious thought. And yet, at the end, the Yoruba submit this imperious icon to the social leavening of the call-and-response context. That forces all, leader and led, entourage and master, to recall the revelatory proverb: one tree cannot make a forest.

Kneeling

> The kings are worshiped by their subjects, who believe that they come
> from heaven, at a distance and on bended knees.
>
> —G. B. Ramusio, *Navigazione e viaggi*, 1550[31]

To kneel relates the person to a higher force. Celine Baduel-Mathon enumerates some
of the enactments of the position in the cultures of West Africa: fiancé in the presence
of the father, plaintiff before the court, son approaching father, youths before elders,
the court before the king, person praying to the ancestors or the gods.[32] Such are the
public manifestations of resting on the knees in prayer or reverence. The king kneels
in private. In every instance, to fall upon one's knees indicates dependent relationship. And that relationship triggers an ideal: the person only fully exists when set in
communication with a transcendental source of authority and action; otherwise one
wanders in a maze of endless subjectivity. But should a ruler before whom we kneel
turn evil or corrupt, submission can change to revolution and the followers of an
unworthy king can bring him to his knees. Myriad are the contexts of this act of sup-
plication. Among the Bamana of Mali, when a man accidentally ate food that was
tabooed, the woman who had served the repast in error asked forgiveness on her
knees, holding her hands at the back. The latter gesture signified humiliation. She
knelt to mend a ruined situation.[33]

Among the Agni, an Akan civilization of Côte d'Ivoire, a young man during a formal occasion involving drinking untied his cloth, knelt before his father, and drank
from the goblet that the patriarch held carefully in the hollow of his hand. Farther east
along the coast, coreligionists of the traditional faith of the Ga people, in the region
of Accra, Ghana, knelt to offer to the spirits sacrificial fowls. These were given in twos,
held in both hands, in symbolically balanced double presentations.

Among Egba-Yoruba of the region of Abeokuta, every morning each member
of a traditional compound had to pay his or her respects to the head of the extended
family and his senior wife. A man would prostrate himself (*dobale*) before the leader.
A woman would kneel (*kunle*) or lie upon her right side (*yinrinka*).[34] All three gender-
coded gestures—*dobale, kunle, yinrinka*—traveled the Atlantic to the black Americas.
Here they remain vividly alive in Afro-Cuban *lucumi* worship and Afro-Brazilian
candomble nago.

Certain situations calling for kneeling were of such moment that they blasted
away the normal boundaries of gender and entourage, not unlike the amazing pith
helmet and Mande male robe worn by Wunkirle with her honorific spoon. Even the
king of the Oyo Yoruba, the *alafin*, was expected to kneel before a powerful, titled
woman known as *Iyamode:*

> The king looks upon her as his father, and addresses her as such, being the
> worshipper of the spirits of his ancestors. He kneels in saluting her, and she
> also returns the salutation kneeling, never reclining on her elbow as is the
> custom of the women in saluting their superiors. The king kneels for no one
> else but her, and prostrates before the god Sango, and before those possessed
> [with the spirit of] the deity, calling them father.[35]

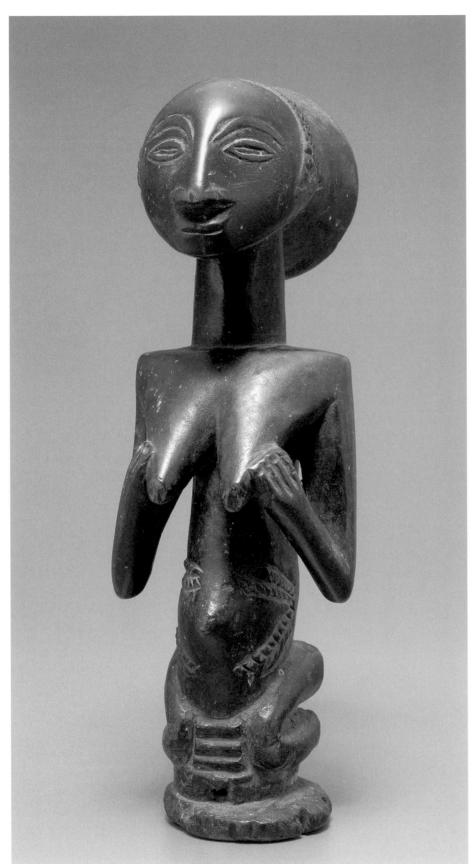

Pl. 19
Kneeling figure
Luba, Democratic Republic of the Congo
19th–20th century
Wood
H. 30.9 cm (12¼ in.)
Gift of Katherine White and the Boeing Company,
81.17.871

Pl. 20
Female figure *(olumeye)*
Yoruba, Nigeria
19th–20th century
Wood
H. 33.8 cm (14 in.)
Gift of Katherine White and the Boeing Company,
81.17.604

Pl. 21
Female figure with bowl for Sango
Yoruba, Nigeria
19th–20th century
Wood
H. 42.6 cm (16¾ in.)
Gift of Katherine White and the Boeing Company,
81.17.595

There is, moreover, a special manifestation of kneeling position that emerges in the Yoruba funeral ceremony known as *ikunle* (literally "the kneeling"). In this vigil members of a recently departed person's family were supposed to spend an entire evening on their knees.

Such exercises, in the greater black Atlantic world, become ritual ordeals or tests of commitment. I remember the night in August 1988 when I was initiated into Palo Mayombe, the strongly Kongo-influenced traditional religion of black Cuba. A young black fellow initiate and I were kept on our knees in an anteroom for more than an hour before being led into the shrine. The pain, after a while, for me at least, became severe. This was a passage of the initiation known as *penitencia* (penance). A priest explained the challenge inscribed within the kneeling: *ponte duro,* roughly, "hang tough"; that is, show you can endure discomfort, if you wish to be one of us. There were other tests that night, all in the kneeling position. At one point a heavy iron kettle with a load of sacred medicine was lowered onto my head while I was blindfolded, kneeling at the altar. As the great weight pressed against my skull, a priest standing somewhere near kept whispering "Aguantalo, Roberto, aguantalo" (Take it, Bob, take it), by way of encouragement.

So important is resting upon one's knees, or bowing low, as a sign of fully respecting the moral imperatives of Earth in Yoruba Ogboni ritual, that the doors in Ogboni shrine architecture are deliberately dwarfed. Everyone who enters is forced to bow to the spirits. A colleague reminds us that the roof to the Dogon *toguna,* or male meeting house, is similarly designed deliberately low, leveling everyone, keeping them seated and bent over. This is done so that "no one can stand up in anger." Saturating the field of African sculpture, kneeling icons are almost always idealized. The face is impassive. The limbs are strong but calmly disposed. Such icons not only impart to a shrine an aura of respect but, in the region of Djenne, Mali, indicate to the postulant what gestures to adopt within the shrine.

Turning to the Luba, we find the motif of the kneeling woman once again a sign of social allegiance and respect. The kneeling woman as icon among the Luba expresses moral rightness deepened with a timeless certainty. Consider as illustration a kneeling figure of a Luba woman with formal coiffure, holding both her breasts (pl. 19). From this stabilizing gesture of respect emerge powerful breasts and shoulders, quietude of mien, and crowning coiffure. Hauteur blends with reverence.

In further kneeling figures (pls. 20–24), we strongly sense how kneeling remains an icon of respect, a test of endurance, and above all, a seal of commitment to the way of the ancestors. To rest on one's knees is to voice with the body a prayerful ideal: every perfect gift is from above.

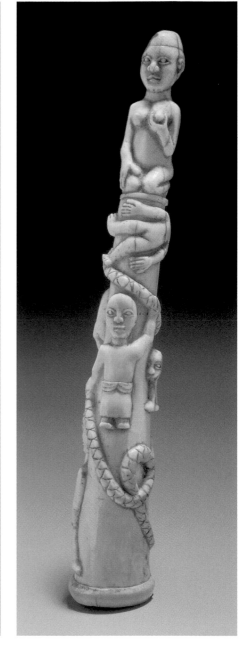

Pl. 22
Thunder god dance wand *(ose sango)*
Yoruba, Nigeria
19th–20th century
Wood
H. 50.5 cm (19⅞ in.)
Eugene Fuller Memorial Collection, 67.91

Pl. 23
Divination tapper *(iroke ifa)*
Yoruba, Nigeria
19th–20th century
Ivory
H. 39.3 cm (15½ in.)
Nasli and Alice Heermaneck Collection, 68.26

Pl. 24
Tusk with relief carving
Loango coast, Kongo, Democratic Republic of the Congo
and Angola
19th–20th century
Ivory
H. 15.6 cm (6⅛ in.)
Gift of Katherine White and the Boeing Company,
81.17.832

Supporting

"Supporting" refers to carrying an object balanced on the head, steadied by both hands. The term also includes carrying a person on the shoulders or upon the back. Balancing requires more poise, for in this case the object rests upon the head of the person without the use of the hands. Supporting is often manifested in African statuary with a cold impassive stare, the seal of nonchalance or "cool." The canon of supporting bears various meanings according to place and culture. Different vernacular observers will see slightly different things even in a single piece of sculpture. Thus three Africans, from widely separated civilizations, were asked to comment on a double caryatid Luba-Songye stool for a leader (pl. 25):

> Ejagham (Nigeria and Cameroon): "They seem to carry something for an important person. The way they carry it is beautiful. They hold it with both hands. The load can never fall."
> Banyang (Cameroon): "This is a heavy load which cannot be carried without both hands, to reduce the weight."
> Suku (Democratic Republic of the Congo): "Our ancestors carried things like that. This pleases me because I have seen my own mother carry things like that, with both hands, taking care that the water in the vessel did not spill."[36]

These views from the inside are instructive, reminding us that weight and delicacy are involved in transporting and that there can be beauty to its unfolding, a beauty that ultimately resonates to the time of the ancestors. Africans also read into the theme of the person supporting a load with both hands upon his head a kind of stop-time rendering of the motion of the body traveling from one point to the next. This is not unlike the ancient Greek interpretation of the caryatid figures of the Erechthem on the Acropolis in Athens: processioneers, maidens who carried sacred objects in the Panathenaic celebration. Supporting is not only drenched with visions of the arrest of important motion but also displays, once again, the idealized flexibility of the human frame. Across tropical Africa women absorb the undulations of the earth in their springlike hips and knees to maintain the absolute stillness of their heads. In addition, the ability to rise with a heavy load on the head is yet another manifestation of the beauty that comes from the stronger power of the youth:

> Let us bend down to work
> We're only young once
> Old age will arrive
> Then when we place a burden on our heads
> We'll find that we cannot manage.
> It is muscular vitality that marks the youth.[37]

But supporting is not just athleticism. It can be a metaphor for responsibility and mind. In the Cameroon Grassfields we witness artistic phrasing of the mystic support of the king by his leopard counterpart in many forms of royal seating. Here the support is figurative and playful, not literal, for we are dealing with thrones that

Pl. 25
Stool
Luba-Songye, Democratic Republic of the Congo
19th–20th century
Wood, metal, pigment, glass
H. 50.6 cm (20 in.)
Gift of Katherine White and the Boeing Company,
81.17.907

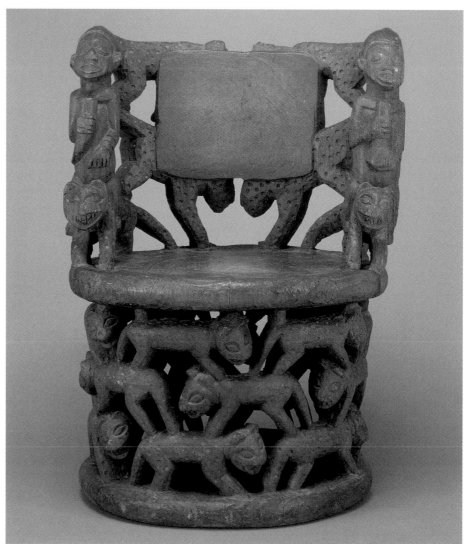

Pl. 26
Stool
Babanki, Bamenda, Cameroon
19th–20th century
Wood
H. 30 cm (11⅞ in.)
Gift of Katherine White and the Boeing Company,
81.17.723

Pl. 27
Throne
Kom-Tikar area, Cameroon
19th–20th century
Wood
H. 82.6 cm (32½ in.)
Gift of Katherine White and the Boeing Company,
81.17.722

rest on the backs of moving royal leopards. How is this virtually pan-African icon of royalty locally nuanced in Cameroon? Among the chiefs of one western Grassfields culture, every leader of consequence is believed to be backed by a secret leopard counterpart. If the ruler dances brilliantly, with striking strength and grace, Bangwa people may say, "Oh ho, he takes his leopard out to dance!" Across the Grassfields and into the Cross River region the leopard connotes daring, physical prowess, impressive running, fighting or dancing. The crosscuts between the impressive athlete-ruler and the power of the leopard are quick and charming in a Babanki stool that is held up by the head of a human and, more playfully, by the ears of a dashing leopard (pl. 26).

Metaphorically resting the body of a seated king on the backs of moving leopards, themselves swarming playfully with their telltale spots, makes the seated king seem protected by countless numbers of the royal denizens of the forest (pl. 27). This is sculptural support by allusion to circles of mystic assistance. Flanking kings on leopardback, royal horns held in right hand, restate the resting of the king on untold reserves of mystic power (pl. 28).

A moving manifestation of literal and spiritual support is a figurated stool that once belonged to a Mambila patriarch in Cameroon (pl. 29). When women experienced difficulty in childbirth, they were brought to this stool and told to sit upon it

Pl. 28
Throne
Kom-Tikar area, Cameroon
19th–20th century
Wood
H. 92.7 cm (36½ in.)
Gift of Katherine White and the Boeing Company,
81.17.721

African Art in Motion   51

Pl. 29
Stool
Mambila, Cameroon
19th–20th century
Wood
L. 46.2 cm (18¼ in.)
Gift of Katherine White and the Boeing Company,
81.17.724

Pl. 30
Farming-animal crest mask *(tyi wara)*
Bamana, Mali
19th century
Wood, brass, wool
H. 87.6 cm (34½ in.)
Gift of Katherine White and the Boeing Company, 81.17.23

Pl. 31
Staff
Akye, Côte d'Ivoire
19th–20th century
Wood
H. 93.9 cm (37 in.)
Gift of Katherine White and the Boeing Company,
81.17.235

and confess whatever sins they might have committed. The release of tension after admission of guilt by this belief unlocks a difficult delivery.[38] When the woman in labor confesses and tells exactly what she has done, figurations on the stool support, in witnessing her action, the healing efficacy of the truth. Two figures, meanwhile—male and female—on one side of the stool physically support the person seated with upraised arms.

The carrying of weight and responsibility blends with the spirit in numerous gems of sculpture. A baby antelope carried on the body of its mother automatically identifies the female of a pair of Tyi Wara maskers among the Bamana (pl. 30). Whereas the victorious shouldering of a chief on the shoulders of a retainer on an Akye "linguist's staff" is nuanced by gestures to the heart and stomach—to inward sources of nobility of mind (pl. 31).

We close among masters of the theme of allegorical support, the Luba. Joseph Cornet compares Luba to Baule art in shared nobility and calm, with "no exaggerated attitude or awkward gestures break[ing] the inner serenity of the faces of the ancestor statues."[39] It is certainly true that the Baule chieftain being carried in triumph on the shoulders of his follower, the follower himself, and the Luba woman supporting a bowl become advocates for submission of self to authority (pl. 32). The Luba caryatid theme can be placed in perspective of time with a number of documents. An engraving from the end of the last century shows the king of the Luba seated on a large, handsomely carved caryatid stool while at the same time resting his feet on

Fig. 8. "Queen Djinga Bandi Sitting before Portuguese Governor," from Giovanni Antonio Cavazzi, *Istorica descrizione de tre regni, Congo, Matamba e Angola* (Bologna, 1687), British Library, London.

the thigh of his wife, thus supported by both statuary and a living person. Availing ourselves of the rich cultural cognation of the Bantu area, one can adduce an even earlier illustration of the living caryatid, dated 1687.[40] I refer to an illustration of Queen Djinga Bandi, received by the Portuguese governor of Angola (fig. 8). She rests upon the body of a follower, who serves as a living caryatid. Granting strength and meaning to the icon of support is the abiding presence of the spirit. Speaking of the Luba, but with insight of far wider application, Jack Flam, novelist and art historian, made this point forever clear:

> The effortless grace with which [the Luba images] carry their burden, the serenity of their countenance (so close to other Luba ancestor figures) and the hierarchy of importance in their body parts, all infer that the caryatid image is meant to be interpreted as a spiritual representation.[41]

Pl. 32
Figure supporting bowl
Luba, Democratic Republic of the Congo
19th–20th century
Wood
H. 49.5 cm (19½ in.)
Gift of Katherine White and the Boeing Company,
81.17.875

Balancing

> **Pride resides in having the load rest easily on the head with an insouciant countenance that reveals no sign of pressure or strain, [while walking] smoothly with the arms swinging free.**
>
> —Sylvia Boone, 1986[42]

To move in utter confidence with an object balanced on the head is one of the accomplishments of traditional Africa. On my first trip to tropical Africa in 1961, I was amazed to see a young man bring sheets and pillowcases balanced on his head into a resthouse room. That summer I observed schoolchildren carrying ink and writing paper casually stashed atop their heads. I saw how balancing was a gift cultivated early in childhood and onward as part of the arsenal of African bodily grace into maturity.

Children in Benin master this talent as they learn to play games:

> *Adigba,* "woman with the burden," is a game played by all small [Beninois]. The children fix twelve wooden sticks in a pile of sand. Then each child, by turns, carries on his knees, with his hands tied behind his back, a cushion balanced on his head, for a distance of about twelve meters....
>
> As he approaches the area where sticks are, he is supposed to pick them up with his lips, never allowing the pillow on his head to fall. The game is very difficult, ventured only by children adept in carrying things on their heads.[43]

This is a beginning level of the skill. The highest levels refer to transcendental equilibrium, ultimately enabling a person to communicate mind itself by the quality of his composure and the importance of the object balanced on his head (pl. 33). Transporting objects on the head without using one's hands occurs with formalized repetitiveness in the sculpture of Africa. There is every reason therefore to sense iconic import.

As to the mystical dimensions involved, one might start off by mentioning that at Akan funerals women sometimes dance with a vessel filled with water balanced on their heads. If the vessel should fall, it is a sign that death was brought by witchcraft. In the same portion of West Africa, priests (*okomfo*) may dance with a shrine—a vessel filled with blessed substances—balanced upon their heads. The association of mind and balance is hinted at in the invocation by which they gloss this act: "Oh tree ... we are calling on you that we place in this shrine the thoughts that are in our head."[44] The spiritual head, filled with fluid and symbolic objects, goes over the literal head. Mind emerges triumphantly redoubled.

Equally dramatic extensions of balancing objects on the head of a moving person occur in the worship of the *orisha,* the deities of the Yoruba people. Just as kneeling can become an ordeal, so transporting on the head without using hands becomes a test of spiritual training and aliveness. Followers of the thunder god, Sango, both in Nigerian Yorubaland and in certain Yoruba-oriented compounds in Bahia in Brazil, must dance upon initiation with a living flame balanced in a vessel on their heads. This logically leads into sculptural renderings of the balancing of the fiery

Pl. 33
Tobacco mortar
Chokwe, Angola
19th–20th century
Wood, brass, beads, string
H. 21.6 cm (8½ in.)
Gift of Katherine White and the Boeing Company,
81.17.913

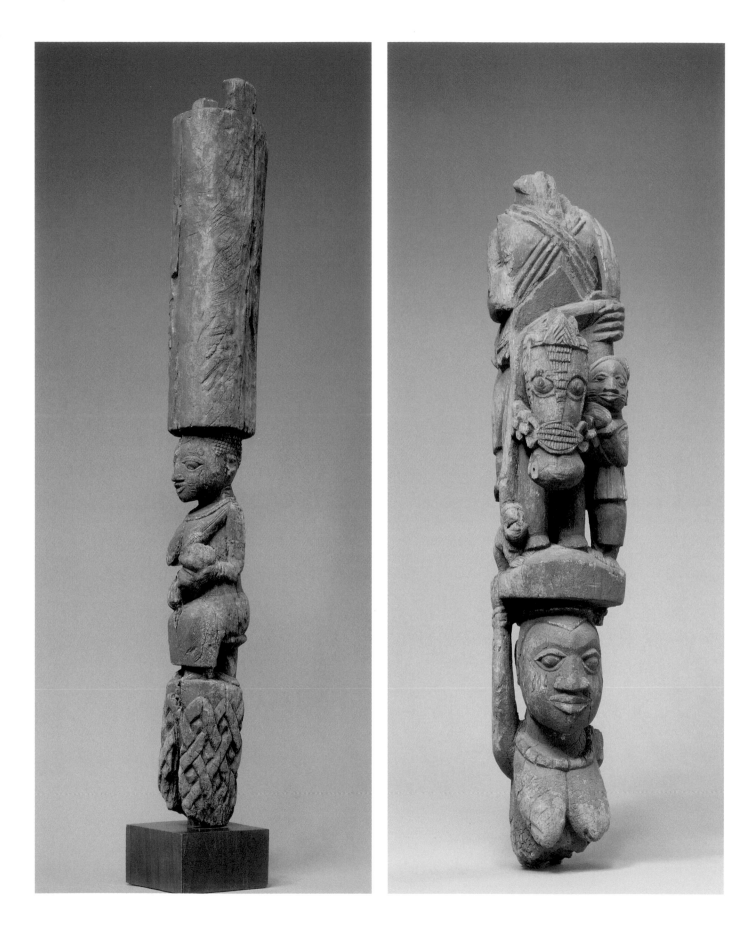

meteorites or thunderstones of Sango (*edun ara*) upon the brow or head of the devotee. The act of balancing puns on architectural support in the traditional Yoruba mind. This leads us to accomplished examples of figurated columns. Witness a carved housepost (*opo fie*) from Efon-Alaiye (pl. 34). It boasts a richly textured base, is covered with interlace, and a central portion depicts a seated wife of an important man (*iyawo oloye*), identified by the double strand of beads about her neck. A strong shaft of wood rests impressively upon her head. This is a senior woman who supports her compound with inherent goodness.

Another column enters into the realm of balancing (pl. 35). It is again from that splendid epicenter of style and grace in Yoruba carving, Efon-Alaiye. A woman with the specially lidded Efon eye supports with her head none other than a fully caparisoned warrior-chief with follower (now sadly reduced to a fragment). Because this striking column comes from Efon-Alaiye, where I did considerable fieldwork, I am able to match this piece to its meaning:

> The mounted figure represents a warrior who fought the enemies of Efon-Alaiye at the time of the Kiriji War [in 1880]. Under him [appears] his wife. This woman was brave too. When her husband went to war, she would be somewhere else, working magic to save him and bring him back alive.[45]

She keeps a world intact. The ruler of Agogo sleeps over his sword, so that his head is always supported by the throne. The legitimacy provided by the sword is here provided by the woman. This is iconic balancing. It is brought to a point of dramatized equilibrium. Yeats himself could be describing this woman who supported her husband and the world that they shared:

> Her eyes
> Gazed upon all things known, all things unknown
> In triumph of intellect
> With motionless head held erect.[46]

Pl. 34
Housepost *(opo)*
Efon-Alaiye, Nigeria
19th–20th century
Wood
H. 110 cm (43⅜ in.)
Gift of Katherine White and the Boeing Company,
81.17.625

Pl. 35
Housepost *(opo)*
Efon-Alaiye, Nigeria
19th–20th century
Wood
H. 56.5 cm (22¼ in.)
Gift of Katherine White and the Boeing Company,
81.17.624

Notes

1. Richard Wright, *Black Power: A Record of Reactions in a Land of Pathos* (New York: Harper, 1954).

2. The late Araba Eko, Isale-Eko, Lagos, Nigeria, January 1972. It is believed that the gods established the correct manner of formal presentation in standing, sitting, and other activities. See G. Gosselin, "Pour une anthropologie du travail rural en Afrique noire," *CEA* 12 (1963), 521. Proper decorum in work gestures are sanctioned in West Africa frequently by reference to tradition and to the world of the sacred: "One thinks specially of the repetition of archetypal gestures mentioned in origin myths."

3. Alade Benhoufewe, Cotonou, Benin, June 4, 1973; Ako Nsemayu, Mamfe, Cameroon, June 8, 1973; Piluka Ladi, Kinshasa, Democratic Republic of the Congo, June 13, 1973.

4. *The American Heritage Dictionary,* 85, 554, 1256.

5. Marcel Griaule, *Folk Art of Black Africa* (New York: Tudor, 1950), 100.

6. Alade Banhoufewe, Cotonou, June 4, 1973; Ako Nsemayu, Mamfe, June 8, 1973; Piluka Ladi, Kinshasa, June 13, 1973.

7. Bruce Glaser, *Minimal Art: A Critical Anthology* (New York: E. P. Dutton, 1964), 155.

8. Kofi Antubam, *Ghana's Heritage of Culture* (Leipzig: Koehler and Amelang, 1963), 71.

9. Harris Memel-Fote, "The Perception of Beauty in Negro-African Culture," *Colloquium on Negro Art* (Paris: Presence Africain, 1968), 58.

10. Araba Eko, Lagos, January 1972.

11. Ibid.

12. F. J. J. Buytendijk, *Attitudes et mouvements* (Bruges: Desclee de Brouwer, 1957), 125.

13. Dejo Afolayan, Nigeria, 1988.

14. Ibid.

15. George Tabmen, Monrovia, Liberia, March 25, 1967.

16. Peter Sarpong, *The Sacred Stools of the Akan* (Accra: Ghana Publishing, 1971), 8.

17. Hugh Goldie, *Dictionary of the Efik Language* (Ridgewood, N.J.: The Gregg Press, 1964), 290.

18. "*Atenase:* The Manner of Sitting," in Antubam, *Ghana's Heritage of Culture,* 114.

19. Ibid.

20. Susan Vogel, "Yoruba and Baoule Art Criticism," unpublished paper, 1971, 5. Vogel cites Pierre Etienne, "Les Baoule et le temps," *Cahiers Orstom ser. sciences humaines* (Abidjan, Côte d'Ivoire), nos. 3, 5 (1968), 1–37. Etienne finds that Baule expend unusual time, labor, and money on bathing and rank this pleasure high among the good things of life.

21. Eva Meyerowitz, *The Akan of Ghana* (London: Faber and Faber, 1958), 31. In addition, Thomas Akyea, on behalf of the Agogohene, added the following information about the queen mother during fieldwork at Agogo, Ghana, on May 19, 1969: "The queen mother is either the sister, niece, or even mother of the king. She is a member of the court panel, and without her presence the court is not full. Any pronouncement or judgment given without her confirmation will not be binding. In her absence no authority can enstool a chief."

22. Henry Drewal, John Pemberton, and Roland Abiodun, *Yoruba: Nine Countries of African Art and Thought* (New York: Harry N. Abrams, 1989), 33.

23. James W. Fernandez, *Fang Architectories* (Philadelphia: Institute for the Study of Human Issues, 1977).

24. Djibril T. Niane, *Sundiata: An Epic of Old Mali* (London: Longman, 1965).

25. Ako Nsemayu, Mamfe, June 8, 1973.

26. From Babatunde Lawal, *Yoruba Sango Sculpture in Historical Retrospect* (Ann Arbor, Mich.: University Microfilms, 1971), 113.

27. Jochen Kohler, "Das Pferd in den Gur-sprachen," *Africa und Ubersee* 37 (1953–54), cited in Jack Goody, *Technology, Tradition and the State in Africa* (London: Oxford University Press, 1971), 71.

28. Alade Banhoufewe, Cotonou, June 4, 1973.

29. Marcel Griaule and Germaine Dieterlen, *Le Renard pâle* (Paris: Institut d'Ethnologie, 1965), 455–56.

30. Robert Smith, "Yoruba Armament," *Journal of African History* 8, no. 1 (1967), 88.

31. G. B. Ramusio, *Navigazione e viaggi* (1550), quoted by Thomas Hodgkin (1960), in *Nigerian Perspectives: An Historical Anthology,* 2nd ed. (London: Oxford University Press, 1975), 127.

32. Celine Baduel-Mathon, "Le Langage gestuel en Afrique occidentale: Recherches bibliographiques," *Journal de la société des africanists* 41, no. 2 (1971), 207, 209, 212, 213, 217, 218.

33. Human Relations Area File: Dieterlen, 118 E-5 (1946–49), FA8, Bambara; Dieterlen, 101 E-5 (1946–49, 1951).

34. E. A. Ajisafe Moore, *The Laws and Customs of the Yoruba People* (Abeokuta, Nigeria: Fola Bookshops), 7.

35. Samuel Johnson, *The History of the Yorubas* (Lagos, Nigeria: CMS Bookshops, 1921), 11.

36. Ako Nsemayu, Mamfe; Chief Defang, Cameroon; and Piluka Ladi, Kinshasa, June 1973.

37. Kwabena Nketia, "Yoruba Musicians in Accra," *Odu,* no. 6 (June 1958), 40, retranslation by author.

38. Gilbert Schneider, correspondence with author, Katherine White Archives, Seattle Art Museum.

39. Joseph Cornet, *Art of Africa* (London: Phaidon, 1971), 192.

40. Jack Flam, "The Symbolic Structure of Baluba Caryatid Stools," *African Arts* 4, no. 2 (winter 1971), 56.

41. Ibid., 57.

42. Sylvia Boone, *Radiance from the Waters* (New Haven, Conn.: Yale University Press, 1986), 126.

43. Charles Béart, *Jeux et jouets de l'ouest africain,* vol. 1 (Dakar, Senegal: IFAN, 1955), 264, "Equilibres avec object sur la tête," translation by author.

44. R. S. Rattray, *Ashanti* (Oxford: Clarendon Press, 1923), 148.

45. Iloro, December 21, 1963.

46. *The Collected Poems of W. B. Yeats* (New York: Macmillan, 1952), 168.

Pamela McClusky

Case Histories

Art Steps from Africa to America

Heroes Go Solitary Walking: Hunters' Shirts

Salif Keita is about to perform in a crowded club in Vancouver, B.C. When his orchestra takes over, a precise complexity fills the air, mixing music from too many sources to identify at once. A spotlight is set on center stage. Someone rushes in and out of it, unleashing a sense of disquiet. Eyes strain through the smoke to sort out the vision. It's Salif Keita, swirling along an unpredictable path. When he does stop to allow his voice to explode, his agitated appearance comes into focus. He wears a bristling shirt and hat, activating a work of art with all the force it implies. No longer immobilized as it is in the museum, captive in a Plexiglas case, the shirt is where it once belonged. On stage, Salif Keita is showing what it's like to come from a line of epic tradition going back eight hundred years. Confidently overcoming the restraints of a largely foreign audience, he sings songs loaded with references from his past. The audience begin to wave their hands gently above their heads in a manner African friends have dubbed "kelp dancing." I wonder how many in the crowd are simply enjoying an unusual albino performer with a tight band, just as I wonder how many museum visitors see the shirt on display as a perplexing oddity. The audience sways while Salif Keita shudders, again and again, sending his shirt into turmoil.

A hunter's shirt visually defies its place in an art museum (pl. 36). Wild boar tusks, antelope horns, wads of dried mud, rusty stains, and bulging packets of leather bring a shadowy dose of forest ingredients into view. Such murky wilderness entered the art museum in stages. First, the shirts were featured in a major exhibition that introduced them as visual feasts but didn't say much about who originally wore them. Soon thereafter, studies began to reveal the original owners as members of a culture whose tenets will not fit into the usual classifications. The shirts brought into focus the strength of Mande people, who share "a space, in some way perhaps a time, and for many, an idea."[1] Among the lessons the shirts have unveiled are the Mande definition of heroes and their unique way of handling knowledge and discussing sorcery.

Pl. 36
Hunter's vest
Maninka, Guinea-Conakry
20th century
Cloth (strip weave), horns *(safele)*, cotton twine *(tafow)*, leather, amulets *(basi)*
L. 80 cm (31½ in.)
Gift of Katherine White and the Boeing Company, 81.17.70

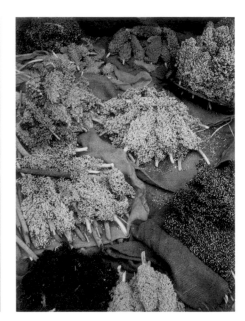

Fig. 9. Left to right: Goats, meal preparation, market ingredients, Burkina Faso, 1969.

It was a greasy, aromatic mass of power.   —Katherine White, 1970

In 1969, Katherine White was made chairwoman of the African Subcommittee of the Museum of Modern Art in New York. She took it upon herself to convince the museum to host an exhibition about African design and collaborated with Roy Sieber, a professor who ably filled the role of curator. She relished being the catalyst: "I bought every juicy thing I could find to push them over the hump and get the enthusiasm going." She undertook a field trip to collect ammunition for her meetings at the museum. During her travels in Burkina Faso, she searched "for cloths among the cabbages, millet heads, woven mats, dainty Arab horses, agile steers with towering horns, sheep painted with blue stripes and magenta dots, even the side show of a python coiling himself around a tiny desert deer" (fig. 9). On the same trip, she traveled to Ghana and found an old man selling "a war dress, a dull strip-weave tunic cluttered with leather sewn amulets containing passages from the Koran, magic leopard's teeth, bells, a string heart, and shriveled sheep's vitals. The chicken blood had blackened stiff the chest and back. It was a greasy, aromatic mass of power. They say, dressed in such, a Ghanaian can face a machine gun in total safety."[1]

Upon her return, White packed a suitcase and went to the Modern. She showed slides and passed around samples of what might be in an exhibit. "I let them handle my enormous paper thin Pheul earrings, 5½ ounces of hammered red-gold elegance, each one packaged African fashion in a brown-and-white man's handkerchief. I showed them a huge Cameroon wall hanging sew-dyed with chameleons, houses, and water patterns.... They lifted an anklet weighing 16 pounds, thick with ornaments, and their hands turned blue from the black bronzy indigo of Nigerian batik. They liked what they saw. The show was on."[2]

In dividing the labor required to mount an exhibition and publish a catalogue, the organizers asked White to survey collections. Throwing herself into a year of documentation, she covered "twenty major institutions, thirty-eight private collections, traveled fifty thousand miles and collected two thousand photographs." She photographed "aprons of porcupine quills from the Pygmies, engraved ostrich-eggshell bottles, and huge three-foot-around feather headdresses from the Cameroons. Necklaces of deer hooves, iridescent beetle wings, human teeth, bird bones, glass and tortoiseshell, anklets of huge flat brass sun discs, and fighting rings from Uganda."[3] She was especially attuned to emphasizing a range of media that would stand out in a museum like the Modern.[4]

A lovely sock in the teeth.   —John Canaday, 1972

African Textiles and Decorative Arts opened in fall 1972, following *Italian Design*. The two exhibitions exposed a stark contrast in what could be considered modern art. *Italian Design* featured specially designed rooms for living as well as objects for daily use such as furniture, ashtrays, and appliances. The curators attempted to bring together the broadest spectrum of divergent Italian design, but Robert Jenson in his review for *Artforum* pointed out one unifying element: "Plastic is the universal favorite of the Italian designers." He quoted one Italian designer who maintained that the material "allows an almost complete process of deconditioning from the interminable chain of psychoerotic self-indulgences about 'possession.'" Jenson followed, "He is right; plastic triggers few associations within us. It has no history and a malleable future.... The designers have created the furniture of an almost perfect human alienation and despair, designed for the forces controlling man, rather than the other way around." He ended by calling the designers "assassins of the human spirit."[5]

On the first floor of the museum, *African Textiles and Decorative Arts* displayed 240 objects to present a broad spectrum of African design. The galleries were darkened, music played, and a *New York Times* reporter wrote of a mixed feeling of well-being issuing from the exhibition, or "a lovely sock in the teeth."[6] In the gallery installations by Arthur Drexler, head of the Design Department (fig. 10), visitors were led down meandering ramps from which floating textiles were suspended just out of reach. Jewelry, hats, combs, and skirts were housed in circling tubes that sent the eye moving in curves. Very little plastic appeared, but a multitude of other media were evident. Occupying an alcove, shirts were beacons of visual ferocity—sprouting projectiles and strips of hide, saturated in smoky colors, stained with sweat and caked with soil, never washed with soap. One can only ask: who would wear such a shirt with pride?

Fig. 10. Installation view from the exhibition *African Textiles and Decorative Arts,* The Museum of Modern Art, New York, 1973.

Fig. 11. Elder hunters at a burial ceremony for a hunter, Kankalaba, Burkina Faso, 1997.

Ah, savage and solitary beast, we cannot finish praising you.

—Bamana salute

Just as the protrusions of the shirt keep people at bay, so the hunter broadcasts an approach to life that sets him apart. Mande explanations of human character distinguish between people who have the tendency to rebel and those who do not. Rebellious people are said to have ample *fadenya,* or "father-childness," with a need to strike out and transform the rules of society. Other people are said to be filled with *badenlu,* "mother-childness," which results in living as quiet, reliable citizens who put the group's needs before their own. Hunters are among the most willful, self-directed, and heedless of social orders. Hunters, warriors, leaders, and sorcerers are said to be like ferocious animals, an impression the hunters' shirts reinforce.

A hunter never gets his fill of solitary walking.

—Seydou Camara, 1976[7]

A hunter walks into a forest wearing a shirt of two distinctive colors: a lighter brown that blends into the early dry season when leaves are falling, and a darker brown for a later season when more earth is exposed. He gets the color from tree barks, and recites incantations as the shirt steeps in dye. The shirt is never washed, but absorbs wood smoke, sweat, soil, and stains, making it better able to hide a human's scent from the hunted prey. As the hunter sets out, the shirt helps him blend into the environment and shields him like protective armor. Active hunters are not the only men to wear such shirts—hunters' bards, warriors, and sorcerers also don them. Shirts loaded with added elements are not worn every day (or when hunting), but are put on when hunters assemble to accept new members into their association, join community celebrations, or attend funerals (fig. 11). A description of such a funeral, or "death diversion," for a fellow hunter takes us closer to the original "gallery" in which a hunter's shirt would be seen. Filling the air of the deceased's compound, a praise singer plays his lute and sings in salute to the gathering hunters. By evening, the hunters settle into seven days of frenetic activity—they sing, dance, and drink, fire muskets, and blow whistles. The noises and songs scare off the spirits of the animals the hunters have killed over the years. Dancers encircle the hunter's widow to assure her of their protection. Late at night, long after other mourners have gone home to rest, a praise singer might begin. Depending on his skill and knowledge, the singer could deliver a one- or two-hour partial recitation of an epic or take two or three nights to deliver a fuller rendition. Songs praise the qualities of the deceased and recall the feats of great hunters throughout history. The mourning hunters will occasionally challenge each other to create extraordinary sights. One might strike the ground with his gun and cause water to flow. Another will swallow flames. As the all-night ceremony wears on, a mourner may boast that he is ready to stick knives into his cheeks, or remove his eyeballs. Audacious behavior goes with the attire. What culture pays tribute to this agent of disequilibrium?

> Give me a skull, man, I have no face-washing-pot,
> Give me a hide, I lack a covering cloth,
> He gave me huge intestines for I had no sleeping cloth,
> He gave me some blood for face-washing-water,
> He gave me small intestines as the belt for my waist.
> Put the big tail in front of me as a room-sweeping brush,
> Give me a leg bone to use as a toothpick,
> Famori, the hunter is coming.
>
> —Seydou Camara, 1977[8]

These two shirts (pls. 36, 37) are under the influence of a culture that resists classification. At the end of the twentieth century, Mande is known as a space, a time, and an idea. In spatial terms, Mande-speaking people are found in regions of West Africa reaching from the headwaters of the Niger River to a heartland in Mali, including sections of Gambia, Guinea-Conakry, Guinea-Bissau, Liberia, Sierra Leone, Senegal, Mali, Burkina Faso, Mauritania, and Côte d'Ivoire. The Mande were galvanized during the era of Sundiata Keita, who founded the Malian empire in 1235 and ruled it until 1255. His praises are continually recited in *The Epic of Sundiata*, perhaps Africa's best known heroic saga.

> Mande may stumble but it will never fall down.
>
> —Cheick Mahamadou Cherif Keita, 1995[9]

The legendary Lion King and founder of the Malian empire, Sundiata is credited with initiating behavior to which Mande people remain loyal. His life story is recounted again and again in many versions of an epic that evolved over hundreds of years. It is recited by musicians, who entertain but also act as historians and confidential advisers to leaders. Along with Sundiata's, other poems and songs specifically created for hunters make up a rich oral culture. Despite the towering influence of this oral tradition, Western scholars were slow to recognize its significance. The Sundiata epic was transferred to written form in the eighteenth and nineteenth centuries; then

colonial writers tended to treat the saga as a source of history, editing out the mythic and supernatural details. When recitations were recorded and transcribed anew in the 1960s, awareness widened. Since then, a wave of studies devoted to Mande sculptors, blacksmiths, musicians, textiles, and epics has emerged. These studies continue to reveal the nature of the ideal Mande hero.

> **The hero is the agent of disequilibrium.**
>
> —Charles Bird and Martha Kendall, 1980[10]

Sundiata Keita defines Mande heroism. An extremely shortened episode from the epic reveals only partly the character of his heroism. Often related in a song called "Simbon," it tells how Sundiata is hexed at birth and remains a cripple, crawling like a reptile until the age of seven. Responding to his mother's despair, he asks for an iron staff that has been forged seven times, and tries to lift himself up. When the strong iron staff bends under his weight, he asks his mother to fetch a branch of a custard apple tree. He struggles to his feet and stands for the first time. Now filled with astonishing strength, he uproots an entire baobob tree with his bare hands and lays it at his mother's feet in tribute. He makes the bent staff into a bow, with which he hunts buffalo and elephants. For the rest of his life, Sundiata stands tall against every obstacle. He gains a reputation as an unequaled hunter, a king among kings, and the lion who possesses all the secrets of the wilderness.

Many nuances lace his sudden transformation from crawling boy to towering hunter. He combines the iron rod and the tree, symbolizing how man-made technology and natural powers must be fused to find strength.[11] After suffering from years of ridicule as a cripple, he rises up to confront his detractors and restore the honor of the deprived. Sundiata masters his difficulties to become the vehicle of collective will. In some situations, he triumphs by wielding medicines to dissolve adversity; in others, he is a ruthless rebel, or "adversity's-true-place."[12] In a gesture recalling Sundiata's initial frailty, the Mande greet a hunter by embracing his legs. Sundiata's legend doesn't dwell so much on his physical prowess as on his ability to overcome enemies with wisdom.

> **Wisdom dictates amassing as much information about the natural environment as possible.** —Sedou Traore, 1988[13]

Creatures contribute tusks and claws (detail, pl. 36) to a shirt that speaks of a life largely spent in their wilderness, away from people. Hunters become acquainted with the habits of animals and reptiles after spending days, weeks, and months in their company. They learn to recognize ecological zones; use leaves, roots, and barks of plants; and discern the properties of bones, claws, skins, and organs of animals. More than one hundred years ago, the Manden plateau was home to wild boar, baboons, lions, anteaters, roan antelope, hartebeest, bushback, leopards, hippopotami, buffalo, elephants, giant eland, and giraffes. Each creature had to be tracked and treated differently. A delicately pointed horn that repeatedly stands out on one shirt came from the duiker antelope, called *sineri*. Prized as prey, the duiker lives in the forest but wanders alone onto farm plots to graze. Wary and shy, it can be coaxed

Pl. 37

Hunter's shirt *(donso duloki)*
Mande, Bamana, Mali
20th century
Cloth (strip weave), teeth, horns, leather, tin, amulets *(basi)*
L. 130.8 cm (51½ in.)
Gift of Katherine White and the Boeing Company, 81.17.70

Pl. 36 (detail)

to stand still. Killing *sineri* requires preparation, caution, and subtle prowess. Buffalo horns on another shirt (detail, pl. 36) declare a different kind of hunting—tracking an animal known for its tendency to rampage and seek revenge.

Horns and teeth on shirts signal other hunter's skills as well (pl. 37). Inner cavities on both become chambers for storing medicines made of ingredients drawn from the forest. A hunter relies on medicines when confronting spirits who might attempt to sabotage his pursuit. Called *jinew*, wilderness spirits inhabit luxuriant pockets of the forest, and live in winds wafting over the savanna or in tall termite mounds. *Jinew* are not considered symbols of other worlds, but are members of this world to be reckoned with. When the hunter travels through their homeland, a spirit may contact him. Some are said to be insistent and adept at psychological torture. They must be engaged not just intellectually but through preparations called *daliluw*.

The best way to know yourself is through your *daliluw*.

—Mande proverb

To become successful, hunters master *jiridon*, or the "science of the trees." Their shirts catalogue the experience of searching for medicinal ingredients in the fertile

Pl. 37 (detail)

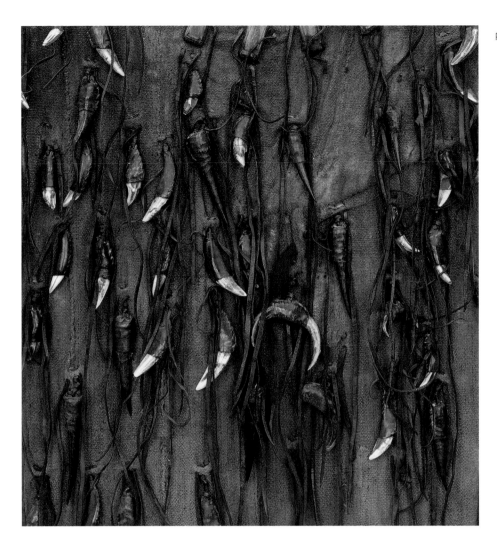

setting of the forest—finding plants, collecting venom from bees and snakes, and extracting tears from animals. *Jiridon* tells how to create medicines by combining parts of various living things. *Daliluw* are the recipes and techniques for mixing these elements. Many observe aspects of herbal chemistry, for example, pounding and boiling ingredients to produce a concentrated solution for curing fevers or bad breath. Other *daliluw* prescribe ritual preparations to activate or control energies said to animate the world. *Nyama*—an unpredictable energy of action—flows through all things and is ever present. *Nyama* can be helpful or hazardous, and hunters attempt to control it through their study of *daliluw*. They become known for their ability to prevent snakebites, cure stomachaches, and cause a person to fall in love.

> **The ashes of what was deadly do not fill an oribi's horn**
> **(the smallest things are often the deadliest).**
>
> —Seydou Camara, 1977[14]

A single amulet on a shirt can have a long process of creation. The tip of the horn (detail, pl. 37) of a bushback antelope is encased in leather. Such an amulet prompts many associations: first is that of the bushback itself, a small antelope with a large

concentration of *nyama.* This energy can manifest itself in fragile creatures of such delicacy and solitude. Clever and intelligent, the bushback is believed to have been specially blessed by the Prophet Mohammed so that on some moonless nights its horns light up and shine in the forest. Tracking and killing the bushback requires respectful ritual steps, as the animal releases a large amount of *nyama* upon death. Praises are then sung for the antelope to redirect its life force.

One example of a recipe for the contents of an amulet shows the complicated steps required by *jiridon.* Putting together a *nyi-ji* (tears) amulet calls for mixing the roots of seven specific plants dug from seven different footpaths with a flower from a baobob tree, a large blossom from a tobacco plant, the cane or staff of a blind man, fiber from a hibiscus plant used to wash a medicine pot, and the washcloth of a woman. All these ingredients are burnt to ashes and then placed in the horn's cavity. A stopper is pierced with an iron staff, and the blood of a white rooster is poured over it. If a hunter wishes to activate the amulet, he withdraws the staff from the horn and points the amulet at an animal. The power forces the animal's tear ducts to flow, obscuring its vision and setting the stage for the kill. Once the animal is slain, the hunter waters the iron staff with its tears.[15]

> **Amulets are, in short, prominent physical manifestations of Mande beliefs about the world's deep structures and the practical access that human beings have to them.** —Patrick McNaughton, 1988[16]

Bulging packets covered in leather are seen on shirts of the Mande and neighboring Asante (pl. 38). This form of amulet announces that a spiritual force has been harnessed and is at work. Most commonly a short prayer, verse from the Koran, or magic square is written on paper, folded, and packed inside the amulet. Blacksmiths and Muslim teachers (*mallam*) choose the inscription to be sealed in secrecy. The notion of writing as an act of recording words for others to consult openly is thereby reversed. Encased in leather, fur, or fiber, the amulet may also enclose the words and prayers uttered by the *mallam.* Asante chiefs and senior officials did not wear these shirts to hunt; instead, they wore them into battle as protection or during installations of leaders to announce that they were prepared for warfare.

> **Fa-Jigi had a magic powder called "wasp sting" in his armpit,**
> **And this powder became a wasp.**
> **If it stings you,**
> **You will run in place.**
> **Jigi had a magic powder called "to-make-unconscious,"**
> **And this was given to the white men.**
> **Eeh!**
> **Fa-Jigi brought a powder called "beware,"**
> **And this became a bee that made excellent honey.**
> **Eeh! . . .**
> **He brought sorcery with him,**
> **Sorcery for saving people.**
>
> —Seydou Camara, 1975[17]

PL. 38
War shirt *(batakari)*
Asante, Ghana
20th century
Cloth, leather, twine, cowry shells, amulets *(basi)*
L. 89 cm (35⅛ in.)
Gift of Katherine White and the Boeing Company,
81.17.454.1

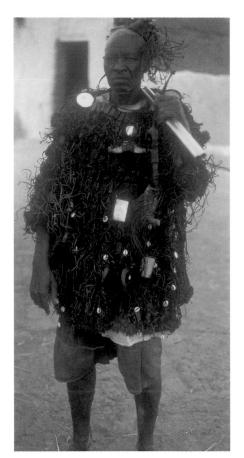

Fig. 12. Numu Tunkara wearing hunter's shirt, Fana, Mali, 1976.

Finding words to approximate Mande thinking is especially difficult when researchers approach the realm of the occult, sorcery, or magic. A fourteenth-century writer quoting an informant who lived in Mali for thirty-five years pointed out the prevalence of herbs for healing, making poisons, and settling disputes over sorcery.[18] European colonial accounts were read with distrust after later researchers discovered how Mande informants handle inquiries about sorcery. Public questioning violates the usual method of transmitting knowledge in restricted conversations. When outsiders delved into secret and potentially dangerous subjects, hunters launched terrifying descriptions of occult practices to intimidate and throw the strangers off track. As intensive studies of Mande art have evolved, researchers continue to caution readers about Mande perceptions of sorcery and the supernatural. Both are approached as neutral, common parts of the environment. To master their potential, and thereby become known as an accomplished sorcerer, is a desired goal.[19]

To be a man is to have many secrets.   —Bamana proverb

Hunters travel far to learn from the wilderness and from others like them. A serious hunter builds a repertoire of *daliluw* during his apprenticeship and his long journeys in search of new information. All of his life is dedicated to acquiring new knowledge, which is reflected in the depth of accumulations on his shirt (fig. 12). Each *daliluw* is the result of a careful, highly private encounter. Unlike the Western notion that knowledge is enhanced if made public, this knowledge is closely guarded. Often the hunter may hear an incantation for a *daliluw* only once and be expected to retain it. Memories of such instruction are stored like documents and recalled with extreme fidelity.

These dead heroes have done more for me than contemporary leaders.   —Banzumana Sissoko, 1979[20]

Epic performances and praise songs for hunters remind everyone of the need for heroic deeds. When hunters gather, their professional praise singer or bard (*donson jeli*) is present, often wearing a shirt laden with amulets. Songs may last one or two hours or take several evenings to unfold. Often playing a string harp-lute, the performer is called upon to teach, explain, and recall historical personalities and events that can motivate people in their current lives.

Shirts like those of the hunters are often worn by the *donson jeli.* Hunters would give singers amulets and trophies of horns, tusks, claws, and teeth to sew onto their shirts. One famous *donson jeli,* who made his living as a performer until his death in 1983, was Seydou Camara (fig. 13). Born into a family of blacksmiths, he was conscripted into the French army and served in Morocco and then Timbuktu from 1937 to 1945. After becoming an apprentice to another *jeli,* he won a hunters' bard competition in 1953. His fame spread in the late 1960s and 1970s as he was heard regularly on Radio Mali and performed at hunters' festivals, funerals, weddings, and baptisms all over southern Mali. Camara also offered his medicines and guidance to people who were ill or anxious about new journeys, marriages, businesses, and hunts.

As hunters brought Camara part of their kill in the form of dried meat, he sang to calm the *nyama* of the slaughtered creature.

> **We are the needles which sew the social fabric**
> **And music is our thread.**   —Salif Keita, 1987[21]

Salif Keita also wears shirts laden with anatomy and amulets to declare his tie to Mande heroism. Reported to be a descendant of Sundiata, he embodies the ethical *fadenya,* breaking down social boundaries as he roams the world with a rebellious voice. The albino child of noble parents, he disregarded his family's position in order to perform. Mande nobility maintain that members of the noble caste should not become dancers, singers, or even public speakers. And as an albino, Salif Keita was considered bad luck, so he left his home to relocate in Bamako. His fame grew there in the 1970s as he sang in the Super Rail Band and Les Ambassadeurs. In recent years, he has struck out in multiple directions to reshape Mande music to fit the world-music arena. Singing songs that again place Sundiata in the spotlight, he lets international audiences hear how ancient and modern Mande heroes approach the world with fearless conviction.

Hunters themselves have been shifting their profile throughout the twentieth century. Hunting is no longer the only avenue for pursuing heroic encounters. Instead of seeking dangerous activities in the bush, young Malian men now face adversity by moving to large cities or traveling abroad for schooling. In Bamako, the capital of Mali, hunters' associations focus on the pursuit of knowledge from the past. Praise singers who recount history, recite genealogies, and maintain a rich oral tradition have been actively recorded since the late 1960s. And Mande people are producing films that narrate their experiences. *Keita: The Heritage of the Griot,* a film by Dani Kouyate, immerses the viewer in a retelling of the Sundiata epic and evaluates its place in West Africa today. The film follows the path of learning taken by Mabo Keita, a young boy torn between a Westernized schoolteacher and a praise singer who teaches him about the life of his distant relative, the famous Sundiata Keita. The struggle to not forget Mande history takes over the boy's curiosity and imagination. Flashbacks to Sundiata's time show the hunter's shirt in action. The role of the hunter is shifting to one who stalks knowledge rather than game.

> **We are kings in Mande, even if we wash dishes or clean toilets in**
> **other lands. We are like disenfranchised clans when we travel over-**
> **seas; foreigners have no idea how noble we are, how much history**
> **we have.**   —Manthia Diawara, 1998[22]

A successful hunter proudly wore one of these shirts filled with tusks, mud, gnarled leather, smoke, sweat, and innumerable elements (fig. 14). Unveiled in an exhibition for American audiences, such a shirt led to the discovery of a different type of hunter: a hero to be lauded in epics, an antagonist who embraces the wilderness, and a leader in search of knowledge about healing and death. In writing about the upbringing of a hunter, Maryse Conde in the novel *Segu* describes how the master

Fig. 13. Seydou Camara, hunters' singer *(donson jeli)*, Bamako, Mali, 1975.

Fig. 14. Hunter at Samori Toure centennial celebration, Kerouane, Guinea, 2000.

hunter Kemenani transmits his wisdom to Tiefolo. His words evoke the solitary walking commemorated by the hunters' shirts:

> He revealed to Tiefolo the prayers, incantations, and sacrifices that make a man emerge victorious from all his encounters with animals. At first he felt some repugnance about hunting, for Tiekoro had passed on to him a horror of bloodshed. Then he got caught up in it, though even now, whenever his quarry fell to his knees before its final collapse, giving its tormentor a look of utter incomprehension, a chill still went down his spine. Then he rushed forward toward the animal and passionately whispered into his ear the ritual phrases designed to win him forgiveness.[23]

Notes

1. Stephen Belcher, *Epic Traditions of Africa* (Bloomington: Indiana University Press, 1999), 89.

2. Katherine White Journals, 1970, Seattle Art Museum.

3. Ibid., 1972.

4. During the 1960s and 1970s, the Museum of Modern Art was establishing a convention of displaying modern culture that emphasized isolating works of art, predominantly paintings and sculptures, in neutral presentations. The 1930s through 1960s had been a time when curators and designers like René d'Harnoncourt and Alfred Barr experimented with exhibition techniques such as diverse lighting, wall colors, and atmospheric suggestions of alternative contexts for viewing art. By 1968, there was a clear trend toward absolutely modernist settings with minimal didactic or interpretive effort. For a review of this evolution, see Mary Anne Staniszewski, *The Power of Display: A History of Exhibitions at the Museum of Modern Art* (Cambridge: MIT Press, 1998).

5. Robert Jenson, "Italian Design Show at MoMA: A Post Mortem," *Artforum* 11, no. 2 (1972), 85–87.

6. John Canaday, *New York Times,* October 22, 1972.

7. "Manden Mori," sung by Seydou Camara, recorded by Gerald Cashion, 1976.

8. Famori Keita commemoration, sung by Seydou Camara, recorded by Gerald Cashion, 1977.

9. Cheick Mahamadou Cherif Keita, "Jaliya in the Modern World: A Tribute to Banzumana Sissoko and Massa Makan Diabate," in *Status and Identity in West Africa: Nyamakalaw of Mande,* ed. David C. Conrad and Barbara E. Frank (Bloomington: Indiana University Press, 1995).

10. Charles Bird and Martha Kendall, "The Mande Hero: Text and Context," in *Explorations of African Systems of Thought,* ed. Ivan Karp and Charles Bird (Bloomington: Indiana University Press, 1980).

11. Insight derived from the excellent notes in the California Newsreel 1999 catalogue. California Newsreel is an organization that distributes African films in the United States and provides suggestions for discussions regarding issues embedded in the deep structures of the films.

12. John William Johnson, *The Epic of Son-Jara,* text by Fa-Digi Sissoko (Bloomington: Indiana University Press, 1986).

13. Quoted by Patrick McNaughton, *The Mande Blacksmiths: Knowledge, Power, and Art in West Africa* (Bloomington: Indiana University Press, 1988).

14. Famori Keita commemoration.

15. Gerald Cashion, "Hunters of the Mande: A Behavioral Code and Worldview Derived from the Study of Their Folklore" (Ph.D. diss., Indiana University, 1984).

16. McNaughton, *Mande Blacksmiths.*

17. *Epic of Fa-Jigi,* narrated by Seydou Camara, recorded by David Conrad, Bamako, Mali, September 29, 1975, in *Oral Epics from Africa: Vibrant Voices from a Vast Continent,* ed. John William Johnson (Bloomington: Indiana University Press, 1997), 31–32.

18. Kate Ezra, "Early Sources for Bamana Art," in *Corpus of Early Arabic Sources for West African History,* ed. N. Levtzion and J. F. P. Hopkins (Cambridge: Cambridge University Press, 1966): "Al-Dukkali said to me: 'The people of this kingdom make much use of magic and poison. They take great interest in them and are very exact in them. They have plants and animals from which they compound fatal poisons. . . . They are poisons for which there are no antidotes'" (p. 149).

19. See Barbara Hoffman, "Secrets and Lies: Context, Meaning, and Agency in Mande," and Patrick McNaughton, "The Semantics of Jugu: Blacksmiths, Lore and 'Who's Bad' in Mande," in *Status and Identity in West Africa.*

20. Banzumana Sissoko, a griot called the Old Lion, criticized other griots for singing the praises of the living. Interview by Cheick Mahamadou Cherif Keita, 1979, in "Jaliya in the Modern World," 185.

21. Salif Keita, "Nyanyama," *Folon . . . The Past,* Island Records, 1995.

22. Manthia Diawara, *In Search of Africa* (Cambridge: Harvard University Press, 1998).

23. Maryse Conde, *Segu* (New York: Ballantine Books, 1987), 59.

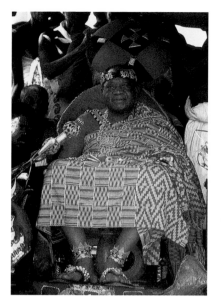

An Art of Persuasion: Regalia from the Asante Kingdom

Ananse the spider often creeps into Asante stories. In this one, his struggle with wisdom serves as a prelude to a kingdom that has a "great passion for persuasive public speech":[1]

One day, Ananse put all the wisdom in the world into a pot and decided to put it out of reach of all men. He would throw wisdom away so that the rest of mankind would be fools. With the wisdom pot on his back, he came across a fallen tree which had blocked the path except for a small gap beneath the tree. Ananse made several attempts to pass beneath the tree with the pot at his back, but to no avail. Kweku Tsen, his son, who was watching silently, at last volunteered a piece of advice to his father, "Put the load on the fallen tree, pass beneath the tree without the load, and pick up the load from the other side," he advised. Ananse complied and succeeded. Yet realizing wisdom was not his monopoly after all, Ananse in frustration smashed the wisdom pot. The pot broke and wisdom spread to all mankind.[2]

Spiders not only talk but dispense wisdom in Asante society. Ananse's son gives advice that deflates his father's greed to indirectly benefit everyone. The skilled use of such stories and proverbs is evident in Asante art, whether it be a ruler's dress or a drummer's refrain. Another hallmark of Asante creativity is its ability to take what looks familiar or ordinary and infuse it with extraordinary insights. Miniature brass sculpture looks merely entertaining but transforms business dealings into daily exhibitions of eloquence. A stool may look like a piece of furniture but be so endowed with sacred qualities that it embodies a nation. Wearing cloth can be a form of rhetoric.

To begin, five rings look like, and are, very common items created in gold. But they demonstrate how the Asante instill meaning in seemingly mundane objects. The first ring depicts a gold peanut (or groundnut, pl. 39)—not a foodstuff one would expect to inspire reflection, but in the Asante world it can refer to a proverb: "If you want to grow something for me, plant groundnuts, not corn" (a wish for a permanent relationship: groundnuts remain in the soil once planted, whereas corn is easily uprooted and destroyed).[3]

PI. 39
Peanut ring
Asante, Ghana
20th century
Gold
H. 3.8 cm (1½ in.)
Gift of Katherine White and the Boeing Company,
81.17.400

79

Pl. 40
Bird ring
Asante, Ghana
20th century
Gold
H. 4.5 cm (1¾ in.)
Gift of Katherine White and the Boeing Company,
81.17.429

Pl. 41
Porcupine ring
Asante, Ghana
20th century
Gold
H. 5 cm (2 in.)
Gift of Katherine White and the Boeing Company,
81.17.401

Ring two features a bird holding a keg of gunpowder in its beak and balancing a cannon on each wing (pl. 40). This represents a common proverb: "The courageous bird Adwetakyi sits on cannons" (a brave man faces all odds; he is always ready to face the enemy).

The third ring erupts in spikes that launch a range of associations (pl. 41). Some people read it as a cocoon; others see the bristling coat of a porcupine. Thus, an array of proverbs can be recounted: "The grub: it does not talk, but it breathes" (a stranger's character is not easily known). "You have become like the grub that has no mouth but it breathes" (said of a quiet but wicked person). "Kill a thousand and a thousand more will come" (remove a porcupine quill and others will fill in; the unified Asante are always armed and ready for action).

A tortoise's small head peeks out of its shell on the fourth ring (pl. 42). Tortoises bring forth a host of proverbs, including: "Tortoise, you are also suffering in your shell" (however secure a person seems, he has hidden troubles); and "When you go to the village of the tortoise and he eats earth, you eat some too" (when visiting another, respect his customs no matter how strange they may seem).

Finally, the fifth ring is a bulbous form best known as a wisdom knot that only a wise man can untie (pl. 43). Another reading, however, could ascribe this proverb: "If you are weaving and the thread gets tangled, use both hands to untie it" (even the wise man needs another's advice to solve a problem).

When worn as part of a complete royal regalia, this handful of rings is joined by bracelets, necklaces, sandals, hats, cloths, staffs, swords, stools, and umbrellas. Each item is selected for display by an Asante who seeks the proper words to enhance a given situation. In a museum's display, a collection of royal art proclaims the visual force of a prosperous kingdom, but doesn't reveal the eloquence that sustained the kingdom.

What the average museum goer sees is a gold peanut, bird, grub or porcupine, tortoise, and knot. But viewers attuned to the proverbs behind the rings begin to see the wisdom in the ordinary. On just one hand, a ruler is able to convey concepts for further discussion:

> the longing for a lengthy relationship,
> a readiness to use force when necessary,
> suspicion about someone's duplicity,
> compassion for another person's insecurity,
> the need for leaders to consult others in making decisions.

While rings introduce the oratory of leadership, miniature sculptures show how metaphoric speech once fit into daily Asante life. Miniature sculptures cast in copper alloy served as goldweights, placed on scales as a counterbalance to piles of gold dust. Sales transactions thus became small-scale momentary exhibitions. The heads of families, chiefs, and wealthy traders curated these exhibitions as a constant part of doing business. In a special bag (*futuo*), each trader kept his own corpus of weights.

A small handful of weights illustrates the range of images and issues revealed by these everyday sculptures. One of the most common goldweights is one named Sankofa, a bird with a swirling, backward-twisting neck (pl. 44). These are four of its many interpretations: "Pick it up if it falls behind" (whatever mistakes one has made in the past can be corrected). "Go back and pick" (*san*, return; *ko*, go; *fa*, pick: any aspect of culture that doesn't draw from the past to replenish the present and cast a shadow into the future will die).[4] "When it lies behind you, take it" (use the wisdom of the past), or simply, "one foot should be in front of another."

Two men (pl. 45) lean back to greet each other in a weight that evokes another proverb: "They have ended up like Amoako and Adu" (an expression about wasted opportunities: Amoaku and Adu parted in their youth and meet again in old age to discover they are both as poor as when they started).

Pl. 42
Tortoise ring
Asante, Ghana
20th century
Gold
H. 4.1 cm (1⅝ in.)
Gift of Katherine White and the Boeing Company, 81.17.1684

Pl. 43
Wisdom knot ring
Asante, Ghana
20th century
Gold
H. 5.7 cm (2¼ in.)
Gift of Katherine White and the Boeing Company, 81.17.399

Pl. 44
Figurative weight *(abrammuo):* **Sankofa bird**
Asante, Ghana
19th century
Copper alloy
H. 3.5 cm (1⅜ in.)
Gift of Katherine White and the Boeing Company,
81.17.397

Pl. 45
Figurative weight *(abrammuo):* **Leaning men**
Asante, Ghana
19th century
Copper alloy
H. 3.5 cm (1⅜ in.)
Gift of Katherine White and the Boeing Company,
81.17.361

Pl. 46
Figurative weight *(abrammuo):* **Birds-on-tree**
Asante, Ghana
19th century
Copper alloy
H. 7 cm (2¾ in.)
Gift of Katherine White and the Boeing Company,
81.17.362

A mass of birds cover a tree (pl. 46) to suggest: "The woodpeckers hope the silk-cotton tree will die" (if the tree dies, grubs will fill the rotting wood and give the woodpeckers more food; one man's downfall is another man's gain).

The leopard with emphasized spots (pl. 47) conveys: "When the rain falls on the leopard it wets the spots on his skin but does not wash them off" (a man's nature is not changed by circumstances).

The scorpion (pl. 48) signifies: "The scorpion does not bite with his mouth but with his tail" (the enemy might not fight you openly but undermine you secretly).

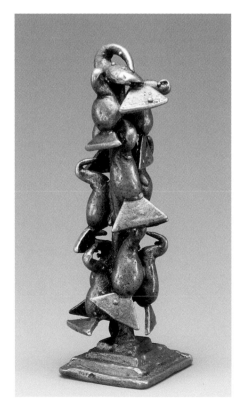

A deer with long horns (pl. 49) means: "It is always too late to say, 'Had I known'" (a deer with horns so long they injured other animals asked his friends to push them in, but remembered too late that he needed horns to defend himself).

A shield (pl. 50) suggests: "Though the covering of a shield wears out, its framework still remains" (although the head of the family may die, the family endures).

A woman carrying a bowl on her head (pl. 51) is a reminder: "As long as the head remains, one cannot avoid carrying loads about" (as long as people live, they never stop worrying).

Gold fueled the Asante rise to prosperity, and goldweights were one outcome. Some of the richest gold deposits

Pl. 47
Figurative weight *(abrammuo):* **Leopard**
Asante, Ghana
19th century
Copper alloy
H. 3.2 cm (1¼ in.)
Gift of Katherine White and the Boeing Company,
81.17.390

Pl. 48
Figurative weight *(abrammuo):* **Scorpion**
Asante, Ghana
19th century
Copper alloy
H. 2.9 cm (1⅛ in.)
Gift of Katherine White and the Boeing Company,
81.17.394

Pl. 49
Figurative weight *(abrammuo):* **Deer**
Asante, Ghana
19th century
Copper alloy
H. 3.5 cm (1⅜ in.)
Gift of Katherine White and the Boeing Company,
81.17.396

Pl. 50
Figurative weight *(abrammuo):* **Shield**
Asante, Ghana
19th century
Copper alloy
H. 6.8 cm (2¾ in.)
Gift of Katherine White and the Boeing Company, 81.17.370

in Africa launched a trading network that reached across the Sahara, south to the coast, and eventually to Europe and the Americas. By the fourteenth century, the Akan people of Ghana (from whom the Asante emerged) were making all the equipment necessary to trade gold—scales, weights, spoons, shovels, and gold-dust boxes. Abstract weights based on Islamic standards came first; they were followed by figurative weights as the Asante empire reached its peak of affluence in the seventeenth and eighteenth centuries with the trade in gold and slaves. In five centuries of goldweight production, there may have been as many as three million created to enhance daily business.[5] Weights could also be sent as a message:

> As a white man sends a letter, so do we send these weights to one another. The Crab's Claw. As you know, the crab is a very tenacious animal, and what he once holds with his claw he will never let go; even though it be severed from his body, it will still hold on, until crushed to atoms. If I were to send this to another chief who had done me an injury, he would at once know what I meant without a long palaver.[6]

Weights enhanced the bargaining process between buyer and seller. A Swiss missionary described how the weights worked in the Asante capital of Kumasi in 1875:

> The gold is weighed out amidst very noisy scenes. Each person carries his own weights with him, but those of the vendors would be found too heavy and those of the purchasers too light. Arguments go on for a long time until the correct weight is produced. Only now does the weighing take place....
>
> The weighing of gold can be as delightful as it is tiring, especially in the case of small purchases, for example, when you want to buy fruit or vegetables from the market woman ... a transaction worth a few pennies takes up as much time as one involving several ounces. This can teach a white man patience, but in my case I lost patience again and again.[7]

Such frustrations led the Swiss to introduce silver coinage in the 1860s, but it met with little success, and by 1868 a new proverb was created: "The white man has only one weight." However, soon after, the ancient gold trade fell into decline, and flat coins bearing European monarchs' faces were making inroads. By the 1890s, as the British stepped in to undermine Asante leadership, they brought with them large shipments of silver coins. Elderly Asante say that goldweights ceased to be made by 1905, yet the weights became such appealing collectibles that an industry of producing replicas blossomed and continues to the present.

The temporary exhibitions of proverbial sculpture that goldweights engendered are just one art form mastered by Asante culture. The other, more prominent vision is their royal panoplies, opulent combinations of art worn and carried in processions and festivals. One of the most vivid descriptions of a court panoply was published with color illustrations in 1819 by a young Englishman, Thomas Bowdich, in *A Mission from Cape Coast Castle to Ashantee*.[8] His account is loaded with details of a tumultuous three-month visit, and introduces a dilemma that plagued the next century of communication: the British might admire Asante visual art, but they were ill equipped to listen to the persuasive intentions it carried.

On May 19, 1817, four young Englishmen ended nearly a month's journey of 140 miles from the coast of Ghana to the Asante capital, Kumasi. Thomas Bowdich recorded the "magnificence and novelty" of the scene they were led into. A throng of people greeted them, producing a blinding glare as the sun reflected off masses of gold ornaments. While their eyes were dazzled, their ears were saluted by drums, horns, flutes, and instruments resembling bagpipes. Huge umbrellas, gently pulsing up and down, added bright streaks of scarlet and yellow to the arena. The visitors shook hands with men dressed in silk cloth draped over the left shoulder and layers of gold jewelry. A few wore so many ornaments on their wrists that young boys had to support their hands. After meeting a file of dignitaries, the Englishmen came upon the Asantehene (Asante king), who extended his hand.

Osei Bonsu, the Asantehene, was bedecked in silk cloth and abundant gold ornaments. Every item of his clothing was accented with gold and silver ornaments, from his white leather sandals to his hat. He greeted each of the Englishmen, as did the women of his court. A stool entirely encased in gold was visible under a nearby umbrella. As they were escorted to their quarters, dancers, dwarfs, and mimics entertained them. The Asantehene came to say good night and ask their names again. In the following days, the visitors met with Osei Bonsu and his councilors in a five-acre palace complex with a maze of inner courts, a judicial hall, and official residences. Later, the British mission also dined at the Asantehene's retreat, where they were offered roast pig, ducks, fowls, stews, pease pudding, oranges, and pineapples along with port and madeira, spirits, and Dutch cordials. Bowdich reported, "We never saw a dinner more handsomely served, and never ate better." His observations about Kumasi commended its organization of twenty-seven main streets, spoked to divide the city into seventy-seven wards. Streets that were cleaned daily served as stages for numerous ceremonial events. He admired how relief patterns on residential walls enlivened the surfaces of the city and indicated the rank of the person housed within. Bowdich's color depiction of Adoom Street features a woman seated beneath an umbrella, her produce scales ready to balance goldweights (fig. 15). He recorded his admiration for the work of potters, goldsmiths, weavers, and carvers living in the suburbs of Kumasi.

Bowdich indicates that life around the palace was not usually so quiet, but exuded a sense of intrigue as titled officials moved in and out of the palace, often late at night under torchlight. He also watched the Asantehene appear with his spokesmen, stool carriers, drummers, umbrella carriers, cooks, heralds, sword and elephant-tail bearers, ministers, and executioners. At several places around the city, the king would periodically sit to meet and greet people. He did so from eight-foot-tall platforms of polished clay, covered by a large umbrella and attended by fifty to one hundred courtiers sitting below him.

Bowdich watched the Odwira festival in early September and deemed it to be a harvest "yam festival" (fig. 16). Processions of chiefs and military leaders paraded by the Asantehene with their entourages, accompanied by musicians playing horns and drums. As darkness fell, the processions continued under the light of hundreds of huge torches. Girls bearing silver bowls filled with palm wine enhanced the festival's conclusion the next morning. The final visual mark of the festival was the spectacle of melting down the royal gold ornaments while crowds looked on.

Bowdich's volume was full of such observations of the magnificence and complexity of the court and Kumasi. English critics questioned his accounts and suggested he was exaggerating or struck by delusions caused by reading the tales of the Arabian Nights. The British government paid greatest attention to his reports of human sacrifice and highly visible executioners. From this point on, conflicts between the British

Fig. 15. "Part of Adoom Street" (detail), from Thomas E. Bowdich, *A Mission from Cape Coast Castle to Ashantee* (London, 1819).

Fig. 16. "The First Day of the Yam Custom," from Bowdich, *A Mission from Cape Coast Castle to Ashantee.*

and Asante hinged on misunderstandings of the nature of Asante governance. What the British saw as autocratic rule was actually subject to an inner council of eighteen leaders, including the queen mother, who met to advise the Asantehene. What Bowdich described as a yam festival was a kaleidoscopic history lesson, a time of purification when court cases were heard, tributes offered, oaths sworn, and allegiance to the nation renewed.[9] What Bowdich reported as rampant sacrifice was capital punishment. And what he saw as golden spectacle was often full of unspoken eloquence he was unable to hear.

In his account, Bowdich noted the fact that "the royal stool, entirely cased in gold, was displayed under a splendid umbrella." While in Kumasi, he purchased a stool of a form still commonly made. Through his brief description and collecting of the earliest datable stool, Bowdich brought attention to a fundamental Asante art form. Of all the complex layers of regalia a leader must coordinate, the stool remains crucial. Stools are the ultimate object of leadership, and language connects the two: being "enstooled" means assuming a public position. Learning the depth of associations a stool can embody is an essential step in Asante art history. Unfortunately, the British were unable to recognize the profoundly persuasive force a stool can have.

> **How often I have tried to keep together the power and kingdom of Asante by my eloquence, but they would not have it.**
>
> —Okyeame Kwame Butuakwa, 1895[10]

> **Discussing matters of wisdom, I could hold my own. But this is a matter of might.** —Okyeame Yaw Boaten, 1903[11]

The war ignited by the Golden Stool, which came at the end of a series of conflicts, began the twentieth century with a vivid illustration of cultural blindness. When the British governor arrived in 1900, he entered a Kumasi far different from the city Bowdich had written of in glowing terms. The capital was now riddled with evidence of encounters with British forces. The cityscape was badly scarred; monuments were missing, reduced to ruins, or remade into new structures. A palace complex blown up in 1874 by British forces was rebuilt as a large impenetrable fort. Only rubble remained of an Asante museum built in 1822 for Asantehene Osei Bonsu. Inspired by what Osei Bonsu had heard of the British Museum, the two-story building had housed treasures given to the Asante kings by international delegations of traders and visitors between 1822 and 1874. The British removed most of the objects from the museum before destroying the structure. As soldiers were dismantling it, one reporter, Winwood Reade of *The Times*, described the contents:

> The rooms upstairs reminded me of Wardour Street. Each was a perfect old curiosity shop. Books in many languages, Bohemian glass, clocks, silverplate, old furniture, Persian rugs, Kidderminster carpets, pictures and engravings, numberless chests and coffers. A sword bearing the inscriptions "From Queen Victoria to the King of the Ashantee." ... With these were many specimens of Moorish and Ashantee handicraft, gold-studded sandals such as only the king and a few great chiefs may wear ... leopard skin caps lined with

yellow velvet and adorned outside with beaten gold . . . and a plume of the same metal; saddles of red leather, magnificent canopies or state umbrellas of velvet and satin, baskets or cradles in which Ashantee chiefs are accustomed to be carried on the heads of slaves, with other curious and tasteful things too numerous for me to describe or even catalogue.[12]

While the ruined museum and damaged palace complex were visible scars of conquest, the most egregious insult to the Asante was the banishment of their ruler, removed by the British four years earlier. Just as Bowdich had seen how the vitality of Kumasi was closely tied to Osei Bonsu, so the reigning Asantehene embodied the personality behind the empire. The loss of Prempeh I, the exiled Asantehene, was made more acute by the breadth of his accomplishments at a young age.

Prempeh I assumed leadership of the kingdom in 1888, when he was only sixteen years old.[13] He inherited a monarchy troubled by weak predecessors, civil unrest, and British ambitions voiced by officers like Colonial Secretary Frederick Hodgson, who denounced his rule as "a bloodthirsty despotism." Prempeh dedicated himself to reconciling factions in the kingdom by making agreements with independent European and African forces. He gained a reputation as a leader with *tekyerema de,* "the sweet tongue," and could disarm even his strongest opponents with the proper arguments. His policies relied on negotiating, never going back on his word, and restoring faith in many Asante institutions. As Prempeh's abilities to consolidate the Asante empire became clear, the British desire to dissolve the empire became just as clear. Reports in the British press of barbarous Asante sacrifices reached "an orgy of hyperbole," often based on a misidentification of criminals receiving capital punishment as sacrificial victims.[14]

> That bygones will be bygones.   —Asantehene Prempeh I, 1894

After being enstooled in 1894, Prempeh had a court official write a letter on his behalf to the British governor. His letter of June 28 inserted an old Scottish proverb for good measure:

> I beseech you my good friend, to pray and ask blessings from your God to give me long life and prosperous and peaceful reign, and that my friendship with H.M.G. [Her Majesty's Government] may be more firm and closer than hitherto had been done, that bygones will be bygones, that Ashanti will wake herself as out of a deep sleep, that the hostilities will go away from her, that the evils which the constant wars have brought upon her like destroying our jewels, may die everlastingly from her and that I shall endeavor to promote peace and tranquility and good order in my Kingdom.[15]

The governor was not persuaded by Prempeh's overtures and warned his district commissioner not to be taken in by the good manners and apparent friendliness of the Asante, for they were "artful, unscrupulous, treacherous, untruthful, and utterly unworthy of having any reliance placed on them or their statements."[16] When an Asante delegation of seven spokesmen was dispatched to London to open diplomatic channels in 1894, they were refused an audience. In turn, Prempeh would not allow a British resident to live in Kumasi. At the start of 1896, an expedition forced him to accept a British protectorate (fig. 17). After he acquiesced, the British officers charged him with withholding payment on a loan and arrested him. Prempeh stated, "I would rather surrender to secure the lives and tranquility of my people and country." He was deported to the coast on January 20, 1896, along with his mother and fifty-two chiefs and attendants. At twenty-eight years of age, he had just begun to consolidate a kingdom suffering from years of instability. He would be held captive for twenty-eight years in the Seychelles islands before being allowed to return to Kumasi.

Soon after Prempeh's deportation, British troops set buildings on fire and demolished whole sections of the city. The allure of discovering caches of gold prompted much of the destruction. Beyond buildings, they also blew up many of the sacred trees that gave Kumasi its name (*kum*, tree; *ase*, under). Large broad-leaved trees of the ficus variety were situated along the avenues and streets to punctuate the city plan. They not only provided shade for outdoor gatherings but also marked royal history. The most significant tree was planted to commemorate the founding of the nation in the early 1700s. Subsequently, each new ruler planted a tree to commence his reign and to honor major events. Oaths and offerings would be made under these trees, dwelling places for the spirits of deceased kings. Because trees helped to establish the moral state of the city, it was a serious offense to pick leaves from them. Torn branches were a sign of disorder and death in the royal family.

Kumasi had lost its ruler, palace, museum, houses, and now its sacred trees. On March 13, 1900, the new governor of what was then the Gold Coast colony, Sir Frederick Hodgson, set off from the coastal town of Accra to meet with Asante leaders, who were petitioning for changes in the British occupation. Not foreseeing any trouble, he prepared for a routine visit and traveled with his wife and only twenty men as a military escort. Entering Kumasi on March 25, Governor and

Lady Hodgson were led through an arch as missionary school children sang "God Save the Queen." They reached the British stone fort, which stood in the middle of an open space, to find Asante royalty and chiefs waiting under large twirling umbrellas. Drums and horns sounded. As the governor passed by, each leader rose from his stool to salute.

Sir Frederick met the assembly again on March 28. The Asante leaders formed a semicircle with their stools, arranging themselves in order of seniority. Facing the assembly, Governor Hodgson amazed his audience by demanding that they pay interest on an old war indemnity. His final words delivered so strong an insult that the chiefs fell silent:

> Let me tell you once and for all that Prempeh will never again rule over this country of Ashanti. . . . The paramount authority of Ashanti is now the great Queen of England whose representative I am at the moment. . . . Where is the golden stool? Why am I not sitting on the golden stool at this moment? I am the representative of the paramount power, why have you relegated me to this chair? Why did you not take the opportunity of my coming to Kumase to bring the golden stool and give it to me to sit upon?[17]

No one responded. Without speaking, the Asante all stood up, shook the governor's hand, and filed past him. In the solemn departure, British officials noticed one woman who reached out and touched the medals of the order of St. Michael and St. George around the governor's neck. The woman was Yaa Asantewaa. Four years earlier, her son, chief of the state of Edweso, had been deported with Asantehene Prempeh I. In his absence, she had assumed the rule over Edweso, while constantly arguing for the restoration of the Asante monarchy. After the encounter with the British governor, the Asante called a secret meeting. The sixty-year-old Yaa Asantewaa recounted all the grievances the Asante had against the British and swore never to pay interest. As the men, concerned about their depleted resources, debated the wisdom of going to battle with the British, Yaa Asantewaa stood and declared:

> How can a proud and brave people like the Asante sit back and look while whitemen took away their king and chiefs, and humiliated them with a demand for the Golden Stool? The Golden Stool only means money to the whitemen; they have searched and dug everywhere for it. . . . If you, the chiefs of Asante, are going to behave like cowards and not fight, you should exchange your loin cloths for my undergarments.[18]

To emphasize her point, she fired a gun in front of the chiefs. They responded by planning a war, to be led by Yaa Asantewaa. The conflict officially began three days later, after Sir Hodgson sent a detachment of men to search for the Golden Stool. When the men came back empty-handed, Hodgson realized he was in a dangerous position. The Yaa Asantewaa War, a guerrilla campaign lasting from April to November 1900, is acknowledged to be one of the most determined resistance movements of the colonial era. The British contingent was trapped in the fort and remained there for two months. British relief troops armed with new weapons eventually overcame the

Asante, but it took them many months to capture Yaa Asantewaa. She was sent to join Prempeh and her son in the Seychelles, and lived there in exile until her death in 1921.

The British annexed the Gold Coast as a British colony in 1901 and ruled it until 1957. Two more decades were to pass before the English began to realize why a stool inspired rebellion. Mistaken for a coronation seat, the Golden Stool became a target for British officials, who thought it was a prize to capture and own. But the Golden Stool remains an object of devotion at the core of the collective Asante identity.

To the Asante, the Golden Stool is known as Sika Dwa Kofi, "Born on Friday." Oral tradition traces its origin to a Friday in 1701, when the founder of the Asante nation, Osei Tutu, received the stool. Suddenly, in the midst of a thunder and lightning storm, a golden stool floated down from the heavens, ruled by the Sky God Nyame, and came to rest in Osei Tutu's lap. He turned to his priest, Okomfo Anokye, who interpreted it as the soul or spirit (*sunsum*) of the Asante nation. The gold material was equated with the enduring and vital life force of the sun, which would bless the unity of the Asante nation. Together, these two men formulated the foundation of Asante identity, shifting its focus from a military state to one of an effective government thriving on the trade of the precious metal. A set of seventy-seven laws became associated with the Golden Stool, the most essential being a sense of "common citizenship," which requires every person of the Asante union to place their loyalty in the stool. A cylinder support at the core of the Golden Stool may symbolize the tree planted by every Asantehene to serve as the center of his dynasty. Inside the core cylinder, the priest Anokye placed hair and nails collected from the leaders brought together by Osei Tutu. Brass bells were added to the stool to enable contact with ancestors. Fetters implied a vigilance in keeping the nation secure.

Since it carries the soul of a nation, the Golden Stool is treated extremely carefully. Never permitted to touch the ground, it is always seated on its own European-style chair with an elephant-skin mat. This position signifies that the ruler presides over both human and natural forces. In the course of two centuries, the Golden Stool also became known as a sign of confirmed leadership. When an Asantehene passed away, the stool and other regalia were held in trust until a new leader could be chosen. The new Asantehene could gain access to the treasury and the royal regalia only after being enstooled. Keeping the Golden Stool was the final affirmation of a new leader's position. He did not sit upon the stool, but kept it by his side to embody all the laws and government processes that he would honor.

After King Prempeh's deportation in 1896, the Golden Stool disappeared from sight. It was not seen again in public until 1921, when it was accidentally unearthed and the bells were removed to be sold. When this news circulated, Asante chiefs became concerned that the British might assume control of the Golden Stool. Signs of national mourning—red clay smeared on faces and arms—appeared widely. But this time, the British consulted their new anthropological department in Ghana, led by R. S. Rattray, who would publish many studies in the next decade. He launched his written reports with an attempt to correct "misconceptions, if not total ignorance in the past concerning this object." As a result of Rattray's counseling, the British permitted the Kumasi council of chiefs to try the thieves according to Asante law, and announced that the government considered the Golden Stool to be the property of the Asante nation. Soon thereafter, the queen mother of Mampong sent a replica of her silver stool to Princess Mary of England as a wedding gift with the words, "It may be that the King's child has heard of the Golden Stool of the Ashanti. That is the stool which contains the soul of the Ashanti nation. All we women of Ashanti thank the governor exceedingly because he has declared to us that the English will never again ask us to hand over that Stool."[19]

Despite many similar attempts to let bygones be bygones, the Golden Stool's rightful occupant remained in exile in the Seychelles for twenty-eight years. During his captivity, Asantehene Prempeh I balanced accommodation with efforts to maintain Asante traditions. He learned English and wrote numerous letters and documents, became baptized, and attended the Anglican church. Simultaneously, he directed the affairs of his subjects in a manner true to the Asante judicial system. Every twenty-one days, he celebrated the Adae festival—a day of rest set aside for communication with ancestors who were fed their favorite food and drink. Normally, this observance would take place in a special room where the ancestors' blackened stools were kept as a locus for their spirits. In the Seychelles, no stools had been allowed to accompany the exiled Asante, so Prempeh I improvised a libation ceremony that relied on the same invocations. Although his correspondence was heavily censored, petitions like this one of 1918 state how painful the separation from his home had become:

Fig. 18. Asantehene Agyeman Prempeh I after his return from exile, Kumasi, Ghana, 1926. Basel Mission Archive D-30.6200.3.

> It is now 23 years since we are made prisoners. I the Ex-king Prempeh being taken prisoner together with father, mother, brother and ex-chiefs; and now my father, mother and brother are all dead leaving me alone and about ¾ of my chiefs are dead and the remainder ¼ few are either invalid or ill. We are now very miserable, so we could not express any wish but entrust all our wishes in thy hands to allow us to go to Kumasi.[20]

Six years later, King Prempeh I was finally allowed to return to Kumasi. He was installed as paramount chief of Kumasi in 1926 (fig. 18), but was never allowed to reclaim the title of Asantehene. The British did help to complete a new residential palace at a site known as Manhyia ("all nations should come together"). His return inspired a new wave of Asante art production as leaders became confident that they could revive their ceremonial lives without colonial interference. Goldsmiths and weavers were hired to create new regalia. Secretly, Prempeh I obtained the Golden Stool, replenished it, and had it carried openly in a 1931 procession that set a model for religious inclusiveness. The Golden Stool was publicly seen (for the first time since 1895) at a thanksgiving service at St. Cyprian's Anglican Church in Kumasi. Inside the church, it was placed in front of the altar. "Then Prempeh and the Queen Mother stripping themselves of all their ornaments went and knelt by the altar and gave thanks for all his liberation and restoration to his people. Was Prempeh supplicating the Christian altar, the Golden Stool that was strategically positioned in front of the altar, or both? Prempeh's experience with modernity was an ambiguous adventure."[21]

Prempeh I passed away two years later and was buried as an Asantehene now immortalized in a blackened stool. On January 1, 1935, his nephew was installed with the title of Nana Osei Tutu Agyeman Prempeh II. As the new protector of the Golden Stool, he began reasserting the essential elements of Asante identity. To this day, the Golden Stool remains a seat that is occupied, not owned. In an unbroken line, Asantehenes have been enstooled and continue to sit in state with the stool at their sides. On April 26, 1999, Otumfuo Osei Tutu II became the sixteenth occupant of the Golden Stool. He succeeded his uncle Otumfuo Opoku Ware II, who ruled from 1970 to 1999 (fig. 19).

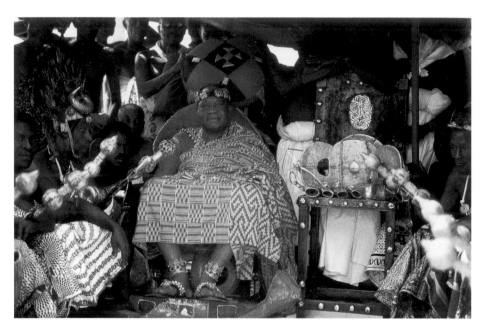

Fig. 19. Asantehene Otumfuo Opoku Ware II seated in state next to the Golden Stool "Born on Friday" (Sika Dwa Kofi), Kumasi, Ghana, 1992.

A stool that is not for sitting but is a national shrine, the Golden Stool demonstrates how a literal reading of Asante art is far from complete. On a heroic scale, the Golden Stool narrates the founding of a kingdom and broadcasts epic messages at every appearance. It serves as a reminder of the laws of common citizenship and of the permanence of the Asante confederacy, and is honored as a sacred emblem that no other nation has ever been able to touch. On an everyday level, personal stools also function as more than furniture.

From mere seats to near gods, stools permeate the social, political and religious life of the Akan. —Herbert Cole and Doran Ross, 1977[22]

Stools indicate special times in a person's life. A child beginning to crawl is given a stool to mark the passage through the dangers of infancy. A girl is seated upon a stool when she is leaving puberty to become an adult woman. A groom will present a stool to his bride to honor their marriage. Day to day, stools are used for household chores like bathing and eating. Each time a person sits on the stool, it absorbs more of the *sunsum*, or spirit, of the owner and becomes linked to the owner's personality and spiritual state. Upon the person's death, the stool becomes a locus for the individual's memory and will be set on its side so that no stray disruption may enter it.

If a leader rises to greatness and is deemed worthy of commemoration, his stool becomes consecrated. After the funeral, the stool is blackened with soot mixed with raw egg, animal blood, and fat, and then placed in a windowless room that is *kronkron*, holy and pure. In this room, an incumbent leader pays respects to his predecessor, offering prayers and libations in return for guidance. Not for sitting, the stool contains the soul of a significant individual. One explanation emphasizes the

Pl. 52
Stool
Asante, Ghana
20th century
Wood
H. 38.7 cm (15¼ in.)
Gift of Katherine White and the Boeing Company,
81.17.338

need to remain in contact with those individuals: "You have your black telephones. You can pick one up and talk to your father in Europe. We have our black stools. We can stand one up, and talk to our grandfather (*nana*) in the Asaman. When you have finished you put the phone down, and when we have finished we lay the stool down. But your father is not inside the telephone, and our grandfather is not inside the stool."[23]

Just as the Golden Stool established the unity of the Asante kingdom, so the stool is a prominent symbol for all political positions. Leaders are not put in office; they are "enstooled." When a leader passes away, "the stool has fallen." On certain occasions, a stool could be appealed to for support. Bantamahene (commander of Asante troops) Awua II in an 1874 battle with the British is recounted as having stood on his stool to cheer his men. Such an act was meant to be "an insult to his ancestral ghosts, to fire their anger and make them fight more vigorously."[24] Certain stool types were once reserved for use by leaders of a particular rank. The Asantehene at one time had exclusive control of many designs, which were not allowed to be sold or used without his permission, but such limitations were relaxed in the twentieth century.

Of the stools in the Seattle Art Museum collection, two stand out as examples of the range in form these objects can take. A circular form is featured on the first example (pl. 52). A proverb, "The halo of the moon circles every human being" (*Kontonkurowi eda amansan kon mu*), is visually apparent in this design. It can be seen as a reminder that the Asante confederacy has the power to control and unite all its people. Or it may signify, as the curving sides frame the central core, that the head of any one person is always surrounded by higher powers. Peter Sarpong also sees the circle as a reminder to a leader that death comes to everyone, even the most powerful king. In response, he should remain humble even though he may have achieved high status.[25]

A roaring lion with a key on his side is featured beneath the second stool (pl. 53). Contrary to Western misconceptions, lions do not roam most of the African continent. They are more common to a savanna than the forests of the Asante environment. Akan proverbs and prayers often refer to the leopard as the "king of the forest," but rarely mention the lion. The sources for the image on this stool thus require investigation.[27] The profile head, the posture, and S-curving tail suggest a non-African source for the depiction. A rampant lion convention comes from the heraldic designs employed by European monarchies. This motif was among the most prominent visual metaphors the Europeans offered. Asante carvers were likely to have noticed the lion on Dutch, Danish, and British sailing ships plying the coast during the gold and slave trades. In addition, to designate alliances, the British and Dutch gave chiefs messenger canes on which the lion could appear. Another, more common source still seen today is the lion, used as a corporate emblem for a commercial trading company. Heraldic crests and trademarks served as symbols to identify the companies selling goods such as cloth and tea.

Two chairs now in the National Museum of Ghana connect the lion with state furniture. Belonging to the Dutch and English governors, both feature lions with crowns guarding royal arms. Sitting in those chairs, the foreign governors would have presided over court hearings that affected many Ghanaians. The bright yellow and silver enamel lion on the Asante stool sets up a role reversal—upholding an indigenous leader rather than a foreign one. Indeed, the lion overtakes the leopard as an Asante symbol of leadership in the twentieth century and underlines the change in power. Asante proverbs regarding the two animals reinforce the lion's prominence: "Only the lion drinks from the palm-wine pot of the leopard" (some chiefs are more powerful than others). "A dead lion is greater than a living leopard" (the lion at its worst is still more powerful than the leopard at its best). "Before the lion, the leopard ruled the forest."

Above all, however, the key placed prominently in the middle of the lion's body puts him in a position of control. Keys and locks as signs of wealth were displayed early in Asante history. Locked chests were said to be "numberless" when the British sacked Kumasi in 1874. The main reserves of the Kumasi treasury were kept in a Great Chest under the direct care of a head treasurer, who was entrusted with a gold key as his badge of office, while the assistant treasurer carried a silver key. Every morning, the Asantehene's bath was accompanied by the rattling of the treasury keys.[28] A stool with a roaring lion and silver key bolsters its occupant with two eminent symbols of power and wealth.

While stools are a basis of Asante heritage, they are less well known than other public art forms of the kingdom: jewelry and textiles. The fame of their textiles in particular inspired Katherine White to visit Kumasi in 1973. The Kennedy Center in Washington, D.C., had asked her to find a *kente*—the distinctive Asante cloth made famous internationally—for the building's lobby, and she agreed to go to the source.[29] As her slides show, Kumasi at that time was home to a royal presence that

Pl. 53
Lion stool
Asante, Ghana
20th century (after 1957)
Wood, enamel paint
H. 42.1 cm (16⅝ in.)
Gift of Katherine White and the Boeing Company,
81.17.545

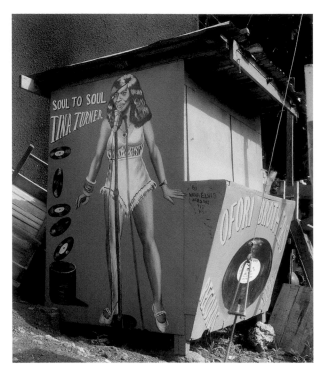

Fig. 20. Record booth with painting of Tina Turner, Kumasi, Ghana, 1969.

continued to thrive, side by side with pop royalty like Tina Turner, whose portrait is seen on the side of a record vendor's booth (fig. 20). Throughout many changes in the twentieth century, the Asantehene, Otumfuo Opoku Ware II, maintained a distinguished history of royal patronage. He had succeeded Asantehene Prempeh II in 1970 and presided over a full court and complex agenda as a traditional leader in Kumasi. White put in a request for an audience.

On the morning of April 24, a messenger from the palace arrived with word that the Asantehene could meet with her delegation:

We changed and eased our way through traffic across town to the palace. Big gates, four soldiers, a driveway of crushed red stone. We walked in, were greeted by a tense man in a business suit—the Asantehene's secretary. We waited outside on the porch. Suddenly a movement from within told us to rise. The Asantehene was there. A very tall man—over six feet, imposing, smiling. Dressed in a white *adinkra,* the cleanest printing job, the finest whipped thread I had ever seen. On both hands were huge gold rings in the shape of a sitting bird with wings spread. His sandals were black leather, the straps of which had triangles of alternating gold and silver, with an ornament on the end. We were so nervous we told our mission before we had been presented with a drink. I managed to remember not to cross my legs. We made (I mean *made*—we were both so flustered we couldn't think) conversation for about twenty-five minutes, after which we minded our manners, signed the guest book, shook all the hands all over again, and departed.[30]

The same dress that rendered White speechless would have an opposite effect in an Asante royal gathering. An audience attuned to looking carefully at the Asantehene's dress would have been able to refer to a number of proverbs, sayings, and allusions provoked by his choices. Gold jewelry and *kente* and *adinkra* cloth were just a few of the many art forms typically owned by an Asante chief. Swords, umbrellas, linguist staffs, caps, helmets, crowns, sandals were also part of royal regalia. As Katherine White set out to create her own set of regalia, she focused on cloth first. She coordinated her visit with a researcher living in Ghana, Brigitte Menzel, who led her to the best sources for *kente.* They traveled twelve miles east of Kumasi to Bonwire, the center for royal weaving established in the seventeenth century. There, the weavers challenged her sense of how collecting should proceed:

April 23, 1973, Bonwire, Ghana
At the turnabout we got out, headed for the shop of James Antobreh. Suddenly he was there behind us and we introduced ourselves. He took us away, down a side street to a compound, where we were put in a bare room, in which stood a cupboard, a battered modern desk, and four chairs. We were seated. Obviously there was a routine ahead of us. Two huge bottles of beer

Pl. 54
Kente cloth (Nkontompo Ntama, "liar's cloth")
Asante, Ghana
20th century
Cotton
L. 316.9 cm (124⅞ in.)
Gift of Katherine White and the Boeing Company,
81.17.466

were brought, opened, poured. I mentioned how interested I was in perhaps finding some old *kente*. "First we do other things, after which you say what you want," I was told. In came a lovely old man, the chief Nana Okai Ababio II, of Bonwire. They chatted between them until Brigitte arrived and we could begin. James was the chief's linguist. Then I suddenly had to make a speech. So I gave a little talk on the Kennedy Center, how beautiful we wanted it to be, how beautiful we thought *kente* cloth from Ghana was, and how happy we were to be there, etc. etc. This was translated to the Chief although I suspected (confirmed later) that he understood it all.[31]

Choosing a cloth was not a direct purchase but an indirect negotiation. White had to follow Asante protocol—stating your purpose comes after proper introductions and time to talk. Eventually, Bonwire weavers did bring inspection samples of many different *kente* strips, each with a distinctive name, according to custom. Their names were reviewed with White, and then she was taken on a tour to see the weavers at work. She debated with several people about which *kente* was appropriate and returned the next day to negotiate. On the same trip, White also spent time seeking out *adinkra* cloth in the town of Ntonso, the center for its production. There she photographed men stamping black dye with a multitude of symbols cut from a gourd, and embroidering the finished cloth strips together. In making her choices, White evaluated the colors, design qualities, look, and feel of the cloths, but remained aloof to their rhetoric.

Both types of cloth have a vocabulary that was once controlled by royalty. *Kente* cloths speak of authority and rank through their carefully inserted patterns, of which over three hundred warp-and-weft variations have been documented. *Adinkra* cloths relay messages through the proverbs and sayings associated with the symbols stamped on them. Dressing as a strategic form of communication requires an encyclopedic memory of symbols and their attendant proverbs and allusions to Asante history. The Asantehene relies on a retainer in charge of his wardrobe to maintain and select clothes for his public appearances. The scope of this encyclopedia is hinted at by just a few textiles from the museum's collection. They have accrued a wealth of messages through the course of the last century.

> Not all people read signs and symbols.   —Abena P. A. Busia, 1999[32]

Sharp turns in a pattern on a blue and white cloth signal a *kente* known as "liar's cloth" (Nkontompo Ntama, pl. 54). It was said to have been worn by a king as a means of questioning the veracity of people who came before him. Another cloth is known as Mmaaban, a mixture of warp patterns implying a unity in strength (pl. 55). Within the variety of patterns are a host of less obvious images assigned names such as ficus tree, donkey's ears, tail of the colobus monkey, lion, vine climber, and belly of the crocodile. A cloth with a strong vertical warp stripe is named Aberewa Bene, "wise old lady" (pl. 56). The name refers both to an exceptional elderly woman of the Asensie clan and to the constant role older women have in matters of traditional jurisprudence. Brief explanations of *kente* only hint at the number of signs and symbols that one cloth can carry. Mmeeda patterns convey a notion of how cloth is used to mark history (pl. 57).

A dictionary translates *mmeeda* as "something unheard of, unprecedented, extraordinary."[33] Other sources rephrase this to mean "something that has not happened before." The British researcher R. S. Rattray recorded it as *asonawa mmada* and said it originated from the name of the first clan to father an Asante king. On this historic basis, the Mmeeda pattern was worn by the person who activated *kente* for an international audience. Kwame Nkrumah was a force in world politics as he led the first successful transition from colonial to independent government in twentieth-century Africa. A goldsmith's son from an Akan group called Nzima located on the coast, Nkrumah drew on Asante visual and verbal arts for his style of leadership.

Nkrumah wore a Mmeeda *kente* cloth on February 12, 1951, the day he was released from a year's prison term for sedition against the colonial government. His party had won overwhelmingly in elections held four days before his release. At the

Pl. 55
Kente cloth (Mmaaban, "unity is strength")
Asante, Ghana
20th century
Cotton and silk
L. 194 cm (76⅜ in.)
Gift of Katherine White and the Boeing Company,
81.17.459

Pl. 57
Kente cloth (Mmeeda, "something that has not happened before")
Asante, Ghana
20th century
Cotton and silk
L. 235 cm (92½ in.)
Gift of Katherine White and the Boeing Company,
81.17.434

triumphant moment, he fully embodied the ethic behind Mmeeda—"it has not happened before"—by choosing to wear it on a highly charged day when all eyes focused on his victory. A more recent amplification of the term *mmeeda* holds it to be "a symbol of ingenuity, perfection, innovation, uniqueness and exceptional achievement."[34] Wearing an Mmeeda cloth was an omen for the next decade of Nkrumah's career as he led Ghana to independence on March 6, 1957, became its first president in 1960, and went on to found the Organization of African Unity.

> *Mmeeda:* **Something unheard of, unprecedented, extraordinary.**
> —Asante dictionary, 1933

Nkrumah wore and chose *kente* strategically. When he waved from the balcony following the euphoric announcement of independence, he wore a cloth called Adwini asa, "my skill is exhausted" or "I have done my best." The monumental *kente* he presented to the General Assembly of the United Nations in 1960 was called Obaakofo Mmu Man, or "one head cannot go into council" (two heads are better than one). A cloth created to honor him personally was entitled Fathia Fata Nkrumah, "Fathia and Nkrumah make a perfect couple." (Fathia was Nkrumah's Egyptian wife, and their marriage was seen as an example of African unity.) On many occasions, he wore a cloth called Oyokoman, named for the clan of the Asantehene, perhaps as an appeal to the royal court to align itself with state policies. Nkrumah also borrowed the Asantehene's prerogative to reward deserving supporters with gifts of *kente,* and he expanded the pool of recipients; highly publicized gifts of *kente* to Muhammad Ali, W. E. B. Du Bois, and Julius Nyerere established it as a cloth of liberation.

Kwame Nkrumah matched his use of textile rhetoric with poetic speech. In late 1960, he hired a royal spokesman to enhance his oratory. Knowing the Asante recognized that "words have to be oiled, tenderized, and embellished to facilitate digestion," he coordinated all his speeches with this skilled Akuapem spokesman.[35] Okyeame Boafo Akuffo was appointed as the first poet of the newly formed nation to provide a prelude of appellations whenever Nkrumah spoke. This innovative use of oral poetry on the radio, in parliament, and at public appearances was said to both make and break Nkrumah. Symbolic language enabled him to build an air of mystery surrounding his power, but it contributed to his downfall when he relied too heavily on *bo akutia*— the ability to chide or scold someone publicly without mentioning a name. And when he banned press stories opposing his policies and songs that he considered critical, it showed he had underestimated how others could also use poetic words as weapons.

By the time Nkrumah was removed from office in 1966, he had helped launch *kente* as a cloth that stood for ideas extending beyond Ghana. His choices reinforced the colors red, green, yellow, and black as indicative of African leadership. The Ghanaian flag he adopted features an expressive color symbolism: red for the blood of those who died in the struggle for independence, gold or yellow for the country's mineral wealth, green for the rich forest, and black for the star of freedom for all Africa. These same hues spread over twelve of the flags adopted by newly independent nations on the continent. Eventually, *kente* evolved into "one of the most familiar of African arts and one of the best known of all African words."[36]

In America, *kente* has emerged as a potent symbol of identification with Africa, in some ways close to its original meaning of a cloth whose "distinctive design still reflects the ideas of strength, wealth, power, and superior social status."[37] A *kente* cloth, or its representation, is an expected visual key for an African American graduation or other ceremony honoring people for their accomplishments. Other uses of *kente*, however, have disturbed Ghanaians, who see a distinctive cloth being marketed as a commercial symbol for all things African (fig. 21). "Kente is now the Motherland, reinvented, packaged and made palatable for mass consumption."[38] Widely available in machine-woven, roller-printed, and machine-made forms, *kente* has become an honored feature at many events, but its pattern names and production quality are not well known. One Ghanaian author explains his attraction to the original woven form: "The slow, deliberate kente weaving process is analogous to life. Further, even in its apparent enduring majesty, the softness, malleability, and ultimate fragility of kente captures the inevitable vulnerability of human beings.[39] A cloth still meticulously woven by hand in Ghana, for specific purposes among the Asante, is now admired for other purposes internationally (fig. 22). When Nelson Mandela toured the United States and Bill Clinton visited Ghana, reporters noted the use they made of *kente*, but not the pattern names they wore.

Fig. 21. "Access to Africa," Ava Van de Water, *Floridian Times* (1993).

Fig. 22. Weaver at Bonwire, Ghana, 1973.

The Adinkra War was a victory for the Asante, but at a great loss.

—Koo Nimo, 1999[40]

Adinkra cloth received its name from a victory over a king of Gyaman named Kofi Adinkra, whose disrespect and arrogance toward the Asante were confirmed when he

Pl. 58
Adinkra cloth
Asante, Ghana
20th century
Imported cotton cloth, pigment, thread
L. 337 cm (132½ in.)
Gift of Katherine White and the Boeing Company,
81.17.472

commissioned a golden stool for himself in the early nineteenth century. After he was defeated, he wore a cloth stamped with a pattern that expressed sorrow for the loss of his freedom and the deaths of his soldiers. This cloth today is translated as *di nkra*, "to part," be separated, leave one another, say goodbye. Named for an enemy who attempted to pirate a crucial symbol from the Asante, the cloth features a maze of symbols likely derived from his court. *Adinkra* cloth is still reserved primarily for funerals. The most famous *adinkra* now in the United States, however, was worn for a different sort of occasion. When forced into exile by the British in 1896, Asante-hene Prempeh I donned an *adinkra* for the photo taken to record his removal from

Kumasi. By doing so, he may have used the cloth to communicate a message by visual means because he couldn't say it in words.[41]

A few hundred *adinkra* motifs have been recorded, but only two hundred or so are regularly used today. Among the dozen symbols with multiple meanings found on one *adinkra* cloth in the Seattle Art Museum's collection are the following (pl. 58):

Fihankra: Circular house signifying safety or security in a home.

Musuyidie: Something to remove evil and bring good fortune, possibly derived from the proverb *Krapa te se okra, okyiri fi* (A good soul is like a cat, it abhors filth).

Pepani amma yenhu Kramo: "Those who claim to be devout Muslims prevent us from knowing the true believers."

Nyame, biribi wo soro na ma embeka mensa: "God, there is something in the heavens, let me reach it."

Dwenini aben (ram's horns): May refer to the proverb *Dwenini ye asise a ode nekorona na ennye na mmen* (It is the heart and not the horns that leads a ram to bully; or, when the horns of two rams clash in a fight, one must give way to another).

Sankofa: For the proverb *Se wo were fi na wosankofa a yenkyi* (You can turn back and fetch it; or, go back and pick—draw from the past to replenish the present).[42]

Although Katherine White could buy *kente* and *adinkra* cloth without difficulty in Ghana, the gold jewelry she desired was not commonly sold in the twentieth century. Fifteenth-century Europeans were aware of the impressive use of gold ornaments from the moment they landed. By 1502, fifteen ships a year are reported to have sailed away with caches of gold ornaments, and over the next four centuries, virtually all the ornaments were taken away to be melted down; very few exceptions survived.[43] As the gold trade diminished in the nineteenth century, the royal ornaments owned by enstooled leaders did not appear for sale. Any attempt to sell them was a breach of property rights and cause for immediate destooling. Unlike *kente* cloth and *adinkra* symbols, widely disseminated since the 1970s, gold jewelry has had less of an international impact. Not reproduced by industrial methods, gold jewelry is available to a limited clientele. Goldsmiths stepped up production in the late 1920s and again around 1935, when Asantehene Prempeh II was enstooled. Ceremonial occasions called for new jewelry to proclaim the importance of the stool that a person occupied. It now appears that the majority of the gold ornaments purchased by White came from a supply dating to this revival period. Departing from her usual thoroughness in recording purchases, she left the history of the gold collection to be pursued.[44]

> One question acts as a key to another. —Asante proverb

Gold pectorals, beads, necklaces, and bracelets, like the rings discussed earlier, often infuse common forms with eloquence.[45] Two large disks known as *akrafokonmu,*

Pl. 59
Soul washer's disk *(akrafokonmu)*
Asante, Ghana
20th century
Gold
Diam. 8.4 cm (3⅜ in.)
Gift of Katherine White and the Boeing Company,
81.17.1685

Pl. 60
Soul washer's disk *(akrafokonmu)*
Asante, Ghana
20th century
Gold, silver
Diam. 11.8 cm (4⅝ in.)
Gift of Katherine White and the Boeing Company,
81.17.414

Pl. 61
Bracelet *(babadua)*
Asante, Ghana
20th century
Gold, silver
Diam. 7 cm (2¾ in.)
Gift of Katherine White and the Boeing Company,
81.17.425

"soul washer's disks," would be worn by a ruler, queen mother, and certain court members to protect the wearer with a radiating pattern that refers to the sun (pls. 59, 60). As the ultimate source of each person's *kra*—the spiritual essence given to a child at birth and removed at death—the sun appears in gold as its earthly complement. Gold ornaments thus became a way of displaying the soul and vitality of the nation. Disks were also worn by *akrafo*, the soul washers, who form a symbolic shield in front of a leader as they walk in processions or sit on formal occasions. Kings frequently employ young soul washers to conduct ceremonies to purify the chief's soul in the course of renewing it. Round beads in a multitude of filigree and appliqué patterns keep the sun disks visible when strung in necklaces, anklets, and bracelets.

Bracelets and armlets could quickly distinguish a person. Known as *babadua*, two bracelets with knobs and angular designs refer to a proverb: "A plantation of *babadua* never stops spreading" (pls. 61, 62). *Babadua*, a tall straggling shrub, both tough and resilient, is often used for the framework in house building and thatching. Such a bracelet is worn by queen mothers to honor their tenacity and fertility. As another piece of protective jewelry, an armlet is less ornament than armor; it dangles thick amulets made of leather sheathed in gold (pl. 63). The amulets, made by Muslims, have Islamic writing inside. A chief gathered such a group around his arm to ward off threats when appearing in public.

Gold beads also form assemblies in which each item contributes to an overall protective force (pls. 64, 65). Many beads are explorations of geometric forms and patterns, but others present a miniature world of common references. Among them are animal teeth to signify a ruler's aggression, talons to indicate fearlessness, bells to summon spirits to encase the wearer and ward off misfortune. Keys are a shape traced to fifteenth-century European trade; they were worn in bunches as a sign of wealth. And a watch emphasized the power of a leader to control time, and thereby events in his domain (pl. 66).

Pl. 62
Bracelet *(babadua)*
Asante, Ghana
20th century
Gold beads, fiber
L. 10.5 cm (4⅛ in.)
Gift of Katherine White and the Boeing Company, 81.17.428

Pl. 63
Armlet *(barurum sebe)*
Asante, Ghana
20th century
Leather, thread, gold leaf
L. 28.8 cm (11⅜ in.)
Gift of Katherine White and the Boeing Company, 81.17.1651

Pl. 64
Beads
Asante, Ghana
20th century
Gold
Diam. (largest): 4.5 cm (1¾ in.)
Gift of Katherine White and the Boeing Company,
81.17.410.1–.11, 81.17.413.1–.4, 81.17.416.3

Pl. 65
Beads
Asante, Ghana
20th century
Gold
L. (largest): 4 cm (1½ in.)
Gift of Katherine White and the Boeing Company,
81.17.418.1–.7, 81.17.419.1–.7

Pl. 66
Watch
Asante, Ghana
20th century
Gold
W. 5 cm (2 in.)
Gift of Katherine White and the Boeing Company,
81.17.409

Speech is not sweet if you strip it of its
garment.   —Asante proverb

One aesthetic impulse underlying much of this regalia
has been discussed recently by Ghanaian scholar Kwesi
Yankah.[46] A pervasive strategy is using the aesthetic of the
indirect, or employing oblique language and actions to
conceal one's intentions so that others must discern them.
Proverbs and sayings are the main tool for indirection—
citing a neutral truism can cause reflection and bring a tense
situation under control. Indirect dress codes also apply, as
witnessed during a subchief's appearance before a court of
elders in Kumasi. He arrived with his cloth inside out, his
sandals reversed, and his entire costume in a state of disorder. By violating the strict rules about dress, regalia, and
behavior, he was able to convey his dissatisfaction with a
decision made by the elders. Without speaking, his appearance commanded immediate attention and set a new course for the proceedings. In a more personal vein, a
woman may wrap a cloth around her waist with a terminal knot to convey the innu-
endo "a fool follows behind me," alluding to a co-wife.

The audience is not just the spectator but the co-creator.

—Koo Nimo, 1999[47]

Asante art was originally created for an audience that constantly fit proverbs into
speech. Recently, when the first woman dean of the University of Ghana named a
dormitory, she reduced an old proverb—"The hen knows when the sun comes up but
waits for the cock to crow about it"—to "Cock a doodle do" and had it placed over
the entrance. Asante rulers continue to wear regalia that communicates with Ghanaian audiences. When the president of Ghana, Jerry Rawlings, described an appearance with Asantehene Otumfuo Opoku Ware II, he said, "Sometimes salt does not
seem to speak," referring to the power this ruler wields over his audience without
uttering a word.[48] On April 26, 1999, before a capacity audience at Kumasi stadium,
the sixteenth occupant of the Golden Stool was enstooled. Asantehene Otumfuo
Osei Tutu II has been lauded as a promising leader because of his unrivaled knowledge of Asante statecraft.

Offered in the hope of creating a vital reception for Asante art, this brief lesson
spoke of the unique role of a golden stool, the messages conveyed by cloths, and the
eloquence found in a peanut.

Notes

1. Kwesi Yankah, *Speaking for the Chief* (Bloomington: Indiana University Press, 1995), 1.

2. Ibid., 45.

3. The proverbs cited here have been drawn from Peggy Appiah, *Why the Hyena Does Not Care for Fish and Other Tales from the Ashanti Gold Weights* (London: Andre Deutsch, 1977); Timothy Garrard, *Akan Weights and the Gold Trade* (London: Longman Group, 1980), chap. 6; R. Sutherland Rattray, *Ashanti Proverbs: The Primitive Ethics of a Savage People* (1916; reprint, Oxford: Clarendon Press, 1969). Additional readings have been enriched by many conversations with Daniel "Koo Nimo" Amponsah, 2000–2001.

4. Interpretation by Koo Nimo, presentation, Seattle Art Museum, March 1999.

5. Garrard, *Akan Weights.*

6. Yaw Atwereboanna, 1903 document in Liverpool Museum, cited in ibid., 301.

7. Johann Gottlieb Christaller, cited in Garrard, *Akan Weights,* 273.

8. Thomas E. Bowdich, *A Mission from Cape Coast Castle to Ashantee* (London: John Murray, 1819).

9. For a discussion of the fuller dimensions of the yam festival, see Agnes Aidoo, "Political Crisis and Social Change in the Asante Kingdom, 1867–1901" (Ph.D. diss., University of California, Los Angeles, 1975), and T. D. McCaskie, "Asante Odwira: Experience Interpreted, History Constructed," in *State and Society in Pre-Colonial Asante* (Cambridge: Cambridge University Press, 1995).

10. Cited in Enid Schildkrout, ed., *Notes from the Golden Stool: Studies of the Asante Center and Periphery,* 1987).

11. Cited in ibid.

12. Winwood Reade, *The Story of the Ashantee Campaign* (1874), 357–58, cited in Aidoo, "Political Crisis and Social Change," 183.

13. The exact date of Prempeh's birth is debated.

14. Ivor Wilks, *Forests of Gold* (Athens: Ohio University Press, 1993), 225.

15. Letter from Asantehene Prempeh I to Governor Branford Griffith, June 28, 1894, cited in Aidoo, "Political Crisis and Social Change," 616.

16. Letter from Governor Branford Griffith to J. R. Holmes, District Commissioner of the Cape Coast, 1890, cited in ibid., 580.

17. Cited in *The Golden Stool: An Account of the Ashanti War of 1900* (London: Kimber, 1966), 33.

18. Cited in Agnes Aidoo, "Asante Queen Mothers in Government and Politics in the Nineteenth Century," *Journal of the Historical Society of Nigeria* 55, no. 2 (December 1977), 12.

19. R. S. Rattray, *Ashanti* (London: Oxford University Press, 1923), 295.

20. Petition by Prempeh I to Governor Gordon Guggisberg, October 13, 1918, cited in Joseph K. Adjaye, "Asantehene Agyeman Prempeh I and British Colonization of Asante: A Reassessment," *The International Journal of African Historical Studies,* 1989.

21. Emmanuel Akyeampong, "Christianity, Modernity and the Weight of Tradition in the Life of Asantehene Agyeman Prempeh I, c. 1888–1931," *Africa* 69, no. 2 (1999), 304–5.

22. Herbert Cole and Doran Ross, *The Arts of Ghana* (Los Angeles: UCLA Fowler Museum of Cultural History, 1977), 140.

23. Informants cited in Wilks, *Forests of Gold,* "Political Crisis and Social Change," 233–34.

24. Aidoo, "Political Crisis and Social Change," 273.

25. Peter Sarpong, *The Sacred Stools of the Akan* (Accra: Ghana Publishing Corporation, 1971).

26. Obo Addy, conversation with author, Seattle, May 2000.

27. See Doran Ross, "The Heraldic Lion in Akan Art: A Study of Motif Assimilation in Southern Ghana," *Metropolitan Museum Journal* 16 (1982), 165–78.

28. Malcolm McLeod, *The Asante* (London: British Museum Publications, 1981), 78.

29. *Kente* as a term has a sequence of evolving translations. It first appeared in print in 1847 when a "cotton blanket (*kintee*)" was acquired from an Ewe town and taken to Denmark. Three possible meanings:

    1. a term honoring a seventeenth-century Asantehene named Oti Akenten;

    2. a combination of two Ewe words, *ke* and *te,* meaning "open" and "close";

    3. "that which will not tear under any condition."

30. Katherine White Journals, Seattle Art Museum.

31. Ibid.

32. Quoted in "Maternal Legacies: A Weave of Stories," Doran Ross, ed., *Wrapped in Pride: Ghanaian Kɛntɛ and African American Identity* (Los Angeles: UCLA Fowler Museum of Cultural History, 1999).

33. Johann Gottlieb Christaller, *Dictionary of the Asante and Fante Language Called Tshi [Twi]* (Basel: Basel Evangelical Missionary Society, 1933), 303.

34. Kwaku Ofori-Ansa, *Kente Is More Than a Cloth: History and Significance of Ghana's Kente Cloth* (Maryland: Sankofa Publications, 1993).

35. Kwesi Yankah, "The Making and Breaking of Kwame Nkrumah: The Role of Oral Poetry," *Journal of African Studies* 12, no. 2 (1985), 86–92.

36. Ross, *Wrapped in Pride.*

37. Nii O. Quarcoopone, quoted in "Pride and Avarice: Kente and Advertising," in Ross, *Wrapped in Pride.*

38. Ibid.

39. Joseph K. Adjaye, "The Discourse of Kente Cloth: From Haute Couture to Mass Culture," Joseph K. Adjaye and Adrianne R. Andrews, eds., *Language, Rhythm, and Sound: Black Popular Cultures into the 21st Century* (Pittsburgh: University of Pittsburgh Press, 1997), 29.

40. Nimo, presentation, 2000.

41. Asantehene Prempeh I's *adinkra* is in the collection of the National Museum of African Art; see Leasa Fortune, *Adinkra: The Cloth That Speaks* (Washington, D.C.: Smithsonian Institution, 1997).

42. See Rattray, *Ashanti Proverbs,* 264–68.

43. Martha Ehrlich, "Early Akan Gold from the Wreck of the Whydah," *African Arts* 22, no. 4 (1989), 56.

44. White purchased a group of rings, bracelets, and necklaces from Karl Merz, who had married the granddaughter of Bantamahene Kwame Kyem. The Bantamahene died in November 1944, and Merz's wife moved to Switzerland in 1949, taking with her from Kumasi this group of jewelry, among many other items. Correspondence indicates that he was selling the jewelry and wanted the previous owners to be known as Nana Kwame Kyem, Bantamahene; James Adjaye-Kyem; and the Kyem family. Listing the owner as an individual and his family does deviate from Asante ownership law. Most goldwork would properly be described as being the stool property of the Bantamahene, not his personal property. Ownership of gold regalia belonged to the office, not to the individual occupying the stool. Research into this ownership question is now ongoing.

45. For an in-depth discussion of Asante gold, see Timothy Garrard, *Gold of Africa,* (Geneva: Barbier-Mueller Museum, 1989).

46. Kwesi Yankah, "Proverbs: The Aesthetics of Traditional Communication," *Research in African Literature* 20, no. 3 (fall 1989), 325–46.

47. Nimo, presentation, 2000.

48. Gilda Sheppard, interview by author, Seattle, 1998.

Assembling a Royal Stage: Art from the Kom Kingdom

The original owners of the nearly four thousand African objects in the Seattle Art Museum are rarely known by name.[1] Art from one kingdom in Cameroon offers an exception and introduces five owners whose interactions with collectors span the twentieth century. Archival notes and files are full of details about kings who surrounded themselves with artistry. These records offer a perplexing view of royalty—of men who had commanding agendas but were dependent on others, who maintained a private distance from their subjects but allowed outsiders to become confidants. One note embodies these contradictions:

Royal Scepter [see pl. 70]
total length ca. 46"; length of handle ca. 6½"—
wood, copper plate, trade beads, horsetail—
finest example of transformation of the simple fly whisk and its use into a royal insignia of authority—: commemorating the tribal victory of the people of Bekom over the Fulani invaders around 1830—
history: presented by Fon Ndi of the Bekom [Kom] nation in 1933 to Paul Gebauer for dental services, the making of an upper plate and lower bridge, which lasted the old boy until his death but did not restore to him the power of youth he had expected. . . . He had been told beforehand that no miracle would occur beyond the pleasure of chewing kola nuts once more.[2]

It seems an improbable exchange: a royal scepter (or flywhisk) for dental services, a symbol of victory over invaders for the chance to chew kola (not to diminish the stimulating pleasure it provides). The museum's records indicate other occasions when the Fon (king) gave away art—a figure was offered in return for help provided to a king's eighty-eight wives; a throne was given because it was admired in a discard pile. Such accounts introduce the close associations between foreigners and the Fons. This closeness creates a puzzle of references: private details, public records, changing governments, two thorough photographic archives, rumors and newspaper accounts— all merge to form a faceted picture of the Kom kings and their art. Anchoring this inquiry are figures designed to sustain a dynasty.

Pl. 70 (detail)

Over the course of a decade, Katherine White acquired objects that all came
from the same closely guarded royal sanctuary high on a mountaintop in Cameroon.
To do so, she relied upon alliances with Americans living in the vicinity of the Kom
kingdom for up to thirty years. Their accounts of collecting from the hands of the
original owner, the king himself, reveal the level of access they enjoyed. Visiting the
royal palace on a frequent basis, they built a photographic record that enhances their
descriptions of royal life. In the final assembly of objects, White established a ceremonial setting, a stage fit for a king (fig. 23).

A complete array of the symbols known as *ufwu-a-Kom* ("things belonging to the
Kom people") would have been seen only at the palace in the Kom capital of Laikom.
There, atop a mountain slope at 6,300 feet elevation, on a long volcanic spur known
for drenching tropical rains and severe lightning, a dynasty established a dramatic
site from which to rule.

> Laikom was worth the stiff climb and the exposure to its bitter cold
> nights, for it was a jewel of architecture. Artistic rulers made it into
> a showcase of towering buildings and a maze of courtyards.
>
> —Paul Gebauer, 1930[3]

No producer could ask for a more spectacular setting for an auspicious public event. Often shrouded in mist, Laikom was perched high above all other settlements on the Grassfields plateau (fig. 24). Entering the palace was equated with
walking into a human body—the main gate was the mouth; the central square, the
stomach; and the Fon's quarters, the buttocks or foundation of the palace.[4] At the
turn of the century, as many as three hundred wives lived in compounds considered
the limbs of the palace body (fig. 25). The innermost square was reserved for the
sacred core of the Kom—an altar defined by a basalt pillar, a cactus tree, and a stone
throne. The tallest building in the complex was an audience hall, into which only
a select portion of the Kom people would be ushered on their way to a ceremonial
occasion. As they entered, palace retainers monitored their every step, and kept
royal art apart from the commoners. Just as the Fon was aloof from contact, so his

possessions were not to be touched by anyone without special authority. Before dawn, officials would be sent to the sanctuary that housed an entire set of royal family portraits. No one saw them emerge and install the assembly in a corner of the large square.

> **Symbolism captures their minds and maintains their interest.**
>
> —Paul Nchoji Nkwi[5]

One of the most prominent portraits is composed of a life-size female figure standing with clasped hands over a stool adjoining her knees (pl. 67). This memorial figure of a queen mother underwent a drastic change of context at the beginning of the twentieth century. In Laikom, the figure was kept in a repository guarded by palace retainers who permitted only the king's closest councilors to enter. Commoners

Memorial figure of queen mother
Laikom, Kom Kingdom, Cameroon
Mid-19th century
Wood, glass beads, brass, human hair, redwood powder
H. 175.3 cm (69 in.)
Gift of Katherine White and the Boeing Company,
81.17.718

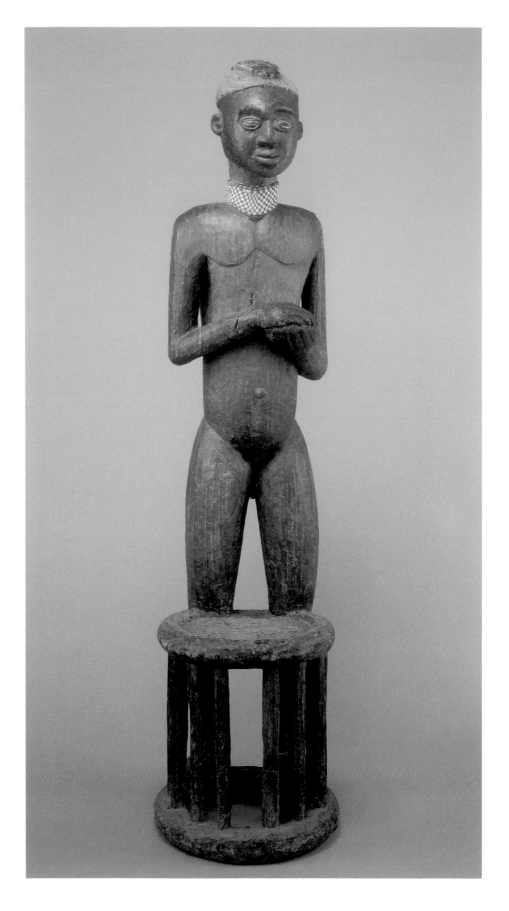

could view the mother only once or twice in a lifetime as part of the installation of a new king, when the queen mother joined a line of portraits dedicated to ancestors whose rule remained unbroken since the founding of Laikom. Her presence was an essential reminder of the female line of descent, which set Kom rulers apart from all neighboring kingdoms.

Kom eyes would read her features with appreciation. Not young or alluring, she is a middle-aged woman of unshakable stability and dignity. Her hair is shaved in a manner common to women of the nineteenth century (fig. 26). Traces of red powder show that she was properly rubbed and coated with camwood as a protective measure. She cups her hands just as royal women do when they clap to greet the king. No sharp features or angles appear in her face, in accordance with a Kom preference for rounded curves. The only exaggerated feature is her ears, which protrude perhaps to signify her role as a woman who listens for ancestral communication. A coating of copper riddled with slight dents becomes a metal sheath over her face. Beauty for the Kom is embodied less in the face than in the body.[6] The figure fulfills an ideal body type, with an ample physique of broad shoulders and long limbs that suggest a woman able to work and provide for her family. The stool at her knees extends to remind viewers of the lineage of rulers whose enstoolment or enthronement she presides over. Around her neck, a beaded necklace in checkerboard blue and white hints at the beading that once covered her body.

In the public setting, the Kom portraits invited ancestors of the past to participate and sanction events in the present. Endowed with impressive composure, the portraits were regarded as capable of controlling behavior. Women, in particular, were believed to have close communication with ancestors. Their covert power could produce reactions in people, while men had to rely on overt power. Figures commemorating the mothers and wives of the Fon had to be present. This queen mother has been identified by the name of Naya, the great-grandmother of Fon Yu.[7] Her strength was imparted to him, the most powerful of all Kom Fons, whose influence on the reputation and extent of the Kom kingdom is legendary.

Just two photographs of Fon Yu are known to exist (fig. 27).[8] Taken between 1905 and 1910, they are the only direct evidence of a remarkable ruler, then nearing the end of his life. Born in 1830, he was known to be ambitious at an early age, and his older brother exiled him for two years to a neighboring kingdom. While in exile, Fon Yu learned to carve. He returned to establish his reign at the age of thirty-five and ruled over the Kom for forty-seven years until his death in 1912—an unprecedented stretch of time (from before the American Civil War until the eve of World War I). In both his photographic portraits, Fon Yu holds sculptor's tools and poses with a memorial female figure whose size suggests that Yu was relatively tall. Lines on his brow mark many years of leadership.

Memories of Fon Yu, the seventh Kom king, loom large. A forceful innovator, he is credited with making bold moves and focusing increasing attention on himself as the main actor in the prestige system. Forty-five villages came under his control for ritual and secular affairs. Laikom became his showcase for architecture as he established how court compounds were to be distributed over the landscape. Known as

Fig. 26. Babungo wife with shaved coiffure rubbed with camwood, ca. 1930–1960. The Metropolitan Museum of Art, Department of the Arts of Africa, Oceania, and the Americas. The Photograph Study Collection. Bequest of Paul Gebauer, 1977, J-26.

Fig. 27. Fon Yu (reigned 1865–1912) posing as carver, with the female figure of the Afo-a-Kom ensemble, ca. 1905–1910.

the king who began and ended wars, he invited noted warriors to drink with him weekly at his palace. Fon Yu is also remembered for swiftly punishing by death those who failed to be hospitable to strangers.[9] To enhance his stature, he surrounded himself with art as symbolic support. A school of carvers produced royal sculpture, implements, and doorposts that set him apart. Portraits of his family sanctioned his right to rule: they underlined the notion that the Fon might be the supreme force in the nation, but he still depended on his family for support. Admiration for Fon Yu's restless enterprise is tempered by memories of his severe tactics of law enforcement, including experimentation with slow poisons.

In 1900, Fon Yu was firmly positioned in Laikom. He aggressively fended off a German explorer in 1889, but by 1904–1905, German expeditions were making the ascent to Laikom. During 1904, a German missionary named Reinhold Rhode acquired a pair of memorial figures—one of them the queen mother—and several other items from the palace. It is not known whether these items were obtained by gift or by coercion. In August 1905, German forces ended a punitive expedition by signing a treaty and enacting a gift exchange with the Fon. Sculptures and masks were taken back to museums in Berlin and Frankfurt. By that year, the Rhode figures were installed in the newly established Museum für Völkerkunde in Frankfurt.

Fig. 28. Performance at Laikom, 1974.

The shift from Laikom to Frankfurt could not have been more radical. In Laikom, the queen figure was situated on a secluded mountaintop, as remote and inaccessible as the Fon. The figure's potency was enhanced by the caution and care exercised by the Kom curators, who watched over the art in secrecy. When displayed, its impression on an audience was enhanced by the sensory overload of music, the excitement of performances, and the effects of abundant food and drink (fig. 28). In the German museum, the figure was stripped from seclusion and brought indoors. A postcard image of the "Cameroon Gallery," issued in 1906, shows the arrangement (fig. 29).[10] The male and female portraits were placed against a wall amid a spray of weapons and a line of masks above. All day, every day, they were on view. No spectacle remained, just isolated objects.

A label for the female introduces a colonial explanation of who she was:

Throne of the Queen, 68½" high. Standing life-size wood figure representing the great-grandmother of the King. Face and hands are covered with copper overlay. The eyes are formed from indigenous resinous substance. Its neck is ornamented with blue and white beads. Both of these thrones were used by the royal pair during festivities and important palavers. Both were held in awe as fetishes by the people.[11]

Calling it a "fetish" throne that a queen sat upon while ruling with her king, the German curators invented a stereotypical role. The queen was no longer a trigger for Kom memories. The curators presented it as a flat statement of colonial fact—Kom kings and queens had their thrones captured and were subjected to colonial rule. What Fon Yu had to say about this queen mother figure is not known. Despite the fact that the Germans had continuing contact with him for the next five years, no dialogue regarding his role as an artistic leader is recorded. The two photographs taken of him were even misidentified for more than fifty years. Fon Yu died in 1912 and was succeeded by his nephew Nggam. German rule did not last long, as British and French forces split Cameroon for a half-century of separate rule beginning in 1915.

The Frankfurt museum sold the queen figure in 1934 to Arthur Speyer, a German collector and dealer. Then, after fifty years in German hands, the queen figure moved to Paris at the height of a growing market for African art. The figure entered the gallery of Charles Ratton, a renowned collector and dealer who had been an advocate of African and Oceanic art since the 1930s. His close associations with the Surrealists bolstered his reputation in artistic circles, but he was denounced for his ties to Nazi leaders when he offered his collection to the Musée du Louvre in the 1980s. Before long, word of the queen figure's availability reached Katherine White, who was collecting with frenzied enthusiasm after 1961. Her description of a visit to Charles Ratton's gallery shows how the queen figure has entered another kind of sanctuary—now guarded by the officials of the European art world. Ratton tests her association with two of the leading curators of African art: William Fagg, then at the British Museum, and Margaret Plass, at the Philadelphia Museum of Art. In a dealer's maneuver, Ratton waits to determine White's serious interest and expertise before bringing out objects that are not in open view:

Paris, April 1966

It was nearly 11. I rushed out and got a cab to 15 rue Marignan. The black glass sign said Charles Ratton—Expert. I rang the bell and tried to calm myself. I remembered him as small, spry, white haired. The photographs of the Cameroon Queen stool had been with me for so long that the sale was for me a fait accompli: finally someone came. I was shown into a room. M. Ratton came, and we went into his office. There she was. I was afraid to look at her—it was a collision of emotion for me. Her face was still gentle, but grosser than I had remembered. The real hair glued on her eyebrows disturbed me a little. She is still, straight, and awkward, but very shy and proud. I began to recover from my fear. M. Ratton kept up a lively chatter. Many of his casual inquiries were tests. "Do you find negroes like their art?" "When is Mr. Fagg coming to Paris?" "How is Margaret?" He found he approved of me as much as he did the last time. "You have good people to speak for you," he said. Indeed, I am lucky.

We made arrangements, said goodbye. He wrapped up a dainty Bakuba paint box for me as a souvenir. It was a pleasant episode. He comes to New York Monday to observe the Rubenstein sale—many of her things were his "achievements," as he calls them.[12]

The queen figure now has three identities. A royal portrait kept in seclusion. A fetish throne in a German museum. A Parisian dealer's "accomplishment." Of international stature, the figure would now enter the living room of a growing private collection in Gates Mills, Ohio. In 1966, the Kom memorial figure became a distinguished feature of Katherine White's assembly. Once unveiled in Ohio, the female figure was reunited with the male from the same royal sanctuary in Laikom (pl. 68). The male figure's exportation was the result not of German incursion but of American alliance. A note in the museum's files provides a glimpse of the association that led to its removal from Laikom:

When Fon Ndi of Kom died in 1954 [fig. 30], his 88 wives were, according to custom, put in charge of an impartial party, in this case Dr. Gebauer. He was in charge for a year—it cost him 6 cows and much palm wine. The older wives were allowed to retire on a small piece of land. The others, young enough to bear children, could choose their next husbands. At the end of the year there was a ceremonial bathing so they could be free of their old lives. This stand was brought to Dr. Gebauer by the new Fon of Kom, Law-aw, as a reward for his work. He said it was the oldest thing they had. Dr. Gebauer said the Fon was aware of the sentimental value the piece would have for the recipient.[13]

We might wonder why the Fon would give to a foreigner what is called the kingdom's oldest thing, a sculpture closely guarded and restricted from sight. For a partial answer we should consider changes in Laikom. Fon Ndi, born in 1866, was instated as king in 1926. He inherited a palace of 252 houses, occupied by 109 wives.[14] His leadership was limited by British colonial policies of indirect rule. One major change

during his reign was the active presence of missionaries. Roman Catholic and Baptist missions had been established in the Bamenda division years before (1838 and 1919), but during Fon Ndi's era, Christians set up schools and hospitals and began to exert new influence, especially on the young men commemorated in this figure.

Not a portrait of an individual, this sculpture is a memorial to a whole system of service that the Fon relied upon. Young men known as *chisendo*s formed an elite group of attendants who assisted with many aspects of palace life.[15] A candidate was chosen between the ages of ten and fifteen if he had an aptitude for learning, regardless of his family's position. At the palace, he underwent at least ten years of intensive training, including instruction in diplomacy, trade, security, and ceremonial and ritual preparations. The trainees were supervised by officers of an organization known as Kwifon, or "voice of the Fon" (fig. 31), an intricate system of government common throughout the Cameroon Grassfields. It was said that Kwifon supported the Fon as a taproot supports a tree.[16] Not seen, but ever present, Kwifon members heard everything going on and could exert unlimited power when necessary. They announced orders, enacted regulations, settled domestic disputes, and inflicted penalties as warranted. Outside the palace, whenever acting in the public eye, Kwifon officers veiled themselves in masquerade so as not to be identified as individuals. Behind the scenes, they acted as a democratic decision-making forum. After being trained by Kwifon officers, *chisendo*s eventually became Kwifon members themselves.

Fig. 30. Mourning the death of Fon Ndi (reigned 1926–1954), with Paul Gebauer (center) taking photographs, Laikom, 1954.

Pl. 68
Retainer figure
Laikom, Kom, Cameroon
19th century
Wood, nails, fiber fragments
H. 77.3 cm (30½ in.)
Gift of Katherine White and the Boeing Company, 81.17.719

Fig. 31. Kwifon group portrait in front of the royal storage house, Laikom, 1970.

Fig. 32. Royal storage house interior, Laikom, 1966.

The sculpture (pl. 68) represents a *chisendo* of high status. As a signal of how extremely close he is to the Fon, he is seated on a leopard stool, a royal prerogative symbolizing the cunning and stealth with which royalty operates. The *chisendo*'s cap also signifies rank. Small holes and nails indicate that his body was originally covered with a beaded coating. Beyond these references, the relaxed display of authority combined with service makes this figure stand out. Symbols of strength are matched by a body that would assume gigantic proportions if he stood. Long arms curve up and end in hands that expand to hold two containers—a gourd and a large bowl. Long legs splay over the seat. In contrast to the endless facets that flicker across the surface of his limbs, his face remains a study in calm, smooth composure. Serenely juggling two vessels while sitting atop a leopard is testimony to the dignity of the *chisendo*.

Photographs record this figure placed on the ground next to other memorial figures, as well as stored in the royal sanctuary guarded by the Kwifon (fig. 32).[17] It would likely have been the task of a *chisendo* to bring out the figure and fill the vessels with palm wine and kola nuts—two essential ingredients for a ceremony, to lubricate and heighten awareness of events as they unfold. This figure has sat through many years of royal ceremonies and testifies to the unique position of the *chisendo* in Laikom.

Fon Law-aw's removal of the figure is a portent of personnel shifts in his palace. Hundreds of *chisendo*s were once in residence, enabling the Fon to guard the cultural center of the kingdom and learn the running of Kwifon government. By the end of his father's reign, missionary schools and national government policies were giving parents new choices for their children's education. While becoming a *chisendo* was desirable in the 1940s and 1950s, by the 1960s formal education was one of the changes forging a path through the kingdom. Steadily, recruitment of *chisendo*s

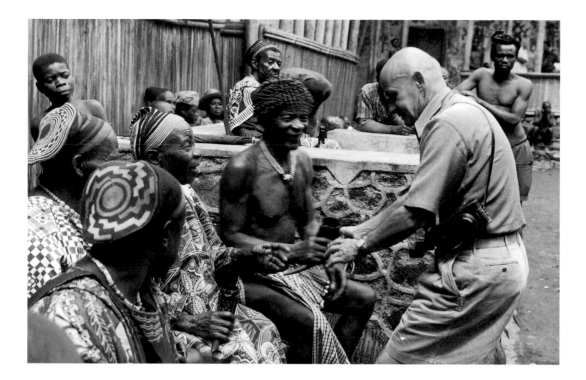

Fig. 33. Paul Gebauer saluting subchiefs, Laikom, 1954.

dropped off, until by 1990 only five were left in the palace.[18] Fon Law-aw gave the *chisendo* portrait to a foreigner whose tenure in Cameroon overlapped this period of change.

> **Henry VIII would have been envious.** —Paul Gebauer, 1979[19]

Paul Gebauer and his wife, Clara, arrived to work at the American Baptist Mission in 1931 and stayed until 1961 (fig. 33). Their legacy of Cameroonian art is embodied in thousands of photographs and hundreds of documented objects now housed in several museums. Katherine White corresponded with Paul Gebauer for years to seek advice about assembling her own selection. She began by buying the male retainer figure from him in 1964. Paul Gebauer speaks of himself as being "prematurely bald, prematurely blunt, and prematurely initiated into the secrets of missionary-politicians."[20] He and Clara became known for sending home candid reports and participating in studies of local art and landscape. Paul's descriptions of Fon Ndi's palace—the Fon seated near the fireplace with attendants nearby, ruling over a kingdom punctuated with ceremony and architectural artistry—are filled with admiration. He launched a study of spider divination that led to a master's thesis, an endeavor that did not sit well with some of his Baptist brothers. His statement of purpose set a course of acceptance that must have been noticed by the Fons he came into contact with:

> We shall not take our culture to them, for they have one of their own. We shall not burden them with our American civilization, because theirs is one of their own.... We shall not laugh at their arts and crafts but encourage them to carry on and to perfect their expression of their appreciation of the beautiful. We

shall not denounce their social and political institutions as sinful and ugly and out of date, for we of the west lack the wisdom to discriminate, nor do we have the right to do so.[21]

The Gebauers backed up this manifesto by establishing a school that was "as informal and individual as possible." They earned a reputation for hiring artists to adorn building projects with sculpture and for being attentive to a succession of leaders throughout the region.

Kom art and ethics were treated differently by Roman Catholic missions. In the 1920s, Kom Catholics were known to unmask Kwifon masqueraders and spit upon them—an opposition that was to reverse later in the century.[22] More pointedly for Fon Ndi, however, Catholic missionaries began encouraging his wives to leave their compounds and marry mission converts. This campaign lasted into the 1940s, and in 1947 reached a crescendo. A Catholic newspaper made a scandal of the issue by publishing "Just Cargo," a nun's description of what she counted as Fon Ndi's six hundred wives. The article included her account of witnessing a girl being thrown on the ground and stepped on by the Fon. This article became the basis for a United Nations investigation, which determined that for the sake of vividness the writer had dramatized Kom custom and made it appear she was describing an actual incident.[23]

Although the United Nations and the Catholic bishop backed off from trying to influence the Fon's private life, a journalist named Rebecca Reyher set out to witness the "heartbreak of polygamy." Her account, entitled *The Fon and His Hundred Wives,* was published in 1952.[24] As part of her journey, she visited Paul Gebauer, who puzzled her with his clear opinions regarding the issue. He commended Fon Ndi's intelligence and his system of governance, and condemned Catholic baptism for its shortsightedness. Reyher proceeded to Laikom, was invited by the Fon to stay at his guesthouse, and talked with him on numerous occasions. Her focus rarely wavered from the plight of runaway wives or from skeptical disapproval, but her account does provide details about the crosscurrents of Fon Ndi's time. Reyher left Africa after two weeks at Laikom and several months in Cameroon and Nigeria, while Paul and Clara Gebauer stayed thirty years. And Paul Gebauer was given a sculpture in thanks for his service to Fon Ndi's eighty-eight widows.

Endowed with two major Kom sculptures, Katherine White continued to look for others. In 1968, she purchased a throne that left Laikom after another long-term American alliance (pl. 69). Gilbert and Mildred Schneider had gone to Cameroon in 1947 as part of the American Baptist Missionary Society and stayed for sixteen years. Stationed for many years fifteen miles from Laikom, they were instrumental in setting up a facility for the housing and treatment of lepers. Gilbert established an extensive archive of photographs and notes of his observations, which led to a doctorate in anthropology upon his return to the United States. His documentary work was carried on by his son Evan, born and raised in Cameroon. Their joint efforts comprise a remarkably thorough record of cultural evolution from the 1940s to the present. During their initial tenure, the Schneiders became close to Fon Lo-oh (ruler from 1955 to 1964) (fig. 34). Gilbert worked so closely with Lo-oh and a Kom adviser and former *chisendo,* Johnson Mbeng, that he was permitted to move around the palace without

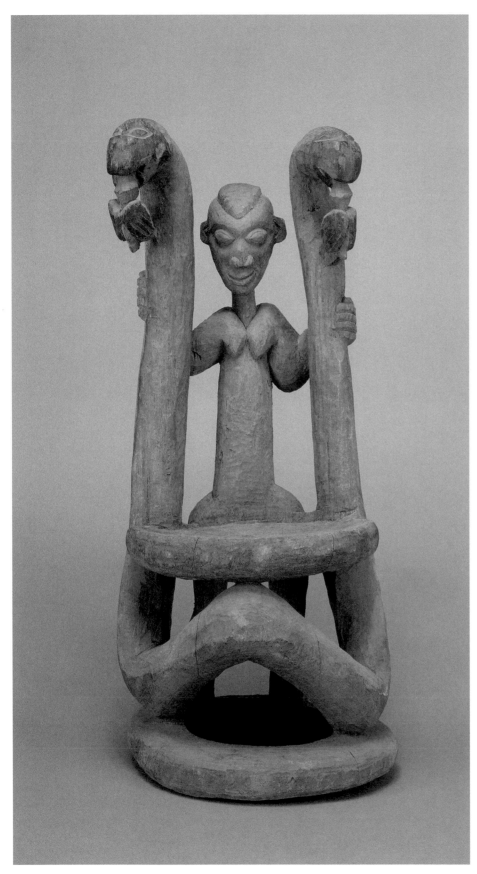

Pl. 69
Coronation throne
Laikom, Kom, Cameroon
20th century
Wood
H. 99.7 cm (39¼ in.)
Gift of Katherine White and the Boeing Company,
81.17.720

escort and to take pictures of royal objects. During one visit, Schneider noticed a figure piled up with other items in a passageway. In a letter to Katherine White, Schneider explains:

> The figure which you now have was in the "discard" category. I voiced concern about the piece and other such items and the Fon immediately gave me permission to take a few items. He gave me that particular piece without any strings attached. He was glad that two people took interest in documenting the royal palace. We should be grateful to have the Kom throne in the States. The royal palace burned in the early 1960s and all the "discard" pieces that remained were destroyed by fire.[25]

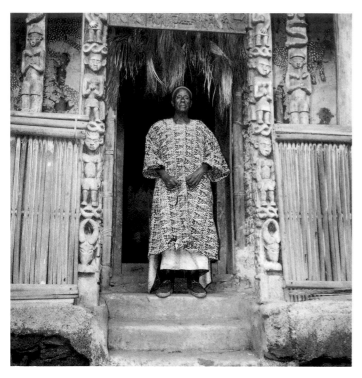

Fig. 34. Fon Lo-oh (reigned 1955–1964) in front of main gathering house, Laikom.

This "discard" visualizes the origin of Laikom. It is a stool whose back is formed by a woman grasping a two-headed snake in her hands; each snake head holds a bird in its mouth. Just as this woman is steadfast in holding this large swirling creature about her, so the story behind the stool unites the Kom as the "people of the snake." Kom people tell and retell the story as their foundation myth.[26] The tale begins in a time when the Kom were settled and thriving in Bamessi. The Fon of Bamessi, however, became upset by the growing population and suggested to the Kom Fon, named Muni, that they each build a house for troublemakers and set the houses afire. Muni agreed and built his house in good faith, but the Bamessi Fon built a house with two doors so that his people could escape the fire, while the Kom people burned. Deeply disturbed by this trick, Muni was ashamed and decided to hang himself, but he also wanted revenge. He told his sister to lead the Kom people away and to look for a new lake that would form from the bodily fluids of his rotting corpse. She was to wait and watch the lake sink and disappear, leaving traces of a python's track. Once the track was sighted, she was to gather the Kom people together and follow the python until it disappeared. The sister carried out this plan, and the snake led the people to the highest mountain peak, where they founded Laikom.

Laikom's perch sets it apart as a capital. Colonial administrators often suggested moving it to a lower, more accessible position in the valley. Fueled by a story of betrayal and survival through allegiance to a female, the Kom maintained the position of their capital. The story is reenacted and reinforced whenever a new Fon is installed. In the process of an installation, a man must acquire new powers that elevate him above all others. Unlike ordinary men, he learns to foresee the future, communicate with ancestors, and triumph over evildoers. He acquires sacred powers and changes his character to prepare for leadership.

During the 1960s and 1970s, one corner of Katherine White's living room was being filled with Kom royal art, rich with significant associations. She continued to purchase elements that would complete the stage appropriate for a Fon. A flywhisk given to Paul Gebauer in 1933 was purchased from him in 1971 (pl. 70). In turn, he gave her two cloths essential to any royal display (pls. 71, 72), and attached a note saying, "This was used as a back drop behind the king when he was holding audiences."[27] No stage for a king or major ceremony in the Grassfields was without *ndop* cloths. The textiles present slightly fuzzy white lines against a deep blue-black background. This effect of scratchy lines, resembling a chalk drawing, is derived from the process of sewing the fabric in preparation for resist dyeing. Connecting the Kom to their neighbors, *ndop* cloths have been imported from adjacent kingdoms ever since they became a necessary backdrop for royalty after 1914.[28]

On ceremonial occasions, *ndop* defines spaces for a stage—a place for the ruler to sit and display regalia, for performances to be given, or for assembling ritual objects. Designs on *ndop* broadcast patterns full of royal references. The first *ndop* features meandering stripes and V forms, known as a python pattern for the creature who established the trail to Laikom. The second is loaded with birds, pinwheels, and a web of crossing lines to suggest the work of a spider, a creature the Kom hold in high regard because of its ability to burrow into the ground and thereby communicate with ancestors. Such communication is the premise for a form of divination that makes use of ancestral wisdom. With the stage now well set, Katherine White bought gowns and caps to dress an audience member appropriately to see the king (pls. 73, 74).

Eager to share her accumulation of palace art, in 1973 White sent several pieces to an exhibition entitled *Royal Art of Cameroon* at Dartmouth College's art gallery. Featured on the front cover of the exhibition catalogue was a figure similar to the queen throne. Known as the Afo-a-Kom, it touched off an international controversy over stolen art. By the end of 1973, the figure was on a plane to Cameroon, but not before giving rise to abundant stories of intrigue and ethical violations. The sensational news coverage took liberties, but in the aftermath many insights were gained into the Kom people's perceptions of royal art. Years later, the anthropologist Eugenia Shanklin sorted out what she calls the odyssey of the Afo-a-Kom and concluded that it is an object lesson for Kom and Americans alike. She identified two interpretations of the events: the American version (Americans as good guys) and the Kom version (Kom outwits America).[29]

> Forever forget your uncomfortable appearance in this sophisticated technology whose achievements tend to overlook human consideration.

—Cameroon Ambassador François-Xavier Tchoungui, 1973[30]

In the American version, the *New York Times* played a key role by breaking the story of a theft. According to the *Times,* a figure called the Afo-a-Kom was stolen from a royal Cameroonian sanctuary in 1966, and then smuggled out of the country before being sold in a New York gallery. American Peace Corps workers noticed it on the cover of the 1973 exhibition catalogue and contacted a former *Times* reporter living in Cameroon. In researching the story, the reporter was told that the Afo-a-Kom was an object of sacred status whose disappearance was wreaking havoc in the kingdom.

Pl. 70
Royal scepter or flywhisk
Laikom, Kom Kingdom, Cameroon Grassfields
19th–20th century
H. (head) 15.2 cm (6½ in.)
Wood, copper, beads, horsetail
Gift of Katherine White and the Boeing Company,
81.17.732

Pl. 71
Ndop **cloth**
Cameroon
20th century
Cotton (strip woven with sewn resist)
L. 246 cm (87 in.)
Gift of Katherine White and the Boeing Company,
81.17.778

Pl. 72
Ndop cloth
Cameroon
20th century
Cotton (strip woven with sewn resist)
L. 558.8 cm (220 in.)
Gift of Katherine White and the Boeing Company,
81.17.774

Pl. 73
Man's garment
Cameroon
20th century
Cotton with appliqué and embroidery
L. 116.2 cm (45¾ in.)
Gift of Katherine White and the Boeing Company,
81.17.769

Pl. 74
Hat
Cameroon
20th century
Cotton (crochet), cowry shells
H. 14.3 cm (5⅝ in.)
Gift of Katherine White and the Boeing Company,
81.17.759

Widespread famine, impotence, fighting, and despair were attributed to the figure's absence. Cameroonian children were said to be collecting money for its return. In all, twenty-two articles appeared in the *New York Times* beginning in October 1973.

Sympathetic American government officials, a corporation, and a private collector pooled resources to return the sculpture to the Kom. A delegation was quickly formed and a plane loaded in December with government representatives, reporters, and the sculpture in a first-class seat. Upon the delegation's arrival, Cameroonian functionaries put obstacles in their path as issues of national politics arose. Among those witnessing the events was Evan Schneider, who documented the occasion. Already so familiar with the Fon and the lay of the kingdom, he recorded in photographs the layers of responses among the Kom audience. The delegation attended seven welcoming ceremonies in seven days, the final one held by the Fon at Laikom (fig. 35). The delegates received gifts of stools and robes during a joyous ceremony, but they were escorted onto the plane to fly home the next day. As an American delegate concluded, "It was simply two different sets of people seeing the same thing in different ways."[31]

The Kom version begins with a letter from an American asking the Kom adviser Johnson Mbeng to steal two statues from the sanctuary where the Afo-a-Kom had been kept. Mbeng, not pleased by this suggestion, showed the letter to Fon Nsom, who proposed that they, a tiny kingdom, try to trick the giant American nation into returning what was rightly theirs. Mbeng wrote letters to Americans inventing a story of famine, impotence, and mourning caused by the removal of the Afo-a-Kom. In fact, when the statue disappeared, the Fon did not express concern about it. And because only a privileged few ever saw the statue, and then only once a year, the Kom people as a whole did not miss it—there was no widespread mourning.

When the American delegation returned the statue, the Fon was put to a test of his diplomatic abilities. The Minister of Information stepped in to claim it for the nation of Cameroon (established as a united republic in 1972). He announced that the government would make the statue a symbol of national unity and send it around the country until the proper home could be determined. The minister placed it on view in the window of the Office of Tourism with a sign saying "This statue is worth 15 million francs in America." Fon Nsom challenged the government's claim to ownership with his own ingenious response to the situation:

Fig. 35. Fon Nsom (reigned 1967–1974) with *ndop* cloth in background, 1974.

> The Fon had done one funny thing when we entered the office. He was shown a chair at the side of the room and he refused it, saying he wanted to be directly in front of the Minister. So he sat there while we interpreted all the things that had been said for him. Then he said, yes, thank the Minister and tell him that he was glad this thing is for the whole of Cameroon. Then he insisted that we ask the Minister this question: "If I cut off my ear or pluck out my eye, would it belong to Cameroon or to me?" The Minister said, "If you remove your eye, it is still your eye, it does not belong to Cameroon." And the Fon said, "Yes, exactly so, and the Afo-a-Kom is still my Afo-a-Kom." The Minister said the Fon should not be comparing the eyes, the ears, with the Afo-a-Kom.[32]

When the minister spoke of sending the Afo-a-Kom on a tour around Cameroon, the Fon stated he would have to stay with it wherever it went. The minister asked, "What are you talking about? You want to stay here?" In reply, the Fon said he had been living in Yaounde in a hotel for three days with free food and a free bed. He would stay. Soon thereafter, the minister placed a few calls. By the next day, the Afo-a-Kom was on its way back to Laikom, where it was greeted with jubilation (fig. 36).

Fig. 36. Crowds viewing Afo-a-Kom, 1974.

In the aftermath of this two-sided story, lessons emerge. Fon Nsom, known in Kom for his fondness for intrigue, was able to assess an American weakness for sensational news. He and Johnson Mbeng adopted the stereotype of a poor kingdom unable to cope without its sacred statue. Jumping on an opportunity to save the situation, Americans responded with amazing swiftness. They were less aware of the complex Kom realities: that a theft from palace storage indicated there were not enough retainers to maintain security; that a Fon is required to negotiate his status in a modern nation state; that a sculpture like the Afo-a-Kom is seen differently by various Kom audiences—as a familiar portrait of Fon Yu by palace officials, and as an awesome reminder of royal power by commoners, but not a sacred god able to cause famine.

In turn, Kom people learned how much Americans value royal sculpture and began making as many copies as possible. Local rumors commended the cleverness of the Fon. Among commoners, the Afo-a-Kom was said to have caused havoc in America by walking around at night and destroying other objects placed near it. The return of the sculpture, in this rendition, was not a gesture of generosity, but was provoked by the need to export the destructive figure.

Fewer than ten years later, the Smithsonian Institution decided to mount another exhibition of Cameroonian objects, *The Art of Cameroon*. Once again, Katherine White's collection was prominently placed on view along with the Afo-a-Kom. Fon Jina Bo II (ruler from 1975 to 1989) had agreed to the loan and relied upon his retainers to carry it out.

Afo-a-Kom toured the United States but again became a beacon for misunderstanding. When the figure was returned by a Smithsonian representative, it was

Fig. 37. Fon Jina Bo II (reigned 1975–1989) at his enthronement with the royal figures, October 1, 1979.

greeted with disappointment. It seems an American impostor, acting as an agent for the Smithsonian, had already been to Laikom. He had promised the Fon a sum of money, a trip to the United States, and the seven vehicles that would bring the sculpture back to Laikom. The Fon, pleased with these plans, had given the man carvings as gifts to take back to the United States. When the true Smithsonian representative arrived, bringing the Afo-a-Kom in a crate and a $300 loan fee, the reality fell far short of the Fon's falsely raised expectations of what was possible from America.

> I have since realized that I am like a wor m since I became Fon of Kom.
> —Fon Jina Bo II

Negotiating with museums is just one of the difficulties a Fon faces. Jina Bo II, the first Fon to be quoted in publications, began his rule with a test of confidence in the process of "becoming Fon" (fig. 37). One Kom scholar, Paul Nchoji Nkwi, describes a situation in late 1974 when contradictory forces were pulling at the kingdom.[33] On December 13, the previous Fon, Nsom Ngwe, brought a case against his heir, Michael Mbain. Mbain was tried for selling three masks from the royal compound. He was brought before the Fon, and the police threatened to imprison him, but he insisted on his innocence. Senior palace retainers led the charges against him, insulting and jeering him for his misdeeds and rudeness toward the Fon. Three days later, however, Fon Nsom Ngwe died unexpectedly. Michael Mbain underwent the initiation process, much of it privately enacted, which stressed his new functions and responsibilities. He emerged as a man transformed seven days later. Those same retainers who had denounced him earlier now called out his praise names as he took the identity of a Fon named Jina Bo II. As Nkwi reports, "The entire enstoolment process was believed to transform an ordinary mortal into an immortal being having power over life and death."[34]

Fon Jina Bo II is one of many leaders presiding over kingdoms that have survived, but not thrived, in the late twentieth century. Ongoing conversions to Christianity and Islam erode his base of spiritual authority. State government agents strive to dismantle the powers of the Fon in order to obtain access to lands under his authority. Customary Kom laws disregard political agendas and have led the Fon to question:

> What makes my land my land? Is it that piece of paper or the fact that I am Fon of Kom? . . . I have since realized that I am like a worm since I became Fon of Kom. I am like a worm in the midst of ants. On my right, the "tiny chiefdoms" are biting me, on my left the Senior Prefect and his gendarmes. Everywhere around me, there are pressures. The land is no longer mine.[35]

Kom royal sculptures have been removed from their original owners over the course of this century. In an art museum, the intricacies of the Fon's role are a remote consideration. On the streets of Cameroonian cities and kingdoms today, the reality of the legacies left by such kings have a far greater impact.

Chiefs, more chiefs, always chiefs.   —Jean-Marie Teno, 1999[36]

The documentary film *Chef!* by Jean-Marie Teno concludes the century with a startling look at a ruler within the context of his own family. Teno narrates his changing expectations as a past chief is honored while his own great-uncle is installed as a chief. Two art forms punctuate the film. First is the cement statue commemorating King Kanga Joseph II, who was born in 1900 and ruled for fifty years. Teno observes that this king sought to develop his community by "straddling two traditions with no preparation and no training." His concrete image presides over a busy intersection. "All alone at the end of the street, he will watch the concrete and beer ads invade his kingdom." A great chief, he is saluted by masquerades whose importance he preserved. But, Teno says, the masks are symbols that "fewer and fewer understand." The masquerades fade away as images of urban distress pervade the film. Questioning the role of such leaders in contemporary culture, Teno stresses the need to ask "Who comes first, the people or the chief?"[37]

The Seattle Art Museum's stage for a Fon of the Kom kingdom is fairly complete. Most of the objects were gifts from Fons to Americans who worked for years in Cameroon. Memories and photographs provide a record of close associations and meanings, but the stage is still missing the key actor—the patron who inspired the art and the only person ritually prepared to use it. In Laikom recently, the Fon remains the lead curator and principal guard of his own ongoing collection (fig. 38). In this role, he extends the kingdom's art in new directions. As part of a visitors center, a pole has

Fig. 38. Fon Yibain (reign 1989–) at the palace, Laikom, 1999.

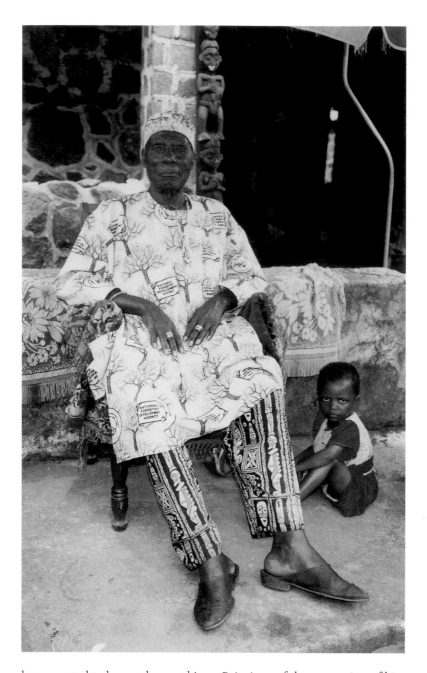

been erected to honor the past kings. Paintings of the succession of kings appear on the palace walls. Just as the Fons adapt their collections to remember the past and attract new visitors, so does the museum. Fon Yibain, the current ruler, was consulted as the museum planned its display of a stage fit for a Kom king. He designated Gilbert Mbeng Lo-oh, named for an American and Kom ancestor, to act as his emissary and conduct interviews with retainers and current members of the Kwifon (defined by Lo-oh as the sacred and administrative arm of the palace). Before bringing the results of his work to Seattle, Mbeng Lo-oh promised "startling revelations about customs and especially myths surrounding Kom art." Thus, the museum will learn from this venerable kingdom as it guides a royal past into the present.

Notes

1. This circumstance changed with a collection of Maasai art in January 2000.

2. Paul Gebauer, note attached to an accession card created by Katherine White.

3. Paul Gebauer, "Architecture of Cameroon," *African Arts* 5, no. 1 (1971), 46.

4. Eugenia Shanklin, "The Path to Laikom: Kom Royal Court Architecture," *Paideuma* 31 (1985), 111–50.

5. Paul Nchoji Nkwi, "A Conservation Dilemma over African Royal Art in Cameroon," in *Plundering Africa's Past,* ed. Peter Schmidt and Roderick J. MacIntosh (Bloomington: Indiana University Press, 1996), 108.

6. Eugenia Shanklin, "The Odyssey of the Afo-a-Kom," *African Arts* (1990), 62–69.

7. Christraud Geary, *Africa: The Art of a Continent* (New York, Guggenheim Museum, 1996), 155.

8. The two photographs of Fon Yu, both taken by Adolf Diehl, are given an approximate date of 1905–10.

9. Eugenia Shanklin, "Missionaries and Witchcraft Beliefs in Kom, Cameroon," in *The Message in the Missionary: Local Interpretations of Religious Ideology and Missionary Personality,* Studies in Third World Societies, no. 50 (Williamsburg, Va.: College of William and Mary, 1994), 56.

10. Reproduced in Tamara Northern, *Royal Art of Cameroon* (Hanover, N.H.: Dartmouth College, 1973), 10.

11. Reproduced in ibid., 12.

12. Katherine White Journals, Seattle Art Museum.

13. Katherine White's summary, based on Paul Gebauer's undated letter to her, Katherine White Archives.

14. E. M. Chilver and P. M. Kaberry, "The Kingdom of Kom in West Cameroon," in *West African Kingdoms in the 19th Century,* ed. Darrel Forde and Phyllis Kaberry (London: International African Institute, 1967), 142–43.

15. Phyllis M. Kaberry, "Retainers and Royal Households in the Cameroon Grassfields," *Cahiers d'études africaines* 3, no. 10 (1962), 282–98.

16. Hans-Joachim Koloss, "Kwifon and Fon in Oku on Kingship in the Cameroon Grasslands," in *Kings of Africa* (Utrecht: Foundation Kings of Africa, 1992), 40.

17. Photograph by Gilbert Schneider of Ngumba House, published in Fred Ferreti, *Afo-a-Kom: Sacred Art of Cameroon* (New York: The Third Press, 1975), 63.

18. Nkwi, "A Conservation Dilemma," 108.

19. Paul Gebauer, *Art of Cameroon* (Portland: The Portland Art Museum; New York: Metropolitan Museum of Art, 1979), 78.

20. Charles Weber III, "The Educational Policy and Mission Schools of the Baptists in British Mandated Cameroon 1922–1945: The Policy and Education Work of Carl Bender, Paul Gebauer, and George Dunger," dissertation on microfiche (1982), Metropolitan Museum of Art, New York.

21. Ibid.

22. Shanklin, "Missionaries and Witchcraft Beliefs," 58.

23. M. D. W. Jeffreys, "Some Notes on the Fon of Bikom," *African Affairs* 50, no. 200 (1950), 241–49.

24. Rebecca Reyher, *The Fon and His Hundred Wives* (New York: Doubleday, 1952).

25. Gilbert Schneider, letter to Katherine White, November 5, 1973, Katherine White Archives.

26. Eugenia Shanklin, "The Track of the Python: A West African Origin Story," in *Signifying Animals, Human Meaning in the Natural World,* ed. Roy Willis (London: Allen and Unwin, 1990).

27. Catalogue card, Katherine White Archives, Seattle Art Museum.

28. Alastair Lamb and Venice Lamb, *Au Cameroon: Weaving/Tissage* (Hertingsfordury, England: Roxford Books, 1981).

29. Shanklin, "The Odyssey of the Afo-a-Kom," 62–69.

30. Ferretti, *Afo-a-kom.*

31. George Spicely, quoted in ibid., 122.

32. Fon Nsom's words were recited by Bobe Chia Fuinkuin, a high-ranking member of the Kom entourage; quoted in Shanklin, "The Odyssey of the Afo-a-Kom," 66.

33. Paul Nchoji Nkwi, "Becoming Foyn: Among the Kom of the Cameroon Western Grassfield," *Paideuma* 36 (1990), 235–43.

34. Ibid.

35. Quoted in Cyprian Frisiy, "Chieftaincy in the Modern State: An Institution at the Crossroads of Democratic Change," *Paideuma* 41 (1995), 56–57.

36. Jean-Marie Teno, *Chef!* California Newsreel, 1999.

37. Ibid.

The Fetish and the Imagination of Europe: Sacred Medicines of the Kongo

The word "fetish" can be a gauntlet, thrown down with unsettling force. Europeans came to use the one word to cover a wide range of objects from all over the African continent. Fetishes were everything from necklaces to sculptures valued by Africans for—in Western terms—their power of "enchantment," provocation of "superstitious dread," or capacity to be "animated by a spirit."[1] Outside Africa, fetish assignments have extended to complex issues of value. Karl Marx used the term to call attention to economic fixations. Sigmund Freud adopted it in describing sexual perversion. Recently, fetishism has been applied to Dutch still lifes as well as Hollywood cinema.

As a curator of African art, I receive at least one "fetish" call every other month. I keep track of them in a phone log that started as a way to contain my frustrations over the imaginary diabolical powers that African art inspires. The conversations follow a pattern: "I have a fetish from Africa. My grandfather/uncle collected it when he was working over there and he said it was supposed to give people headaches and my family doesn't want it around the house anymore. When can you come and get it?"

This basic statement is followed by long digressions about the errant uncle or adventuresome grandfather, but then we close in on what makes the owner uncomfortable about the fetish. One contained "slave tears." Another was "evil and nasty" and "too scary for anyone else to handle." Usually, the object comes from an unknown country, and the caller can only describe it as a standing statue. Along the way, my official capacity shifts from art museum curator to exorcist. Just as I am unsuited for this role, so is the sculpture whose job description has been typecast with one word. The exorcism should be redirected, against the process that created a blanket term for images of belief—against the fetishizing of African art.

> It is we who have constructed the world of the fetish, not the original makers, priests or clients of such figures in Central Africa.
>
> —John Mack, 1995[2]   Pl. 77 (detail)

Standing as an anchor image for fetishes is a male figure holding his hands on his hips, most of his body covered with nails and blades (pl. 75). This sculpture is of the type held up as the epitome of the negative, violent model of vengeance that is still a baseline for fetishism. His body has been pounded with nails, poked with needles, splattered with blood, and incantations are uttered over him to provoke illness and disruption in someone's life. As this caricature steps aside, it is replaced with a figure whose personality and job description are shaped over the centuries of an evolving kingdom. First discovered over five hundred years ago, this kingdom tested European leaders' willingness to exchange goods and knowledge. Within the lifetime of one African king, however, trade took on new and terrible dimensions. The fetish was created as Europe closed off the exploration of African thought and chose instead the exploitation of its people.

Faith is as fragile as glass.

−King Mvemba Nzinga, who became Afonso I,
letter to King Joao III of Portugal, 1526[3]

A Portuguese explorer in 1483 was the first to notice water rushing from the Congo River into the Atlantic. Diogo Cão sailed into the mouth of the river but could not continue. He returned to Lisbon in 1484, taking with him four men from the Kongo kingdom. After meeting these ambassadors, the Portuguese king, Joao II, sent a fleet of three caravels to investigate their reports of a royal capital ruled by an African king. By December 1490, a group of priests, stonemasons, carpenters, and women set out with gifts and building materials to establish diplomacy and a settlement. The caravels arrived at the port city of Mpinda on March 29, 1491, to be greeted by the chief of the province, who was quickly baptized and renamed Don Manuel. Within days, the Portuguese began their walk inland to the capital city of Mbanza Kongo, perched atop a plateau in the Crystal Mountains. Escorts led them into the large city and through a maze of densely planted trees surrounding the approach to the king's quarters.

The expedition found King Nzinga a Nkuwa seated on a raised wood throne with ivory inlay, while around him were assembled his queen, wives, nobles of the court, and chiefs of the provinces (fig. 39). Leopard and civet furs were draped around the king; his arms were laden with bracelets of copper; and his garments were woven of raffia. The leading Portuguese emissary approached him, knelt, and kissed his hand. King Nzinga responded by taking a handful of earth, pressing it against his heart and then against the Portuguese. Porters brought forth gifts from the king of Portugal—brocade, velvet, satin, silk and linen, silver and gold jewelry, trinkets, plate, and a flock of red pigeons. Kongo musicians played ivory trumpets, "producing a sound so melancholy that its like has never been heard."[4] They repeated their song twelve times to honor the twelve generations of kings since the kingdom's beginnings. The next day, the king sent privately for the Portuguese to devise a plan for his baptism, which required the swift construction of a church. Two months later, before a huge gathering of onlookers, Nzinga took the baptismal name Joao I, and his son became Afonso I. A rush of other title holders followed their lead.

Pl. 75
Standing figure *(nkondi)*
Kongo, Democratic Republic of the Congo
Late 19th–early 20th century
Wood, iron, imported nails, fiber, beads, glass, feathers, chalk
H. 80.5 cm (31¾ in.)
Gift of Katherine White and the Boeing Company, 81.17.836

Fig. 39. The arrival of the Portuguese before the king of
Kongo in 1491, from Filippo Pigafetta, *A Report of the
Kingdom of Congo and of the Surrounding Countries . . .*
(1591).

When members of the Portuguese expedition returned to Lisbon, young Kongo
nobles went along to carry gifts of ivory and raffia cloth for the king. They also brought
the news of a vast country with a distinguished government in place for nearly 150
years.[5] The founder of the kingdom, Ntinu Lukeni, had gained renown as a judge
whose fairness in establishing laws and dispensing justice formed a central identity
for the people. Portuguese observers noted the presence of regional governors and
ranks of civil servants convening in numerous courts within the palace. Most chroni-
clers also described a large open plaza known as the court of justice, where an enormous wild fig tree shaded the king as he heard disputes and reviewed his troops.

More Portuguese emissaries came to Mbanza Kongo in 1493 and 1504, bringing ample supplies of vestments, crosses, and religious books. Undoubtedly, one of
the first to handle them was a member of the court who took extreme notice of all
things Portuguese. His curiosity was a major force in an era of remarkable leadership.
Mvemba Nzinga Afonso I assumed the throne after his father's death in 1506 and
ruled until 1543. Not long after his coronation, he loaded a ship bound for Lisbon
with gifts. He sent along his son and several nobles and requested that King Manuel
put them in schools and dispatch more missionaries and technicians.

Indeed, Afonso I became famous for his commitment to Christianity and
education—he studied theological texts with Portuguese priests and made Catholicism the state religion. Reports to the king of Portugal describe him as "the apostle
of the Congo," commending his skills in preaching, his exercise of justice, and his
punishment of those who worshiped idols. Despite the fact that only his household
firmly supported the move, he destroyed a "great house of the nkisi-fetishes" in
Mbanza Kongo.[6] A rendering of Afonso's destruction of the idols depicts a fire con-
suming a bundle of fantastic creatures with curling tails and fearsome faces (fig. 40).[7]

He presented metal crucifixes to all his chiefs and promoted the images of the saints to replace other charms. Evidence suggests that Afonso adopted Christian arts as another, possibly more direct, route to contact gods and ancestors. Afonso also learned Portuguese, thus launching the first correspondence between sub-Saharan Africa and Europe. His vision for exchange between the countries was selective—he was pleased to supply copper, but didn't want outsiders to find his sources of silver and gold. He was glad to have Portuguese priests, books, medicines, and skilled laborers, but didn't want them to interfere with his laws or courts. When Portuguese priests and artisans did arrive, Afonso had them build mission schools and churches, and add new housing and tree-lined streets to the capital. He even improved the diet by introducing new plants provided by the Portuguese—guava, lemon, orange, maize, sugar cane, and manioc flourished in the fields.

When a Portuguese caravel was blown off course and landed in Brazil in 1500, world history shifted. The mines, coffee, and sugar plantations being established across the Atlantic required workers. Portuguese interest in the newly discovered African kingdom swiftly focused on the search for labor. Among the Kongo, people captured in warfare, criminals, and debtors were held as slaves but were entitled to earn or be granted freedom over a generation or two. African slaves of this type preceded a flood of others taken by the Portuguese. In 1512, a fateful request was made by Portugal's King Manuel to King Afonso. Manuel sent five ships carrying more missionaries, technicians, soldiers, books, tools, and furniture than ever before. His ambassador outlined many forms of assistance that Portugal was ready to offer. In return, Manuel asked that Afonso fill the ships with ivory, copper, and slaves and allow his agent to gather regular payments of such commodities. Afonso agreed, and thereby opened the door of the slave trade. Fostered by members of Kongo nobility who sought to increase their own wealth and status, the slave trade started slowly but reached a torrent within one lifetime. By the 1530s, five thousand people a year were being shipped from a port on the Congo River. In 1600, the number reached fifteen thousand a year. Overall, the shipments from this region grew to account for forty percent of the ten million or more Africans forced across the Atlantic between 1500 and 1870.[8]

Afonso sent letters to two successive Portuguese kings, increasingly objecting to the slave trade. He received word that his son Henrique was consecrated as a bishop by Pope Leo X in 1518 (no African would attain such a rank in the Church

Fig. 40. "The King of the Congo, Afonso, Converted to Christianity, Orders Idols to Be Burnt," from Theodore de Bry, *Petits Voyages* (1603).

for another four centuries), but when Afonso tried to communicate with the pope about his disagreements with Portuguese practices, his emissaries bound for Rome were detained the minute they arrived in Lisbon.

One letter written in 1526 to King Joao III of Portugal expresses Afonso's distress over a trade that had grown into a massive force, disrupting his base of control and the entire population:

> Each day the traders are kidnapping our people—children of this country, sons of our nobles and vassals, even people of our own family.... This corruption and depravity are so widespread that our land is entirely depopulated.... We need in this kingdom only priests and schoolteachers, and no merchandise, unless it is wine and flour for Mass.... It is our wish that this kingdom not be a place for the trade or transport of slaves.
>
> Many of our subjects eagerly lust after Portuguese merchandise that your subjects have brought into our domains. To satisfy this inordinate appetite, they seize many of our black free subjects.... They sell them ... after having taken these prisoners [to the coast] secretly or at night.... As soon as the captives are in the hands of the white men they are branded with a red-hot iron.[9]

Another letter singles out priests who became slave traders and set an example for others:

> In this kingdom, faith is as fragile as glass because of the bad examples of men who come to teach here, because the lusts of the world and the lure of wealth have turned them away from the truth. Just as the Jews crucified the Son of God because of covetousness, my brother, so today He is again crucified.[10]

Afonso I's letters continued with appeals that turned personal in 1539 after ten of his relatives sent to Lisbon for a religious education disappeared en route. It later emerged that these relatives had indeed been turned over to a slave trader who shipped them to Brazil. Afonso's letter of December 1540 ended the communication from an extraordinary king, the only African author whose written record emerged from this region for four centuries. After his death in 1543, the Kongo kingdom maintained a base of power but faltered as the chiefs of the provinces built up their own wealth by conducting slave raids. As the chiefs bolstered their positions, the kingdom's centrality weakened, and titles became a sign of commercial abilities. British, French, and Dutch vessels had joined the Portuguese by 1600. The king's forces were defeated by the Portuguese in 1665, and the capital city of Mbanza Kongo was deserted.

Turning to the artistic record of this exchange, we learn that many pieces are missing from the picture. While reports of the baptism of Kongo leaders mention idols being burned, they do not describe them in any detail. As replacements, Portuguese priests of the fifteenth century brought images and practices to lead the Kongo into Christianity. With their conversion, the Kongo were supplied with crosses, crucifixes,

Fig. 41. Jan Sanders van Hemessen, *St. Sebastian*, central panel of triptych, ca. 1525–1566, oil on wood. © Musées de la Ville, Paris.

and religious books created for Portuguese Catholics. It is not known how much influence these Christian visions had on Kongo sculpture. The crucifixion was bound to be prominent—a man's figure pierced by stakes. Images like that of St. Sebastian, whose torso is riddled with arrows, were common (fig. 41): fifteenth-century Portuguese were heirs to "an impressive iconography of macabre bodily imagery which visualized mutilation as a means of achieving power or authority over life."[11] In services, the drinking of Christ's blood as food to sustain the soul of the world would have reinforced the notion of the divinity that can come from suffering. As "idols" were burned, was a new form born that reworked European icons? Was the "fetish" a combination of Kongo and Christian beliefs and images? The answer is obscured by the indiscriminate use of the term "fetish," and the rare occurrence of the Kongo word *nkisi*.

> Some have a Lion's Tail, some a Bird's Feather, some a Pebble, a Bit of Rag, a Dog's Leg; or, in short, any Thing they fancy: and this they call their FITTISH, which Word not only signifies the Thing worshipped, but sometimes a Spell, Charm, or Inchantment.
>
> —William Smith, 1744[12]

European descriptions of the seventeenth and eighteenth century often label African art as fetish, regardless of what form it takes. Derived from the Portuguese word *feitico*, meaning "witchcraft," and the Latin *fasticium*, "artificial," it became a standard catch-all phrase applied from coast to coast throughout Africa; the usage lingers in many dictionaries. Traders carried the term with them and resorted to it whenever they could not interpret the values placed on certain objects. In the course of trade, they perceived the African valuation of inanimate objects to be the basis of a false and flawed economy. Dutch traders in particular promoted the concept that African trade currency was tinged with irrationality, whereas coins were an appropriate symbolic form derived from the abstract nature of God. The broad net cast for the fetish built up a European projection of Africa's inabilities and helped to justify exploitation and eventual colonization.

The term *nkisi* took two more centuries to be defined by Kongo sources, but it began appearing in European accounts in 1650. Evangelical Capuchins moved through parts of the provinces in the mid-1650s and burned as many figures as they could, often with expressions of outrage.[13] One of the earliest references to a Kongo nail figure (*nkisi nkondi*) comes in 1668, when chronicler Olfert Dapper in *Description de l'Afrique* states that people of Loango drive nails into an "nkisi kikokoo," a wooden statue of a seated man. By 1700, another account mentions a fetish called *nkondi,* in the form of a man "one meter high" who detects thieves.

> **The first thing that comes their way ... they exalt to the dignity of a "Genius."** —G. W. F. Hegel, 1837

In the influential text *The Philosophy of History,* G. W. F. Hegel reestablishes the notion of African objects as impulsive creations in discussing how Africans worship "the first thing that comes their way. This, taken quite indiscriminately, they exalt to the dignity of a 'Genius'; it may be an animal, a tree, a stone, or a wooden figure." He goes on to explain, "What we properly understand by Africa, is the Unhistorical, Undeveloped Spirit, still involved in the conditions of mere nature."[14] Throughout the nineteenth century, however, the term "fetish" was employed to challenge Europeans' confidence in their superior rationalism. It became a needle to probe vulnerable areas of confusion—how things are assigned values, and how knowledge influences belief. Karl Marx in *Capital* writes about commodity fetishism—when money becomes a form of exchange that no longer refers to the object as a product of men's hands and labor. He forecasts the time when "everything desirable, from sex to social status, could be transformed into commodities as fetishes-on-display that held the crowd enthralled even when possession was beyond their reach."[15] Into the early twentieth century, Sigmund Freud and a host of psychiatrists and sociologists began to map the sexual fixations lurking behind the scenes of everyday European life. Clients were found to be dependent on articles of clothing (shoes, gloves, underwear) and parts of the body (hair, feet) for stimulation. The fetish was applied to a pathology deemed perverse, but common.

> **All of a sudden, without any transition, they saw appear on their savage waterway European steamships of the nineteenth century.** —Camille Coquilhat, 1888[16]

While the use of the term was expanding to suit European needs, actual African objects called *nkisi* were about to come under siege. Ignoring the earlier discovery of a kingdom and its capital, and the ships making the Atlantic crossing over the centuries, the Congo region was recast in the nineteenth century as the most untouched portion of the Dark Continent, where people were "given over to cannibalism, human sacrifice, judgements by poison, fetishism, wars of plunder, slavery, polygamy, polyandry, and deprived of all unity in government, science, writing and medicine."[17]

In the name of another round of discovery and progress, the lower Congo region became home to what a recent investigative monograph deems "the vilest scramble for loot that ever disfigured the history of the human conscience."[18] The period began in 1885 with the opening of the "Congo Free State," a creation of King Leopold of Belgium, whose groundwork was laid by the famed explorer Henry Morton Stanley. In an exercise of virtual rule, Leopold managed a state as large as Western Europe (sixty-six times the size of Belgium) without ever setting foot there.

With support from American and European leaders, Leopold authorized a regime to extract resources from the Congo. Ivory was the object of desire until 1890, when John Dunlop, an Irish inventor, devised the inflatable rubber tire, an invention that was to fuel the development of the automobile and launch the twentieth century. Rubber tapped from wild trees in the Congo was needed to supply the industrial world's newfound appetite, but it was only through arduous and unwelcome work that rubber was extracted. Agents for Leopold had to fill quotas and instituted extreme measures to force laborers into meeting them. Family members were held hostage until tapping was done. Troops shot everyone in sight if villages refused to supply the agents with enough rubber. When European overseers demanded proof that reluctant workers had been killed, people's hands were cut off and smoked as evidence. Porters were forced to carry sixty-five-pound loads along narrow paths over vast distances. Local revolts were suppressed by troops equipped with an American invention of 1870—the Maxim gun, a semiautomatic weapon that unleashed bullets in streams.

Horrified witnesses to the atrocities began appealing to King Leopold and major Western newspapers to account for the terrifying conditions. By 1904, the scandals were sending shock waves through Europe. Artists in Paris filled anarchist newspapers with political cartoons attacking missionaries and colonial forces. One cartoon depicts a man pounding a nail into a figure; the caption says he is nailing "to get his god's attention" (fig. 42).[19] In response, Leopold operated a public relations campaign, founded on deception and bribes to editors and reporters, which kept much incriminating evidence hidden until 1906 when photographs began to appear.[20] By the time of Leopold's death in 1909, the record of this holocaust was mounting. From 1885 to 1920, in certain regions entire populations declined by fifty percent or more. By some estimates, at least ten million people died from mass murder, torture, and epidemics, which flourished among malnourished and traumatized people. In the later period of Belgian rule in the Congo, however, textbooks portrayed Leopold as a leader who did not deserve criticism, and spoke of "how the Belgians, by acts of heroism, managed to create this immense territory."[21]

DIEUX NÈGRES

Ils sont obéissants comme des Saint Guirec dont notre catholique Bretagne est pourvue. Pour que son Dieu s'occupe de lui, il le lui fait sentir à sa façon...

Fig. 42. František Kupka, "Dieux nègres," L'Assiette au beurre (1904).

Thousands were burned in triumphal holocausts.

—Wyatt MacGaffey, 1993[22]

In this atmosphere of conflict, missionaries were quite active. Protestants took evangelical ventures into the interior beginning in the 1870s and were followed by Belgian Catholics. Missions promised chiefs certain protections if they joined their faith. Christians welcomed the ceremonial burning of thousands of figures as a sign that paganism was failing and resistance to European powers was weakening. Kongo figures now in museums are among the few survivors of an artistic complex still in place at the turn of the century. An 1893 Dutch missionary bulletin is a rare account of how an object was collected for shipment: "This fetish was held in such high esteem that it might only be transported in a hammock, as the Blacks obstinately refused to give it up to Europeans except for a very high price. Later, French soldiers seized it and gave it to a traveler, who sold it to our Rotterdam friends."[23]

Superstitious belief . . . is hydra-headed in its virility.

—John H. Weeks, 1914

To most European observers, the Kongo nail figure was a fetish with a destructive mission. One chronicler of the Kongo, John H. Weeks, spent thirty years gathering his description of habits, customs, and religious beliefs. His first publication, *Among Congo Cannibals,* appeared in 1912 and was followed in 1914 by *Among the Primitive BaKongo.* His account of a nail fetish supports his contention that "a superstitious belief in charms, amulets, mascots, etc. is most difficult to eradicate: it is hydra-headed in its virility":

> The most powerful and most feared of all the fetishes in the catalogue belongs to the medicine-man who has the mbanzangola fetish. . . . If a person desires to cause pain, disease, or death to another, he goes to a medicine man of this fetish order, and, having paid a fee, he drives in a nail or knife where he wants his enemy to feel the pain. A knife-stab in a vital part means a painful death to the man's enemy; a nail in the shoulder, elbow or knee means excruciating agony in one or another of those joints, and indicates that the man does not want to kill his enemy, but only wishes him to have rheumatism, abscesses, or such minor ailments. These fetish images are often stuck over with nails, knives and other sharp instruments. This is probably the only fetish image in connection with which there is no "white art" practiced—it is neither a protective fetish nor a curative one, but is always used to inflict pain.[24]

Several hundred years of European speculation about the Kongo fetish came to an end just as Weeks's publication was being distributed. Beginning in 1912, Karl Edward Laman, a missionary of the Swedish Covenant Church, decided to take a radically different approach. Instead of writing about the Kongo, he sent them an invitation in the Kikongo language. Just by using Kikongo, Laman set himself apart from Belgian efforts to eliminate publishing in a language that bolstered Kongo identity. Any "intelligent person who knows how to read and write" was asked to use his "own manner of speaking and reasoning" to respond to a detailed questionnaire about Kongo culture and institutions. Laman planned to print and translate this literature for missionaries and coming generations. Sixty-eight Kongo responded, all aligned with one Protestant mission or another. Ten went beyond the scope of the questionnaire and conducted their own field research. After seven years, Laman had in his hands 429 notebooks, a unique archive of Kongo culture at the beginning of the twentieth century. Laman estimated that ten thousand manuscript pages returned with him to Sweden in 1919. He prepared a monograph using extracts from the notebooks, carefully identifying each author. Although this manuscript was never published, Swedish authors issued a series of four short monographs between 1953 and 1968 that turned "probably the most remarkable body of ethnography by Africans" into a text in which the African authors are "almost unrecognisable."[25]

An nkisi is a chosen companion, in whom all people find confidence.
–Nsemi Isaki, 1910

Only in 1974 were the earlier Kongo writings finally made available, fifty-five years after being assembled. Two American scholars, John Janzen and Wyatt MacGaffey, published an anthology of the primary texts translated into English. At last Kongo words revealed notions far different from what European writers called a fetish. Nsemi Isaki, writing in 1910, explains *minkisi* (plural of *nkisi*), or sacred medicines, in these excerpts:

> Nkisi is the name of the thing we use to help a man when he is sick and from which we obtain health; the name refers to leaves and medicines combined together. . . . An nkisi is also a chosen companion, in whom all people find confidence. It is a hiding place for people's souls, to keep and compose in order to preserve life (breath). But the help in healing is why people are especially grateful for minkisi. . . .
>
> Minkisi differ in form and nature because the sufferings in the human body differ. The minkisi, in like manner, are as diverse and as many as the many, many illnesses in the land. . . . The ingredients put in the nkisi are categorized like the diseases in the body in order to help the nkisi in its work. . . . Nkisi Nkondi receives wedges, or "nails" made of vegetable matter if the person driving them has no iron ones. Lacking an iron wedge, a nail will be driven into the statue to "bind" it. It is believed that because of the wound that has injured Nkondi, he will become angry quickly and go "tie up" the person identified in the divination. . . . The medicines are the ingredients; their strength comes from each individually and from their being joined together. Each ingredient has an action upon man and the bringing together of these forces is what heals a person.[26]

Kongo authors overturn the European vision of fetishes aligned with irrational superstition. They cite Ne Kongo as a cultural hero who carried the first healing medicine (*nkisi*) with him from heaven. He prepared the medicine in an earthenware vessel set on top of three stones or termite mounds. His actions founded the expertise that a healer (*nganga*) developed to dispense medicines. The healer's therapy involved the proper mixtures of plants and elements, and the healing ingredients were then placed in the *nkisi,* which served as a container. The *nganga's* operation also incorporated theatrical dance and music. In the course of this ritual, a "war" or moral struggle would be declared against ancestors, spirits, and people whose powers cause misfortune such as illness, epidemics, or crop failure. Each *nkisi* required a special initiation—with words, songs, and gestures—before the owner could use it. Without that instruction, we cannot know the purpose of a specific *nkisi.* The distinctive type of figure with nails bears the general name of *nkondi.* Fu Kiau Bunseki offers a dual translation of *nkondi,* based on two classes of the Kikongo language. First, *nkondi* is a device, record keeper, or tool for dealing with *mambu,* or social issues. Second, it identifies someone who is a hunter, dealer, or spy.

Equipped with Kongo words—some from the turn of the century and others from recent discussions, we can surround an *nkondi* with more of the original reading than ever before. But that reading is not definitive, because no one knows where, by whom, or why each figure was created. Definitions are adapted to suit social changes, and so "knowledge of them must be acquired piecemeal, often in the form of an extended invitation."[27] Very few of the sculptures taken out of the Congo were collected with the associated pattern of belief that surrounded them. For the Seattle Art Museum collection, there is no African record of ownership or documentation. A host of dealers in New York, Paris, London, and Los Angeles sold the figures to Katherine White in the 1960s and 1970s, before it was recognized that Kongo explanations for their use could be obtained.

> **Beneath the shadow of a tree ... the court of judgement, *kiazala kia mfundusulu*, was arranged.** —Fu Kiau Bunseki, 1980[28]

Nkondi appear to have been kept apart in their own house, placed in a corner and approached only with the guidance of the *nganga* or priest/diviner. Seen in the very few pictures taken of *nkondi* in the Kongo region are small houses that form the setting for the *nkondi* (fig. 43). A visit would not be lightly undertaken, but was likely to be decreed at the conclusion of a trial, described as a central focus of Kongo life by Fu Kiau Bunseki (fig. 44):

> Under this tree experts investigate the issue, its ramifications, and its effects on community life. The debate is carried on dialectically through diverse songs, slogans, proverbs, mottoes, questions and answers followed by comments. The accused [is] seated within the circle. Any community member is allowed to ask questions to the accused. The main goal of this procedural investigation is to understand social problems and conflicts through the accused and therefore [to] try to find a remedy to cure him as well as the entire community.[29]

Such trials were considered a cornerstone of the kingdom and were full of arguments accented with proverbs and songs. The accused's experience was said to be a form of dying from the humiliation of being interrogated about a crime. After suffering through a trial, rebirth was granted the winner, who would be anointed with white clay to show exoneration. Opposing parties might agree to end their hostility or vow to settle a dispute. The argument (*mambu*) or tribunal was over. To finalize such cases, a visit to the *nkondi* was expected.

Pakalala: **ready to attack and defend.**

Pakalala is one of the *nkondi* figure's many postures. Meaning to stand with hands on hips, it is the stance of a wrestler prepared for whatever may come at him—ready to attack an enemy or defend a righteous person. In Kongo word associations, *paaka* means to cut meat into pieces, just as an *nkondi* takes apart subtle issues. *Paaka mambu* is the total summary and complete capturing of an issue, which the *nkondi* is about to deliver.

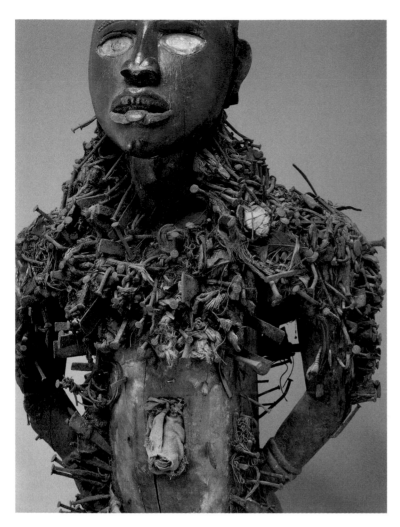

Pl. 75 (detail)

Bibaaku: demolish and divulge.

Inserting nails or blades into the *nkondi* to tie down an agreement or lawsuit is called *bibaaku*. The act summons the figure to watch people adhere to legal covenants. It activates the figure to bring destruction to those who do not fulfill their end of a pact, oath, or treaty. Hundreds of people's trials and mistakes are held firm on this figure's body as a reminder of personal and specific needs of community members (detail, pl. 75). It is the *nkondi*'s duty to fix the client's intentions to remain true to his words of agreement, but also to attack if the agreement is not respected. The *nganga* assists in this process by binding a bit of the client to the nail or blade. Some are asked to lick the nail, adding their saliva as a signature to their agreement. Others might tie on a cloth or string to remind the nail what to do. As the nails accumulate, they become a document covered with intricate details of the many people who have made pacts and decisions in the *nkondi*'s presence. The overall effect was said to produce astonishment in beholders, convincing them of an extraordinarily capable force.[30]

Nganga: priest/diviner.

Keeping track of the precise history of each insertion was the duty of the *nganga* (plural = *banganga*), described as a kind of traffic policeman for the desires and tensions in the lives of his clients. His appearance was often as distinctive as the *nkisi* he worked with. Colored marks and stripes of chalk covered parts of his body, and circles of white chalk surrounded his eyes. Most *minkisi* bear traces of chalk derived from white porcelain clay found under the water or in streambeds, where the dead reside and imbue the substance with their presence. The whiteness applied to the *nganga* may refer to his clairvoyance in contacting this world. John Weeks writes that in place of normal clothes "his dress consists of the softened skins of wild animals, either whole or in strips, feathers of birds, dried fibres and leaves, ornaments of leopard, crocodile or rat's teeth, small tinkling bells, rattling seedpods, and anything else that is unusual and wearable."[31] *Nganga* dressed to impress clients as a kind of "show business" that set the stage for a complex of actions designed to assist individuals and public authorities.[32] Many specialized in particular treatments: some were adept at discovering wrongdoers; others were skilled in resolving conflicts between lineages; and many were curers who prescribed medicines and ritual orders designed to counter any illness. Taking a massage and steam baths, drinking medicine, and hearing confessions were among the measures an *nganga* might recommend for his clients. Some *nganga* were known to wear hats made of red parrot feathers, which may once have rested atop the head of this *nkondi* (pl. 75) with a blaze of jagged color.

Mooyo: **the belly/life.**

The belly of this *nkondi* has been emptied; only a scrap of cloth is left as a hint of what originally covered the navel. A pack of medicines composed by the *nganga* would have filled this hole and been sealed in place with resin, and then a mirror placed in the center. Such medicines gave the figure life, or as Robert Farris Thompson says, a vitality "like a live radio with a working antenna." Without the medicines, the figure has lost its compass and is unable to act. *Minkisi* were portable shrines for the souls or spirits they referred to.

Four other figures illustrate how the mooyo could be configured. The first is seated, with medicines projecting from his navel and the shoulders of his jacket (pl. 76). His gun, uniform, and pith helmet may signal the presence of a European soldier. Sealed behind glass are a host of ingredients that float in a foggy enclosure just out of view. A standing figure whose arms are absorbed into a swollen belly clearly displays his role as a container for medicines—the head twists off (pl. 77). Sitting cross-legged, another holds his hand to his chin in a pose suggesting a person of reflection, lost in thought about how to guide others with his mind (pl. 78). The Kongo phrase "we leave this matter in your lap" refers to the person who is seen listening and thinking on behalf of others.[33] Holding his belly with his left hand and a cane of authority with his right, another Kongo man stands attentively (pl. 79). Medicines coat his face and helmet, but not his body.

Dikenga: **the turning.**

Fu Kiau Bunseki in 1969 first wrote about underlying principles of Kongo art. He clarified a notion that had flourished beneath the surface, beyond European understanding, for more than four hundred years: "The sign of the cross was not introduced into this country and into the minds of its people by foreigners. The cross was known to the Kongo before the arrival of Europeans, and corresponds to the understanding in their minds of their relationship to their world."[34] Bunseki introduced the notion of the *dikenga,* a sign or cosmogram for seeing the progress of a man's soul as akin to the path of the sun (fig. 45). Four moments of the sun are equated with four end points of a cross in a circle. He names the four moments: (1) *kala,* rising, beginning, birth, or regrowth; (2) *tukula,* ascendancy, maturity, responsibility; (3) *luvemba,* setting,

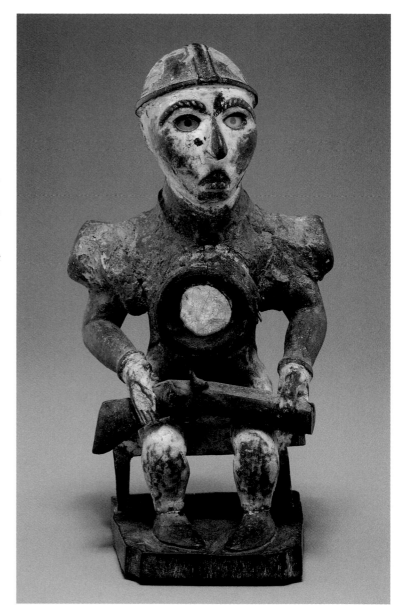

Pl. 76
Seated officer
Kongo, Democratic Republic of the Congo
Late 19th–early 20th century
Wood, mirror, glass, chalk, camwood powder, clay, labels
H. 24.2 cm (9½ in.)
Gift of Katherine White and the Boeing Company,
81.17.835

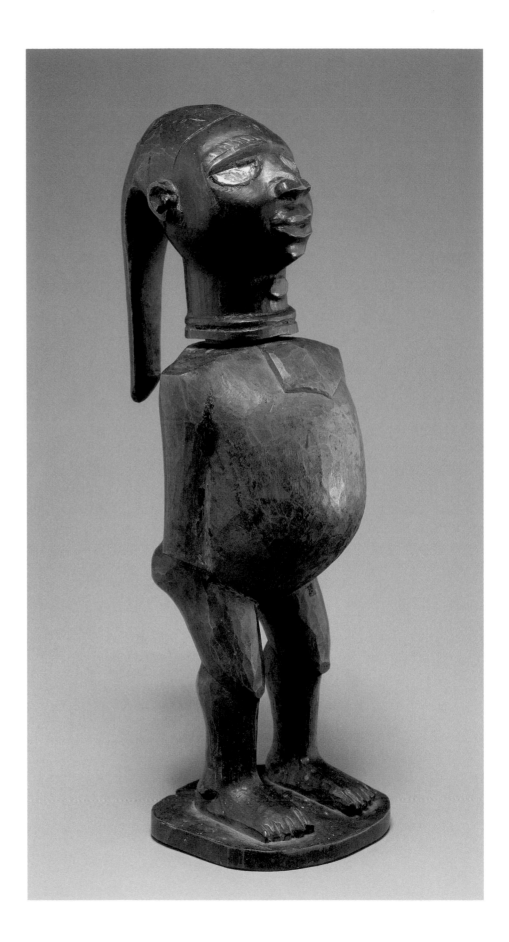

Pl. 77
Standing figure
Kongo, Democratic Republic of the Congo
20th century
Wood, glass, metal
H. 30.1 cm (11⅞ in.)
Gift of Katherine White and the Boeing Company,
81.17.841

Pl. 78
Seated man
Kongo, Democratic Republic of the Congo
20th century
Wood
H. 13.8 cm (5½ in.)
W. 6.0 cm (2⅜ in.)
Nasli and Alice Heermaneck Collection, 68.54

Pl. 79
Standing figure
Kongo, Democratic Republic of the Congo
20th century
Wood
H. 19.7 cm (7¾ in.)
Gift of Katherine White and the Boeing Company,
81.17.839

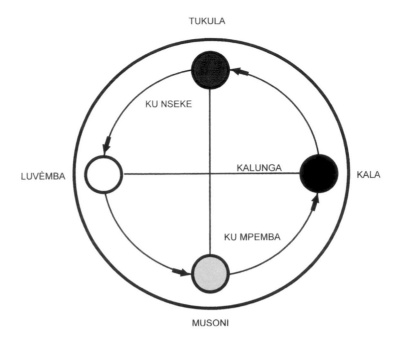

TUKULA

KU NSEKE

LUVÈMBA   KALUNGA   KALA

KU MPEMBA

MUSONI

Fig. 45. Diagram of *dikenga,* four moments of the sun, after the writing of Fu Kiau Bunseki.

handing on, death, transformation; and (4) *musoni,* midnight, existence in the other world, eventual rebirth.[35] All souls are constantly cycling through these four stages, just as each day goes through its stages. Early morning mists are the dying embers of the cooking fires of the dead, who pass away just before the dawn of the living. The *dikenga* sign can also be read as a map: the world of the living and dead meet in the middle horizontal line called *kalunga.*

Turning and circling are found in a woman with child (pl. 80). She sits on an honorary platform incised with pinwheel images that rotate. Her legs form a circle to suggest the cycle of one's life and the revolution of the day from one world to the next.

A *dikenga* sign is a potent document. An *nkondi* figure was likely to witness its impact as a cross was marked on the ground to create a ritual space for oath taking. "The person taking the oath stands upon the cross, situating himself between life and death, and invokes the judgement of God and the dead upon himself."[36] In other circumstances, the *dikenga* declared abilities to lead: "To stand upon this sign meant that a person was fully capable of governing people, that he knew the nature of the world, that he had mastered the meaning of life and death."[37]

Kalunga: ocean, door, and wall between two worlds.

The *nkondi*'s eyes shine, reflecting light from mirrors placed above them. Mirrors, in their shimmering qualities, are reminders of *kalunga,* the shining water that forms a thin barrier between the living and dead. That barrier is crossed by souls and the sun each day. To move into the world below is to enter a time of regeneration, when one's soul can purge itself of the impurities acquired in life and emerge ready to be born into the next existence, washed clean. Looking at the water, or into the *nkondi*'s eyes, we glimpse a miraculous world waiting to welcome the tired soul (detail, pl. 75).

Out of humiliation can stem grandeur.   –Fu Kiau Bunseki[38]

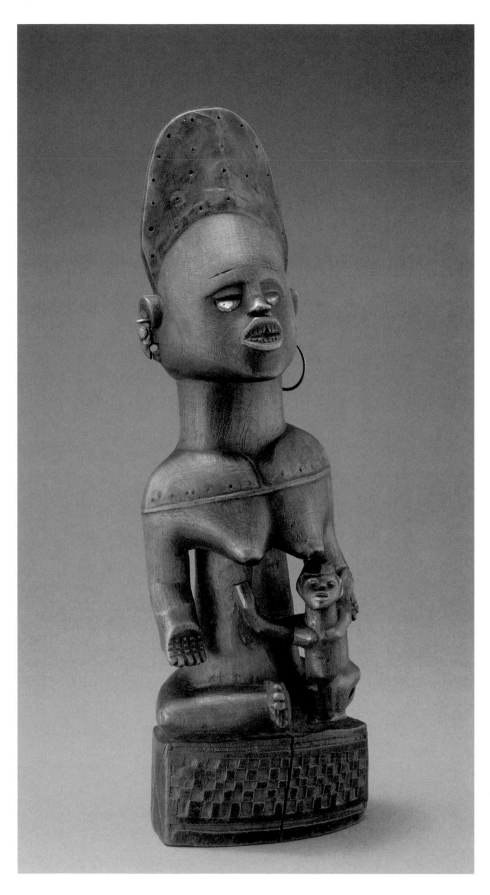

Pl. 80
Mother and child
Yombe, Kongo, Democratic Republic of the Congo
Late 19th–early 20th century
Wood, glass, metal
H. 9.9 cm (3⅞ in.)
Gift of Katherine White and the Boeing Company,
81.17.838

Most Kongo sculpture was collected at the turn of the twentieth century, when the prospects for understanding by outsiders were bleak. One European observer sets the tone of the time: "Kongos have no religion or system of worship; vague superstition takes the place of the former; and the arrangement of charms of the latter. There is no idolatry or attempt to communicate with a Divine Being."[39] The European writers were partly blinded by the need, in the colonial mind, to step in and establish religion where there was none. Another reason is described by Wyatt MacGaffey, scholar of the Kongo, who points out that writers then thought of culture as a collection of traits, not as a system of thought. They were not encouraged or inclined toward abstract thinking themselves, so they deemed the native populations incapable of it.[40] The blinders were so firmly fixed that the Kongo explanations of their own ways of composing the world went unseen. Meanwhile, for centuries, the Kongo maintained a system of *minkisi,* a religion of medicines, common principles of moral conduct, and an orientation to the relations between the land of the dead and the houses of the living.

The large thunder of people's icons.

–Robert Farris Thompson, 1992[41]

Kongo-derived sights and sounds have been an inspiration for African American creativity for centuries. Listen to the samba in Brazil, watch the rumba in Cuba, or tune into the jazz of North America and you are immersed in art forms with Kikongo names and elements. Travel around Cuba, where "underground Kongo practices wired the island," and go to Havana, known as Kuna Mbanza, "to town over there." As cosmograms are drawn in chalk on the earth, priests restate the Kongo *dikenga,* a site where "spirits seat themselves on the center of the sign as the source of firmness."[42] In Haiti, watch for *paquets congo,* bundles containing references to visual codes, puns, and spirits from the Kongo. Attend a ceremony in Rio de Janeiro and you may see Kongo influences mix with Roman Catholic notions of the Latin cross. Examine an Umbanda altar in Uruguay or Brazil for Kongo traces in the mixture of images. Peer inside a large three-legged iron cooking pot in Cuba, Miami, or New York—the assembled ingredients can constitute an *nkisi* much as they would in Kinshasa (fig. 46).

Like a tornado hidden in an egg.

–Fu Kiau Bunseki, 1978

Fig. 46. *Futu nkisi mbuki* (bundle of medicine for a healer), Kinshasa, Democratic Republic of the Congo, 1972.

A walk through African American communities reveals one of the most enduring points of connection to a Kongo aesthetic. Yards and graves display an organic link in a host of choices people make. Considered an opening remark to the person passing by, a yard can itself be transformed into an *nkisi* governed by a concern for protection and completion of the soul's journey. The circles, crosses, diamonds, and spirals of the cosmogram are reconfigured in pinwheels, tires, things that roll on and on. Bottles hanging from trees flash in the sun, luring provocateurs inside to be captured. Tinfoil, mirrors, and lightbulbs reflect light, hinting at the charge of the spirits who wait beneath the shiny surface of the water's edge. Commonplace objects grow empowered by associations. A snail shell placed in the yard or on the grave is a punning reminder that immortality is in evidence—the Kikongo word for snail shell, *zinga,* also means "to live long." Outward simplicity but inner complexity became a hallmark of African American spiritual expression by necessity, but also finds inspiration in Kongo precedents. Bunseki recounts that the first *nkisi* given to Man was Funza, incarnated in unusual twisted root formations. "When you see a twisted root within a charm you know, like a tornado hidden in an egg, that this nkisi is very, very strong—you cannot touch it, only nganga can touch it."[43] African American healers were known as "root persons," respected for their recipes of earth, feathers, forest woods, and many other things, but most significant was a root known as High John the Conqueror.

    Let me be the bad guy.   −David Hammons, 1986

    Kongo impulses have been taken into the streets of New York by the artist David Hammons, whose work conjures many obsessions of the art world. After moving to New York, Hammons found that "everybody was just groveling and Tomming; anything to be in the room with somebody with some money. There were no bad guys here, so I said, Let me be the bad guy, or attempt to be a bad guy, or play with the bad areas and see what happens."[44] He often worked outside galleries, turning his attention to vacant lots in Harlem. Empty Night Train and Thunderbird bottles started appearing on the tips of branches, and metal rings were seen adorning trees like necklaces. Finding tornadoes of meaning in the dirt and discards of life, he created installations using human hair collected from local barber-shop floors, chicken wings found on the street, and bottle caps salvaged from barrooms (fig. 47). On a landfill in lower Manhattan, he constructed *Delta Spirit* out of discarded sheets of metal and surrounded it with an enlarged yard show of doll shoes, bottle caps, feathers, cowbells, wind chimes, and old wheels. The installation was situated by the Hudson River, near the edge of the water's shiny surface, and was a gathering place until it mysteriously disappeared in a fire. In a move made famous by another artist, he collected enormous elephant droppings from the circus and offered the resulting elephant dung sculptures for sale on the streets. Then he sold snowballs. Like the Kongo king who used dirt to signify greeting, David Hammons finds significance in elements that seem simply made but carry complex associations.

    Colonel Frank called this one fetish no. 3.   −Renée Stout, 1989[45]

Fig. 47. David Hammons, *Money Tree,* 1992, gelatin silver print, H. 41.9 cm (16½ in.). Gift of Greg Kucera and Larry Yocom, Seattle Art Museum, 97.77.

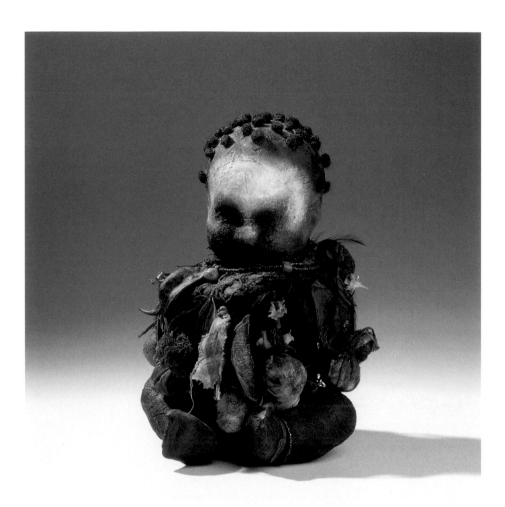

Fig. 48. Renée Stout, *Fetish no. 3,* 1989, mixed media, H. 24.1 cm (9½ in.). Private collection. © 2001 Renée Stout.

Fig. 49. Page from Renée Stout's notebook for *Fetish no. 3,* 1989, ink on paper, H. 28 cm (11 in.). Collection of the artist. © 2001 Renée Stout.

When Renée Stout was ten years old, she saw her first *nkondi* at the Carnegie Museum of Art in Pittsburgh. Kongo imagery and medicines led the artist to create a sequence of sculptures and installations that immerse the viewer in *minkisi* placed in an American context. Her studies guide her work, but she gains admiration for reclaiming African aesthetics and doubling their power through invented realities and personal experiences. In *Fetish no. 3,* Stout takes the image of a doll/child, inspired by her work with three-year-old children (fig. 48). "In working with them for the past four years I've seen a lot of innocence, which, to me, seems to ward off evil."[46] Her dolls imply a role reversal, as they deviate far from the convention of miniature people to play with, and instead project strong personalities with layers of Kongoized identity. In a posture much like that of the woman and child seen in pl. 80, the figure in *Fetish no. 3* sits with her legs in a circle. Stout attaches bundles of her own hair to the head and covers the features with kaolin chalk. She is also known to place inside her works grave dirt, powdered High John the Conqueror root, and other ingredients to ensure that the figure is imbued with the presence of her ancestors and her own being. In another role reversal, Stout plays on the old version of the fetish as a memento brought back from trips to exotic lands by the invented Colonel Frank. In a report about his observations, the fetish is described according to old ethnographic style,

RENEE
STOUT
1989

"FETISH NO. 3"   (1989) $9\frac{1}{2} \times 7 \times 6\frac{1}{2}$ MIXED MEDIA.

COLONEL FRANK CALLED THIS ONE FETISH NO 3. SINCE IT WAS THE THIRD
FETISH HE'D RECEIVED FROM THE PEOPLE OF IBN ISLAND. THEY TOLD HIM
THAT IT WAS VERY EFFECTIVE IN WARDING OFF EVIL BE CAUSE OF THE FORM
IT TOOK. THEY SAID THAT BABIES WERE BORN TOTALLY INNOCENT THEREFORE
THEY WERE ABOVE EVIL THOUGHTS AND DEEDS. ON IBN ISLAND, ANY HOUSEHOLD
THAT DID NOT HAVE A BABY UNDER TWO YEARS OF AGE HAD A FETISH LIKE
THIS ONE TO GUARD THE HOME AND ITS INHABITANTS FROM EVIL AND CORRUPT-
ION. ONCE A BABY REACHED THE AGE OF TWO YEARS HE GOT HIS FIRST
HAIRCUT. THE HAIR WAS THEN GATHERED UP AND TAKEN TO THE ISLAND
WITCHDOCTOR WHO WOULD CREATE LITTLE HAIR BALLS BY ROLLING A SMALL
AMOUNT OF HAIR BETWEEN HIS TWO PALMS. HIS WIFE WOULD THEN
CREATE A BABY'S FORM OUT OF CLAY COVERED WITH CLOTH AND ATTACH THESE
BALLS OF HAIR TO THE HEAD. THE SPIRIT OF THE BABY'S YOUTH AND
INNOCENCE WOULD BE BESTOWED UPON THE FETISH THROUGH THE HAIR
BALLS AND EVEN THOUGH THE CHILD WOULD GROW UP THE HOUSE
WOULD STILL BE PROTECTED

3

full of imaginative notions (fig. 49). The work echoes the fetish phone calls to museums about unnerving curiosities brought back by adventuresome uncles.

Fetishism cycles on, evolving from a word invented by Europeans to disparage African art, to a label applied to Western sexual and economic fixations, to a pun in American art. It is employed as well by African artists who take up the gauntlet of the term. Trigo Piula, in a painting of 1988 entitled *Ta Tele,* puts a Kongo figure on display before an African audience. In the belly, instead of medicine, he places a television screen, ready to receive images seen behind the figure. A soccer match, a kissing couple, a plate filled with food, a beer commercial, and a view of Earth from space are prepared for broadcast. A small symbol planted in the back of each audience member's head indicates what the person desires—a car, a heart, shoes, a meal, clothes, a bottle. As Karl Marx predicted, the fetish for commodities is in full evidence, as advertising promotes the belief that consumer goods can change one's life in important ways.

Mweze Ngangura's film *Pièces d'identités,* released in 1998, considers the value accorded Kongo art in a recent context. It follows the story of a modern-day Kongo king who sends his daughter to Belgium to study medicine and then loses contact with her. Concerned for her safety, he flies to Brussels alone, wearing elements of royal regalia with his dark suit. Observers question why he is wearing such "fetishes." (The regalia happens to be Kuba, but this is a fictional feature film.) When street hustlers steal all his money, the king is tricked into pawning his regalia. A disreputable art dealer then takes control of the "fetishes." Whether the Kongo king can survive on the streets of Brussels without his regalia becomes a test of its power. Does a faith in sacred artistry offer him strength or cripple him in a foreign setting?

Looking back to 1491, we return to this question. The Kongo king Nzinga took a handful of earth and pressed it against his heart to greet a Portuguese visitor. This gesture, interpreted by Fu Kiau Bunseki as signaling his faith in the earth as the ultimate source of medicine, was the first of many offered over the next five hundred years. Kongo art and medicines together provoke viewers to determine whether their faith in creative exchange is "as fragile as glass" or as enduring as earth.

Notes

1. Definitions in the *Oxford English Dictionary*:

a. Originally, any of the objects used by the Negroes of the Guinea coast and the neighboring regions as amulets or means of enchantment, or regarded by them with superstitious dread.

b. By writers of anthropology, used in a wider sense: An inanimate object worshipped by primitive peoples on account of its supposed magical powers, or as being animated by a spirit.

2. John Mack, "Fetish? Magic Figures in Central Africa," in *Fetishism: Visualizing Power and Desire,* ed. Anthony Shelton (London: Lund Humphries Publishers, 1995), 65.

3. From a letter cited in Adam Hochschild, *King Leopold's Ghost* (Boston: Houghton Mifflin, 1998), 13.

4. Suzanne Preston Blier, *Royal Arts of Africa: The Majesty of Form* (London: Lawrence King, 1998), 211.

5. The word "kongo" signifies a socially organized space and has been applied to the people of the region of the Lower Congo River, from the Atlantic coast of Central Africa and extending inland to the current Kinshasa. In the twentieth century, the approximately six million Kongo people were distributed among the Republic of the Congo (formerly French Congo), the Democratic Republic of the Congo (formerly Belgian Congo, then Zaire), and Angola. For clarification of who is and was Kongo, see Wyatt MacGaffey, "Kongo Identity 1483–1993," *Nations, Identities, Cultures,* ed. V.Y. Mudimbe (Durham and London: Duke University Press, 1997), 45–58.

6. Anne Hilton, *The Kingdom of the Kongo* (Oxford: Clarendon Press, 1985), 62.

7. Theodore de Bry, *Petits Voyages* (1598).

8. Statistics about the numbers of the slave trade are continually being reconsidered.

9. Hochschild, *King Leopold's Ghost,* 13.

10. Ibid., 14.

11. Anthony Shelton, "The Chameleon Body: Power, Mutilation and Sexuality," in *Fetishism,* 22.

12. William Smith, *A New Voyage to Guinea* (London: Nourse, 1944).

13. Anne Hilton, *The Kingdom of the Kongo,* (Oxford: Clarendon Press, 1985), 195.

14. Georg Wilhelm Friedrich Hegel, *The Philosophy of History* (1899; reprint, New York: Dover Publications, 1956), 99.

15. Karl Marx, *Capital: A Critique of Political Economy,* vol. 1 (1887; reprint, New York: Vintage, 1977).

16. Captain Camille Coquilhat (deputy to Henry Stanley), *Sur le haut Congo* (Paris: J. Lebegue, 1888), 483.

17. Ibid.

18. Hochschild, *King Leopold's Ghost.*

19. The caption reads: "Dieux nègres: ils sont obéissants comme des Saint-Guirec dont nôtre catholique Bretagne est pourvue. Pour que son Dieu s'occupe de lui, il le lui fait sentir à sa façon."

20. One of the most vehement American writers drawing attention to the atrocities of this time was Mark Twain. In *King Leopold's Soliloquy* (1905; reprint, New York: International Publishers, 1961), he re-creates an imaginary rant by King Leopold against the Kodak camera: "The kodak has been a sole calamity to us. The most powerful enemy indeed. . . . I was looked up to as the benefactor of a down-trodden and friendless people. Then all of a sudden came the crash! That is to say, the incorruptible kodak—and all the harmony went to hell!" 68.

21. Quoted from 1959 textbook, Hochschild, *King Leopold's Ghost,* 299.

22. Wyatt MacGaffey, "The Eyes of Understanding: Kongo Minkisi," in *Astonishment and Power* (Washington, D.C.: Smithsonian Institution Press, 1993), 33.

23. *Nederlandsche Zendingsvereeniging Zendingsblaadje*, no. 234 (November 6, 1893), cited in *Astonishment and Power,* 35.

24. John H. Weeks, *Among the Primitive BaKongo* (London: Seeley, Service and Co., 1914), 225–26.

25. *Art and Healing of the Bakongo Commented by Themselves: Minkisi from the Laman Collection,* trans. and ed. Wyatt MacGaffey (Stockholm: Folkens Museum, 1991).

26. John M. Janzen and Wyatt MacGaffey, *An Anthology of Kongo Religion: Primary Texts from Lower Zaire,* University of Kansas Publications in Anthropology, no. 5 (1974), 35–38.

27. Wyatt MacGaffey, "Complexity, Astonishment and Power: The Visual Vocabulary of Kongo Minkisi," *Journal of African Studies* 14, no. 2 (January 1988), 188.

28. Fu Kiau Bunseki, *African Book without Name* (privately printed, 1980), 41.

29. Ibid.

30. MacGaffey, "The Eyes of Understanding."

31. Weeks, *Among the Primitive BaKongo,* 217.

32. MacGaffey, "The Eyes of Understanding," 52.

33. For a discussion of gestures and poses as found in classic Kongo sculpture, see Robert Farris Thompson, *Four Moments of the Sun* (Washington, D.C.: National Gallery of Art, 1981).

34. Quoted in Janzen and MacGaffey, *Anthology of Kongo Religion,* 34.

35. Fu Kiau Bunseki, 1969, quoted in Janzen and MacGaffey, *Anthology of Kongo Religion,* 34.

36. Wyatt MacGaffey, cited in Robert Farris Thompson, *Flash of the Spirit* (New York: Vintage Books, 1983), 108.

37. Fu Kiau Bunseki, quoted in ibid., 109.

38. Quoted in Robert Farris Thompson, "The Grand Detroit N'Kondi," *Bulletin of the Detroit Institute of Arts* 56, no. 4 (1978), 207–21.

39. W. Holman Bentley, *Dictionary and Grammar of the Kongo Language* (London: Baptist Missionary Society, 1887), 503.

40. Wyatt MacGaffey, *Modern Kongo Prophets: Religion in a Plural Society* (Bloomington: Indiana University Press, 1983), 125.

41. Robert Farris Thompson, "Betye and Renee: Priestesses of Chance and Medicine," in *The Migrations of Meaning* (New York: INTAR Gallery, 1992), 19.

42. Robert Farris Thompson, *Face of the Gods: Art and Altars of Africa and the African Americas* (Munich: Prestel, 1993).

43. Fu Kiau Bunseki, interview by Robert Farris Thompson, October 1978, cited in *Flash of the Spirit,* 131.

44. Quoted in Kellie Jones, "David Hammons," *Real Life Magazine,* no. 16 (1986), 2.

45. From a page of Renée Stout's notebook, 1989, ink on paper, reproduced in *Astonishment and Power.*

46. Renée Stout, quoted in Michael Harris, "Resonance, Transformation, and Rhyme: The Art of Renée Stout," in MacGaffey, *Astonishment and Power,* 123.

A Sculpture Hungry for Aggression:
Ivwri Figure

The *ivwri* figure commands a step back, with its rotted mouth, gaping fangs, and human torso blending into a four-legged creature (pl. 81). The surface is pitted and covered with splotches of red and white. Forcefully, it defies a convention evident in most sculptures from West and Central Africa. Humans and animals, while depicted separately in sculpture, do not often mix. To join bodies with a beast is to make a sculptural statement with unnerving potential.

That potential is expressed in Ben Okri's novel *The Famished Road.* In a vivid description of this kind of union, a hybrid character attacks all senses:

> I saw before me in that new spirit world a creature ugly and magnificent like a prehistoric dragon, with the body of an elephant and the face of a warthog. It towered before me. It was more graceful and less heavy than an elephant, but its tread more resounding. Its face was incredibly ugly. A devourer of humans, of lost souls, of spirits, of all things wonderful, this creature opened its dreadful mouth and roared. Beneath me the tree began to change. Suddenly it seemed the tree was no longer a thing of wood. It became a thing of quivering flesh. The wood rippled slowly into flesh, transforming beneath me. The monstrous creature drew closer and its foul breath knocked my consciousness around. . . . And then the transformation of the wood into flesh became complete and I was suddenly blasted by the earth shaking bellow of a wild animal beneath me. I was overpowered with the odour of its animal virility. Tossing and shivering, shaking its head, and bellowing again as if the sound in some way made its transformation more permanent, I realized that I had made a terrible mistake, and that I was riding on the back of a wild animal, awoken from a fetishistic sleep.[1]

The rare union of human and animal in the *ivwri* sculpture is especially perplexing because there is no clear dominance. Is a man riding a wild animal that has overcome his body, or is a monstrous creature in the process of devouring humans?

Pl. 81

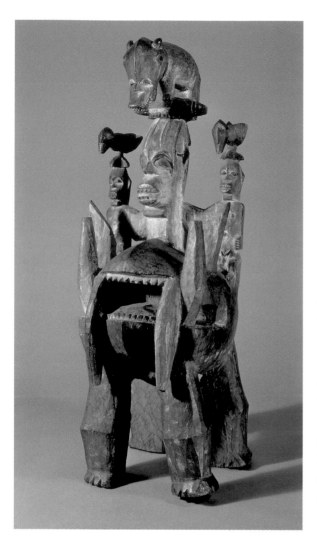

Fig. 50. *Ivwri* figure, Urhobo, Nigeria, 19th century(?), wood and pigment, H. 70 cm (27½ in.). The Trustees of the British Museum, London, 1954.AF.23.428.

Looking for answers about the creation of this hybrid, we step back more than one hundred years to the Delta province of Nigeria.

The people virtually lived their government.

—Obaro Ikime, 1969[2]

When this sculpture was created in the late nineteenth century, the Urhobo were proving an impediment to British plans for the region. The Urhobo stood in contrast to their neighbors, the Ijo and Itsekiri, who maintained highways of trade along what became known as the "oil rivers" of the Delta region. Relying upon an Itsekiri ruler to keep commercial interests flowing, one British major commended the Itsekiri as "the most intelligent and intractible" and "best mannered of all" in the Niger Delta. Meanwhile, he denounced the Urhobo as "shy and timid, treacherous and rude."[3] Urhobo government baffled the British officers, who couldn't find the "head" of a clan or village, let alone of all the Urhobo people. In acts of passive resistance, the Urhobo spent twenty years fending off British ideas of government, preferring to rely on a council of elders who dealt with matters of importance in open discussions. Fiery and eloquent speakers were admired, but authority was diffuse, and no clan attempted to unify control over all. Behind the scenes in most of these discussions, a sculpture like this was invoked for assistance. The confidence it fueled in Urhobo men frustrated the British and remained an enigma for most of a century. Then in the 1970s, an *ivwri* sculpture came up for sale and put cross-cultural perception to a test.

How can anything so hideous be art?

—Katherine White, 1975[4]

Usually quick to make decisions, Katherine White hesitated for months over the purchase of a large carving she described as "ugly, crusted like a poisoned skin." She received a call in February 1975 from a gallery owner who said he had a Nigerian figure like one in the British Museum (fig. 50). Her first reaction was negative: "There it was, under a blanket, no less. Unveiled, it was indeed a large, impressive piece. Over 36 inches, while the BM [British Museum] one is 27½. A big, vast, hard piece, but somehow lacking warmth, without ambience. It wasn't for me."

Several months passed before White reconsidered. By June, she was wavering over a trade to obtain it and worried "on and off, in all my half-awake hours, and driving in cars, and in peaceful gaps in conversations. What to do." Later in the day, she exchanged five pieces for three, plus a sum. "We spent about three hours running back and forth, using one IBEJI [her California car plate] for transport." But she admitted, "that shrine keeps worrying me. I toned it down by washing off some of those glaring white spots. It looks better. I will photograph it tomorrow and send pictures around. The two I could find in books did not have sacrificial patina at all. And this one is so thick."[5]

Does it mean ferocious speed or swift ferocity?

—Leon Underwood, 1947

Until the 1970s, illustrations of Urhobo art were rare, and what was known of its meaning was minimal. Two similar figures appeared in publications with captions that stretch for answers. Leon Underwood described a sculpture in the British Museum with a "fanged maw" and leopard legs painted with spots. His caption asks "Does it mean ferocious speed or swift ferocity?" He sees the central figure as a divinity or spirit, attended by baboonlike figures with human-faced birds on their heads, and concludes, "The subject of the piece seems, with its tribal totem above to be based on fleet ferocity."[6] Relying on visual analysis alone, he deems it a spirit able to sprint and eat at the same time.

Rather an impersonal machine.   —William Fagg, 1964

A second comparison is William Fagg's description of a carving from the neighboring Ijo in the Metropolitan Museum of Art (fig. 51). He states that it "is not for the cult of a god, spirit or ancestor, but is rather an impersonal machine for the control of the life force, and for its direction towards particular ends such as success in war or the recovery of lost goods. Its essential part is the massive quadruped which is variously said to be an elephant or a leopard and may combine the features of both. Surmounting the monster is a human figure representing the owner."[7] What is hinted at here goes beyond a visual hunch, and is backed up by consultation with a colleague who did brief fieldwork in two areas of Urhoboland.[8]

In August, White's photographs of her sculpture reached Perkins Foss, who had lived for two years in Urhoboland working with the Nigerian Department of Antiquities. At the time, he was writing his observations as a graduate student at Yale University. He immediately called White, who noted on her object card: "'That's an important piece,' he said over the phone, sounding beside himself with enthusiasm. He gave me a lot of information about it. Including the component of the patina (yam, chicken and dog blood, gin, and kola) and the symbolism of the red and white dots. Also, he analyzed the parts of the sculpture. And he gave me the town of origin. He will send me a photo of a similar piece in a shrine context and I will send him two 8-by-10s for his dissertation."[9] Foss's dissertation of the next year, entitled "The Arts of the Urhobo Peoples of Southern Nigeria," featured an illustration of the sculpture in White's collection and provided an Urhobo vision of how something so hideous can be honored by a culture.

A magnificent metaphor for aggression.   —Perkins Foss, 1976

Foss commended the Urhobo's southern clans for evolving a "complex image that is a magnificent metaphor for aggression." His work transforms a crusty carving

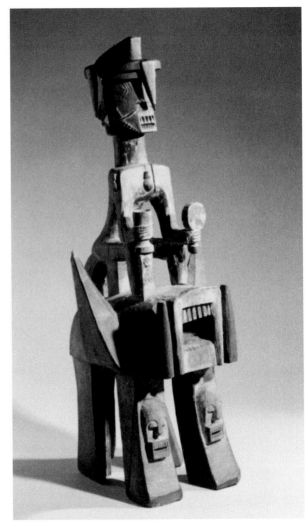

Fig. 51. Efri figure, Ijo, 19th century, Nigeria, wood and pigment. H. 64.8 cm (25½ in.). Metropolitan Museum of Art, New York, the Michael C. Rockefeller Memorial Collection, Purchase, Matthew T. Mellon Foundation Gift, 1960 (1978.412.404).

Ivwri *Figure*   171

of a hybrid beast into a complex sculpture able to "establish otherwise unobtainable levels of compassion and peaceful coexistence in Urhobo society."[10] Hideous in form but therapeutic in effect. Created to inspire wrath and to control anger. Associations unfold and require us to consider an *ivwri* from an Urhobo point of view.

> **Warning: being worried by hunger brings vexation**
> **Hunger makes you say what you do not understand.**
>
> —Urhobo praise poem[11]

Hunger is emphasized visually by a gaping mouth framed by large incisors (pl. 81). This mouth has overtaken the bottom half of the human figure, whose torso rises above. "Ivwri," the name the Urhobo have given this type of sculpture, is experienced as a quality of male character. Just as this figure has an overactive alliance with a beast in his belly, so all men must learn to deal with the force of aggression in their lives. While aggressive tendencies need to be nurtured for a man to succeed in life, they must also be carefully monitored and controlled to be effective. Feeding this image underlines the need for male personalities to check their hunger for confrontation.

> **My Ivwri, here is chalk, oh!**
> **Chalk for children,**
> **Chalk for long life,**
> **Chalk for young-body.** —Urhobo praise poem[12]

The *ivwri* can be fed every four days, following a weekly cycle in which every fourth day is a day of rest. Two foods are favored: a locally produced gin and white chalk, still seen in spots on the sculpture's surface. Supplies of kaolin chalk are dug from riverbeds where water and land meet. Derived from this point of transition, chalk is considered a sign of otherworldliness and religious purity. And chalk has a calming effect on the eyes of the central figure, guiding the lids toward composure. Camwood, a reddish powder derived from a vegetable dye, serves as a sign of rebirth and the role women take in maintaining life. Bites of food from the owner's meal may also be fed to the *ivwri*—the residue might account for the crust that covers the top and inside of this figure's belly. Food is offered so that the *ivwri* will curtail an outbreak of aggression. An *ivwri* can also stir up the owner, inspiring his warrior instincts to defend his family and community.

> **Here is your cutlass, Ivwri.** —Urhobo praise poem[13]

Four human heads are pinned beneath the feet of the crowning central creature. This *ivwri* is designed to take heads as well as protect them. Theft is a core concern for the Urhobo. An *ivwri* can bolster the boldness of a highway robber, but it can also curb losses to thieves. In its ultimate protective stance, an *ivwri* would be charged with warding off attempts to take people as slaves. Until 1930, Urhobo towns were raided by neighbors, who abducted individuals and families; at times, entire populations were uprooted. An *ivwri* formed a locus for a powerful emotional need— protection against the loss of family members and a whole community.

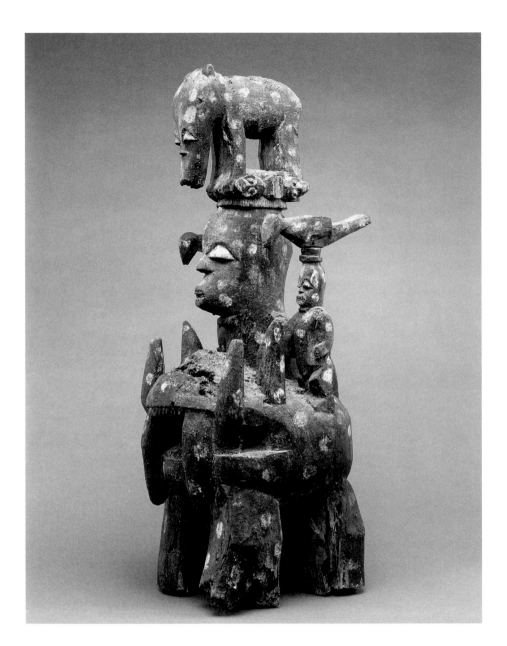

Atarhe: speaking out.

At the moment of birth, an Urhobo male child will announce to the world whether he has a calm or troubled character. Further signs of that character accumulate as the child grows. If he cries constantly, is unable to share, or tends to resent even the smallest misunderstanding, then a frustrated parent might take the child for diagnosis. A diviner could confirm that the child is plagued by a troubling *ivwri*, in which case a small image is placed around his neck.

From that point on, the young man keeps an *ivwri* image as a personal shrine on the family altar and serves it regularly. When he moves into young adulthood, the image goes with him to guide his behavior. Some men live with their *ivwri* as a constant companion, envisioned as a presence that stands quietly and supportively by their side. One elder indicates what can happen if the need for an *ivwri* is not detected early:

Pl. 81
Ivwri **figure**
Urhobo, Nigeria
Late 19th century
Wood, pigment, nails, chalk, deposits
H. 91.5 cm (36 in.)
Gift of Katherine White and the Boeing Company,
81.17.532

Fig. 52. *Ivwri* figure in meeting hall, Ughievwen lineage, Urhobo, 1969.

Suppose I borrow your pen. Tomorrow you return and ask for the pen. Unfortunately, I have to tell you that I have lost it. But I promise to buy you another one. I do so; you return the next day and I give it to you. But you complain that this isn't your pen. I show you that it is exactly the same. You still complain that it isn't *your* pen. So I go out and buy a much more fancy, expensive pen, and bring it to you at your house. You still complain that this isn't *your pen,* and you ridicule me to your friends for having lost your pen. Next day I get five pens, all better than the one you originally loaned me. Still you complain that none of these is your pen, and that I am responsible for having lost it. Whenever you see me for months to come, you complain that I was the one who lost your pen. You are having serious trouble from your ivwri, and these problems will continue until you have an image carved for your use.[14]

Larger-scale *ivwri*, like the one in the Seattle Art Museum, result from a consultation between a diviner and a patron. The two work with an artist to create an image of the proper size and scale to suit the individual. A new owner receives the finished *ivwri* from the diviner after engaging in a tug of war to take ownership. Next, he must face challenges from all other *ivwri* owners in town. They taunt him with a gauntlet of weapons and words in praise of war and aggression and wait to see whether he has sufficient force to command his new *ivwri.* If he loses the *ivwri,* he is deemed unready to own it.

Ivwri that tip the scales indicate a prominent owner. This *ivwri* is one of four likely to come from the same clan by the same artist. A near duplicate *ivwri* was photographed in 1949, then again in 1969 in a meeting hall built by thirty-two villages (fig. 52). Spoken of as an elder *ivwri,* it probably once belonged to a warrior in the second half of the nineteenth century. After his death, the family would have fed the *ivwri* to commemorate the owner and ensure his protection. As the figure was handed down by his descendants, the *ivwri* could evolve into a senior sculpture by being transferred to a collective meeting hall.

The Urhobo hall as a setting for the *ivwri* was quite unlike the museum's stark gallery. There it was given a "wing" made of wood and raffia, a reminder that the figure was not inert or stationary, but able to travel to survey trouble and potential enemies. From its space at the back of the hall, the *ivwri* also visualized aggression's role in social settings. During debates, an *ivwri* personality is volatile. A commanding speaker may be inspired by an active relationship with his *ivwri.* He may build a reputation as one who is adept at arguing—an admirable trait. But if he becomes too stubborn or contentious, if his words are too sharp, composure is lost and he can throw a meeting into chaos. Then it is said that the disruptive person is "having trouble with his *ivwri*" and needs to acquire an image or feed one well.

> The Urhobo hold on to images tightly.
>
> —Perkins Foss, 1997[15]

The museum setting is completely unlike the original *ivwri* display in another fundamental way. An *ivwri* was rarely viewed, in contrast to the sculptures and masquerades with a public presence. Perkins Foss found that it could take months, even years, to be allowed to view *ivwri* images in personal and collective shrines. Figures of this scale might be carefully guarded in meeting halls. Just as major shrines, like land, are not owned by an individual, so it is with large *ivwri* that have achieved senior status. No one person would be able to sell it. How this sculpture made its way into the marketplace is not known.[16] One active avenue for exporting art in the 1970s was European transport companies, whose huge containers arrived full of oil-rig parts and left packed with art. This *ivwri* is among very few that exist in Europe and America.[17]

> Ota gbinowe (will the future be good or bad)?
>
> —Bruce Onobrakpeya, 1988[18]

The need to know more about *ivwri* is still fueling research. Perkins Foss continues to update his work, and an Urhobo graduate student, John Tokpabere Agberia, wrote a full dissertation on the subject in 2000. Bruce Onobrakpeya, a contemporary artist of Urhobo ancestry, has recently founded a center in Urhoboland to promote local and international exchanges. He designed the building as a mini-Guggenheim, with ramped circular spaces, but modeled the program after the Haystack Mountain School in Maine, where the artist spent a residency in 1976.

Onobrakpeya often uses modern media to relate older stories to living issues. When a new Nigerian constitution was being drafted, he created a print entitled *Will the Future Be Good or Bad?* (fig. 53). The print was inspired by the story of a man who goes to the spirit world and sees a spirit flying over the head of a speaker standing before an assembly. The spirit holds white chalk and a sword in each hand. When the man returns to earth, he consults an oracle about the meaning of the scene. He is told that if the deliberations of the assembly reflect wisdom from the group's past, they will be rewarded with white chalk. If their decisions are selfish or corrupt, or they are unwilling to learn from their mistakes, the sword of destruction will be employed. The troubled man is directed to apply this lesson to his life. One hundred years before, the question "Will the future be good or bad?" would have been handled by consultations with a council of elders and an *ivwri* sitting near by. Today, Urhobo art continues to explore ways to acknowledge the effect of aggression. An *ivwri* still needs to be fed.

Fig. 53. Bruce Onobrakpeya, detail of *Will the Future Be Good or Bad?* 1978, plastograph, from *Spirit in Ascent*, Ovuomaroro Gallery Production, 1992.

Ben Okri's narrator, who awakes to find himself seated on a beast that brings the *ivwri* to imaginary life, survives the encounter. He returns to life, marked by the hold that a volatile monster can have over a man's life:

> The beast backed off, giving a vicious snort as if it had burst open a channel through centuries of bad dreams. Then it began with an awkward canter, picked up speed and jumped about the place, tossing its head, attacking the invisible monster. . . . It charged towards a thick cluster of bushes at such speed that I was thrown off and it was lucky I landed on grass and vegetation or I would certainly have broken my neck. I heard the wild beast returning, snorting, pounding the earth. I jumped to my feet, as if from a feverish torrent of nightmares. Completely forgetting my hurting ankles, I ran out of the forest, and fled like a child.[19]

Notes

1. Ben Okri, *The Famished Road* (New York: Anchor Books, 1991), 247.

2. Obaro Ikime, *Niger Delta Rivalry: Itsekiri-Urhobo Relations and the European Presence 1884–1936* (New York: Humanities Press, 1969).

3. Ibid.

4. *Praise Poems: The Katherine White Collection* (Seattle: Seattle Art Museum, 1984), 28.

5. Katherine White Journals, Seattle Art Museum.

6. Leon Underwood, *Figures in Wood of West Africa* (London: John Tiranti, 1947), xlvi.

7. William Fagg and Margaret Plass, *African Sculpture: An Anthology* (New York: Dutton Vista, 1964), 34.

8. Wilson Perkins Foss IV, "The Arts of the Urhobo Peoples of Southern Nigeria" (Ph.D. diss., Yale University, 1976). William Fagg consulted with Kenneth Murray, a field researcher whose work in Nigeria during this time was voluminous but remained unpublished. He did brief work in the Ogo and Ughienvwe areas and photographed an *ivwri* that looks remarkably like the Seattle Art Museum *ivwri* in a clan house in 1949. The photo is in the archives of the National Museum, Lagos, Nigeria, negative number 11.107.23.

9. Katherine White Journals, August 1975.

10. Foss, "Arts of the Urhobo," 76.

11. Ibid., 287.

12. Ibid., 283.

13. Ibid., 286.

14. Elder in Efru, Uvwie clan, ibid., 83.

15. Perkins Foss, letter to author, 1997.

16. It is suspected that European pressure may have led to this sculpture being sold. During this era, a large quantity of art was leaving Nigeria for export to dealers in Europe and America. One common practice for acquiring art from runners or company agents was, and still is, "Don't ask, don't tell." Concern for the methods of collecting and their effects on original owners was frequently not considered the dealer's responsibility.

17. Two almost identical *ivwri* have been photographed in the field by Kenneth Murray in 1949 and Perkins Foss in 1969. The only others in public collections are in the British Museum and the Metropolitan Museum of Art.

18. Bruce Onobrakpeya, *Will the Future Be Good or Bad?* (Lagos: Ovuomaroro Gallery Production, 1988), 99.

19. Okri, *The Famished Road,* 247–48.

Forest Spirits Far from Home: Dan Masks

A masquerade is scheduled for the night of the Seattle Art Museum's African gala. Many galleries are transformed into simulated African spaces—one is a street market, another is a nightclub featuring a dance band from the Democratic Republic of the Congo. A huge altar, concealing a live guardian, has been erected by an Igbo artist from Nigeria. On the museum's indoor staircase, an African American fashion show is the attraction of the moment. Slender models in sculptural clothing take mincing steps down marble stairs. A clockwork schedule of events is being monitored behind the scenes. In the midst of the fashion finale, Won Ldy Paye and members of his group, Village Drum and Masquerade, arrive and are directed to their private dressing room. The schedule dictates that they constitute a masquerade in exactly fifteen minutes.

Forty-five minutes later, sharp drumming from deep inside the museum signals their readiness. The rapid-fire rhythm of a *sankpah* drum moves through the stairwells. Doors suddenly swing open and two masqueraders with attendants sweep into what is normally a café, now an arena for performance (fig. 54).

> **We can't create chaos.** —Won Ldy Paye, 1998[1]

This is masquerading far from a Liberian home. Instead of preparing in a forest enclosure, the performers have emerged from a theatrical dressing room with strong lights. Instead of interacting with audiences who regularly host masquerades, they perform for a crowd more likely to hold seats at the ballet, symphony, or opera. Within the museum, a kind of secret society of patrons and staff met in advance for months to eliminate just the kind of chaos that masquerades can embody. Paye has talked with me about the need to adapt his performances to suit an American audience. "Once we had Yavi grab purses in the audience, and fire swallowing and tongue cutting, but we quit doing that because we got strong reactions and realized we can't create chaos in the audience."[2]

For myself, it is the chaos that I crave. Attending masquerades as a child in Liberia supplied me with extraordinary experiences that stand out as pivotal memories:

Pl. 84

Fig. 54. Village Drum and Masquerade with Won Ldy Paye in foreground, Seattle Art Museum, 1989.

Fig. 55. Yavi masquerade at a Vai celebration, Liberia, 1969.

Being left in complete darkness for hours to await a dawn performance. Standing erect listening to waves of people running by so close that I could smell their breath but was never touched. Watching children my own age emerge from the darkness, keeping their backs exposed and their heads solemnly bowed to be accounted for after time away in forest schools. Hearing mothers discover children they hadn't seen in months or years. Watching these same children not break their stern concentration until massive feasts were served. In Liberia, masqueraders had a way of appearing out of nowhere, sometimes accosting people who got in their way, other times remaining aloof until attendants cleared their path. Quite often they accomplished feats that shouldn't have been humanly possible. They were capable of gravity-defying moves, disappearing acts, and tornadoes of frenetic footwork. A masquerade immersed you in events and surrounded you with characters that could never be fully explained (fig. 55).

Won Ldy Paye's gallery performance holds back on illusions, and the museum places masks in a quiet containment field. Without a voice, music, volatility, movement, a mask only hints at what it once inspired. Yet, even as a minimized wooden face, the African mask has had an enormous effect on the history of art in the twentieth century. Some would say the mask helped launch an artistic revolution. Others see the mask performing a remarkable political feat—opening a door onto a field of protest and ensuing struggles between Africans and Europeans.

> **The cannibal gods be praised who give us the courage for salutary massacres.**   —André Salmon, 1912[3]

Two Africanesque faces rendered in one painting have been called an anarchist bomb or Molotov cocktail meant to blast apart artistic conventions of the previous century. In his painting *Les Demoiselles d'Avignon,* Pablo Picasso painted faces with features that turned the notion of beauty inside out (fig. 56). He placed them on nudes looking at three other nudes. If read literally, the composition could be seen as an encounter between two masqueraders and three women trapped in a bordello. Yet this painting has never been taken as a literal depiction. Many see this thoroughly studied work as a breakthrough in Picasso's search for a new formal vocabulary, one that severs the ties between form and content. Others account for the painting's radical force by pointing out how it disrupts the notion of a passive idealized female. The debate still rages over what Picasso was saying by adopting features of African masks.

Fig. 56. Pablo Picasso, *Les Demoiselles d'Avignon* (and detail), 1907, oil on canvas. Museum of Modern Art, New York. Acquired through the Lillie P. Bliss Bequest. © 2002 Estate of Pablo Picasso/Artists Rights Society (ARS) New York.

Fig. 57. Maurice Radiguez, "Le Bouillon de tête," *L'Assiette au beurre* (1905).

In 1920, Picasso denied his faces were inspired by African art, but in 1937, he described a visit to the Musée d'Ethnographie at the Palais du Trocadero to André Malraux, who published the discussion after Picasso's death. Picasso's narration is one of the first accounts of a European reaction to African art in a museum:

When I went into the old Trocadero, it was disgusting. The Flea Market. The smell. I was all alone. I wanted to get away. But I didn't leave. I stayed. I stayed. I understood that it was very important: something was happening to me, right?

The masks weren't just like any other pieces of sculpture. Not at all. They were magic things. But why weren't the Egyptian pieces or the Chaldean? We hadn't realized it. Those were primitives, not magic things. The Negro pieces were *intercesseurs*, mediators; ever since then I've known the word in French. They were against everything—against unknown, threatening spirits. I always looked at fetishes. I understood; I too am against everything. I too believe that everything is unknown, that everything is an enemy! Everything! ... Spirits, the unconscious (people still weren't talking about that very much), emotion—they're all the same thing. I understood why I was a painter. All alone in that awful museum, with masks, dolls made by the redskins, dusty manikins. *Les Demoiselles d'Avignon* must have come to me that very day, but not at all because of the form; because it was my first exorcism-painting—yes absolutely![5]

Precisely what Picasso was exorcising has led to much speculation. Many artists and art historians find it radical enough that he exploded the human figure and face into fractured surfaces. Patricia Leighton asserts that the radicalism doesn't stop with his visual audacity. Picasso might also have intended to catalyze the outrage over French policies toward Africa in the first decade of the twentieth century.[6] In 1904 and 1906, scandals regarding colonial policies and atrocities were breaking in the news, inciting Picasso's friends in Montmartre. Journals and anarchist newspapers like *L'Assiette au beurre* and *Les Temps nouveaux* featured cartoons by artists protesting the pillage and massacres perpetrated on African populations in the French and Belgian Congo (fig. 57). A French audience at the time might have seen Picasso's masklike faces as an attack not only against formal constraints in art, but also against European efforts to control African colonies with abusive force. This double-edged exorcism could explain why reactions to the painting at the time were so volatile, why Georges Braque would say, "It's as if you were drinking gasoline and spitting fire."[7]

For many years, one of the two faces was ascribed to the influence of a Dan mask (see fig. 56, detail). Yet Picasso didn't see such a mask during his first Trocadero visit. None was available for viewing at the Musée de l'Homme until 1931, and no examples were noted in his friends' collections. From 1907 until his death, Picasso owned African art but did not try to distinguish regions or cultures among his holdings (fig. 58). He and Parisian dealers accumulated Bamana, Fang, Pende, Guro and other masks without concern for distinctions or original meanings. Many cultures were considered as one ubiquitous African culture. Masks continued to be admired for their form, but their function was disregarded.

In the United States, Paul Guillaume and Edward Stieglitz were among the first to show African masks, as part of a 1914 exhibition at the 291 Gallery entitled *Statuary in Wood by African Savages: The Root of Modern Art.* The exhibition continued the premise of admiring African formal qualities. At this time, African masks were considered faces to be incorporated into a modernist aesthetic, and were scarcely appreciated on their own terms. Museum catalogues for years relied on generalities and invented motivations.

A 1935 publication from the Museum of Modern Art declared:

Some [masks] that are to be handed down within the tribe from fetish-man to fetish-man are meticulously carved; others to be worn at one circumcision ceremony, then to be thrown away, may be contrived crudely out of soft wood and painted with gaudy colors in some traditional pattern.[8]

And in 1950, another New York museum added:

Contrary to the civilized man's point of view, which rejects pain as a good, the African Negro incorporates atrocious tests of endurance into his life, which in most respects is an ordeal, a sustained, prodigiously complex ritual ended only by death. His conception of the world is so swarming with spirits to be

Fig. 59. Masonic Temple, Monrovia, Liberia, 1969.

propitiated, and customs to be served, that he has no time to consider what he himself is like: hence his masks, which are more common and various than those of any culture, are the least lifelike.[9]

In 1950 came a turning point in the recognition of what an African mask did in an African setting. After spending twenty years in Liberia, a missionary, Dr. George Harley, issued a monograph entitled *Masks as Agents of Social Control.* He gathered the information while collecting more than one thousand masks and witnessing events related to a secret association he identified as Poro. His missionary station happened to be in an area where people relied on masquerading to resolve the complexities of community life. Harley said his work was fueled by a conviction to record the masking tradition then being suppressed by the Liberian government, so much so "that people had given up hope that it would ever function again." The Poro society was "no longer the great educational institution it once was."[10]

The families who controlled the national government viewed masking as a threat to their authority. Liberia was governed from the capital of Monrovia by descendants of freed American slaves who had arrived in 1822. A cultural gulf divided these settlers from indigenous Liberians, as is evidenced in the Liberian Declaration of Independence, which voiced the freed slaves' "desire for a retreat where, free from the agitation and molestation, we could in composure and security approach in worship, the God of our fathers."[11] This god was Christian, worshiped in churches that sprang up along the coast. As for the indigenous beliefs and structures, one Lutheran missionary clearly stated they were not part of their vision: "We not only have to preach the gospel, but break up the whole social fabric and literally create a new civilization."[12] Their model for a strong men's association was the American Masons, emulated in the twentieth-century construction of an enormous Masonic Temple in Monrovia (fig. 59). Societies like the Poro were not openly endorsed. Harley's conviction that Poro ruled as a secret form of government among the Dan has been disputed by later

Pl. 82
Ga Wree Wree mask
Dan, Liberia, Guinea, and Côte d'Ivoire
Early 20th century
Wood, cloth, bells, leopard teeth, hairpins, cowry shells, twine
H. 50 cm (19¾ in.)
Gift of Katherine White and the Boeing Company, 81.17.197.1

184   Forest Spirits Far from Home

researchers, but his work did recognize a societal role for masquerades. Through them, a complex network of diplomacy, trade, and regulation of warfare was administered. Dr. Harley also became the single largest supplier of Dan and Mano masks to American collectors. From the 1920s to 1940s, he sold most of his masks to the Peabody Museum at Harvard. By the 1950s, his sales diminished and other dealers began offering masks from Liberia and Côte d'Ivoire.

> I started hearing rumors of a mask like the Supreme Court.
>
> –Robert Farris Thompson, 1991[13]

The museum's primary Dan mask (pl. 82) comes from a legendary sweep through New York galleries in 1968 by a woman from Ohio. In what she nicknamed the four-day massacre, Katherine White bought a large quantity of African art and took it all back to her home in Gates Mills to evaluate. She invited William Fagg, then Keeper of the African Collections at the British Museum and a leading figure in African art studies, to help her sort out the best from the worst. Much of that impulse spree she later sold, as she educated her eye and increased her knowledge of the art market. However, the Dan mask purchased from Merton Simpson was never questioned. Simpson was building a reputation as a dealer of distinction who saw hundreds of items brought in by African runners and discerned the best of their type to offer in his gallery. It was rare to find a Dan mask with costume elements remaining, but this one was adorned with layers of them. Working on a publication with William Fagg, White knew this mask must be featured. The mask's caption reads:

> Serendipity has brought together Professor Robert Farris Thompson's very well documented photograph, taken a few months ago, and the newly acquired mask in timely fashion during the production of the catalogue. The mask is magnificent and by reason of the panache of its accoutrements, suggests more strikingly than any other mask in the collection the style of the mask in action. Has it not a verve such as even the salons of Paris have not seen?[14]

By 1970, curator Michael Kan selected the mask for his book *African Sculpture* and provides more hints about the character who once wrote it: "The small slit eyes suggest that this is a female mask of the type worn by a *zo* or Dan priest, who is always in attendance when a great Judgement mask is about to render a verdict."[15]

Ga Wree Wree became a featured guest at an exhibition in 1974 that showcased the findings of Robert Farris Thompson. The mask was restored to its full raffia and cloth costume and seated in front of a large-scale photo mural to announce the arrival of a judge from the forest. Thompson wrote about Dan masks with a mixture of his observations and direct quotations from Dan speakers in 1974. He pushed aside the terms in previous descriptions—the "fetish-man" who uses the mask to conduct ceremonies with gaudy colors. After Thompson visited the home of this masquerade, his account, "Gaa Wree-Wre: Ideal Perfect Justice," revealed masks to have a gravity and composure in confronting conflicts:

> Even before I left the capital of Liberia, Monrovia, for the interior in late March 1967, I began to hear rumors of a splendid mask, called Ga Wree Wree.

The mask was described as a perfect face with hairpin embellishments, rich beads and bells, with kaolin across the eyes as a mark of purity and beauty. This mask was also said to speak, as one of the leading traditional judges of the Dan, with a strong and rolling voice, disguised but clear. I was given to understand that Ga Wree Wree never danced, that it appeared without musicians and with a single speaker, every six years, "for cow feasts or most important matters." Impeccable behavior was demanded by this mask, "which could stop a war": "People watch their lips when Ga Wree Wree is about, that nothing is done against tradition."

By luck my visit to Butuo in April 1967 coincided with the visitation of this mask, come to hear an important dispute over land rights. The mask was accompanied by its Laame, who wore kaolin around his eyes, matching the effect of the mask itself [fig. 60]. Laame claimed that the mask had been carved "in the late nineteenth century" by Wehi Tiakangbaye, of the village of Yaogortu. It was called a *go gle* mask. As such, it is only to be addressed as "my lord" (*m de*).

A towering conical headdress (*comoo*), emblazoned with patterning in indigo blue, red, and cowrie embroidery surmounted the mask. The shape of the headdress, emblematic of great beauty, was accompanied by feminine calm of countenance. The eyes were slits, veritable *yeux en coulisse*, emphasized by sharply stylized kaolin-daubed decoration. Above the generous brow was an ornamental band of cowries, symbols of power and prestige. A striking fanlike headdress of metal hairpins surmounted this ornament. It was said that some of these pins had been "forcibly removed from aged women." This was the story: when Ga Wree Wree is out, no one is allowed to wear dress that resembles its costume in any detail; careless old women had stood with hairpins in their hair in his presence, whereupon he swept into their midst, seized their pins, and carried them away as permanent forfeits to his power.

The mask incarnates forest fierceness (leopard teeth, redness, raffia) and human elegance (slitted eyes, kaolin, hairpins, textiles). Lappets of red decorate the sides of the wearer's head, with red referring to killing, to spilled blood. Brass bells and the teeth of a leopard hang from strands of blue beads at the jaws of the mask. These elements refer to the extraordinary final powers of the Go society. Ga Wree Wree wears a striped shawl of indigo around his shoulders and an enormous bell jar skirt of raffia fiber [fig. 61]. The latter element refers to wild growth and forest origins. It is an awesome *go gle*, tempered by feminine grace. The profound authority of its example is furthered by the dignity and strangeness of its motions, which also stir wonderment in the villages where it has appeared.

Go gle are normally seated when they hear a case. The mask does not dance. He walks and sits. Immersed in the voluminous fiber folds, he cannot swiftly rise or descend as ordinary men. He is locked into great weight, suggestive

Fig. 60. Laame of Butuo, Liberia, 1967.

Fig. 61. Ga Wree Wree sitting, Liberia, 1967.

of his transcendental character, of the gravity of his function. I observed the seating of this mask within a forest glen near the banks of the river dividing Liberian Dan from Ivory Coast Dan. With the speaker responding, "a we, a we" (I answer, I answer) to the first and last phrases, the judge chanted in a growling voice the following words:

> Who passes far?
> Who passes?
> You may say: Krua!,
> Final-Decision-Giver!
> You must act: with the consent of the highest mask.
> Rumors!
> Person-Gave-Person-up: indictment!
> Attention!
> You must act: with the consent of the highest mask.
> Rumors!
> Black mask!
> Heeeeeeeeeeeey! Heeeeeeeeeeeeeeeeeey!
> Behold the mask.
> Who passes far?
> Who passes?

He demanded to know who was before him, from what village and for what purpose. He revealed his appellations, Krua, Final-Decision-Giver, Dense Forest, though no one had the right to use them. He broke his chant with syncopic shouts and admonitions, as he began with the cry, "Who passes far, who passes?"

Suddenly the mask rose and began to walk, a bell at the hip clanging in time to his motion. The walk was strange—short steps, tilting gown, pronounced sway, reminiscent of the walk of a heavily feathered aquatic fowl.

The mask reseated itself upon the earth, immediately immersed in an aura of otherworldly deliberation. This Final-Decision-Giver, sifting truth from rumor, promises in the resolution of fierceness and calm, the ability to weave justice from a total understanding.[16]

> **It is said that when masks are lying quietly on the ground one can sometimes hear them "grinding their teeth."**
>
> —Eberhard Fischer and Hans Himmelheber, 1984[17]

Research among the Dan about their masks continued to be published during the 1970s and 1980s. The special case of Ga Wree Wree was noted as coming from Gomaple, where it was recorded as having risen to such high status only in the last few decades. Researchers began emphasizing the fact that the character portrayed by a Dan mask cannot be determined by the face alone. When masks are taken from their forest home, headdresses and accoutrements removed, they are taken off assignment. Without proper costuming and a character to enact, the mask is an anonymous remnant. Such decommissioned masks are what foreign collections primarily own, leaving behind the rich associations that once supported their creation—the spirits who grind their teeth and stride confidently out of the forest are left behind. One Man na Gle bird mask can be admired for its form alone (pl. 83). The crisp cutting lines of an extended beak and dropped jaw offset a sequence of smooth facial planes. Another mask of the same type is submerged beneath a corona of cowry shells, a mane of fur, flaps of cloth, and a headdress of leather (pl. 84). The wood face gives way to the costumed character of mixed media. Holding flywhisks and waving them gently, the wearer of such bird masks would be accompanied by an orchestra as he danced and sang in tribute to two birds: the hornbill, a large bird thought to bring the prized palm nut to the Dan, and the parakeet, known for cracking the nuts open.

> **Dan masks and the spirits they embody, then, deal with virtually all human concerns.** —Eberhard Fischer, 1978[18]

Observers witness a range of Dan masqueraders. Entertainment masks enact short skits and songs, dropping moralizing proverbs along the way. Bold mimes attack propriety with anger. Unpredictable performers ransack villages and punish conceited or overly inquisitive people. "Flaw-finding" masquerades tempt audiences to laugh at them, and then fine those who do. When modern laws and regulations did not work, the spirits left their home in the deep forest and enacted a sacred sense of order. As Gba Daouda stated in 1982, "In the Dan lands, where the sacred masks constitute the unwritten law, their keepers exercise, in deed though not always by right, all or part of the political power."[19] Masked spirits appeared as teachers, judges, messengers, police, dancers, and entertainers. They were expected to settle disputes,

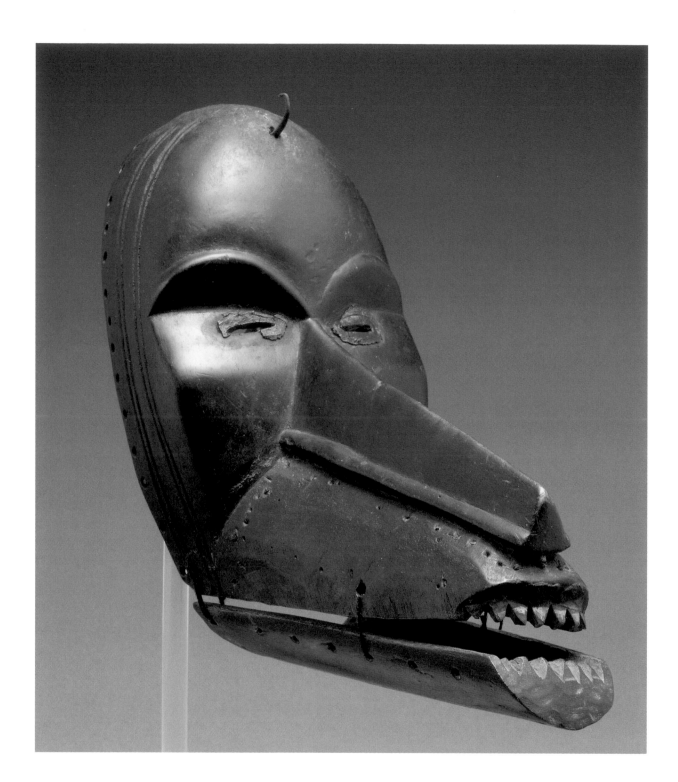

Pl. 83
Man na Gle (Bird) mask
Dan, Liberia, Guinea, and Côte d'Ivoire
20th century
Wood
H. 33.9 cm (13⅜ in.)
Gift of Katherine White and the Boeing Company,
81.17.196

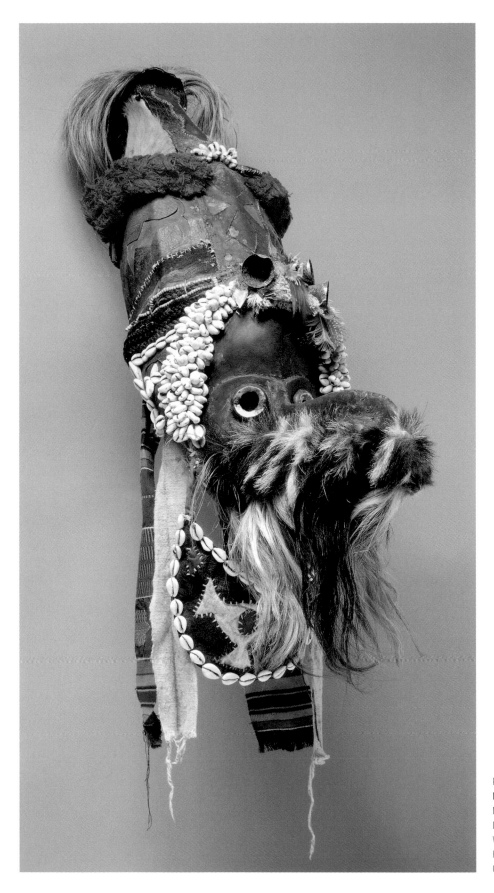

Pl. 84
Man na Gle (Bird) mask
Mano, Dan, Liberia, Guinea, and Côte d'Ivoire
Late 20th century
Wood, cloth, fur, metal, leather, cowry shells
H. 27.9 cm (11 in.)
Gift of Mark Groudine and Cynthia Putnam, 91.210

teach moral lessons, apply and enforce rules, and validate the social control exerted by the council of elders and local men's societies.

> These "African" faces express more, I believe, than just the "barbaric" character of pure sexuality.... They finally conjure something that transcends our sense of civilized experience, something ominous and monstrous such as Conrad Kurtz discovered in the heart of darkness.
>
> —William Rubin, 1984[20]

In the period when extensive fieldwork was accumulating about Dan masking, the Museum of Modern Art opened an exhibition that hardly mentioned what was known about "primitive" art. Focusing minute attention on the activities of European and American artists who drew inspiration from other cultures, it failed to acknowledge what inspired those cultures to create masks. The exhibition publication scrutinized Western primitivism's appropriation of masks, while declaring the originators' use of masks "ominous and monstrous." Masks were not recognized as an art form of gravity and significance.

> There's lots of people who put African art in this big universal, silent story place, keeping it in an ancient era, not giving it active interpretation.   —Won Ldy Paye, 1998[21]

Liberian circumstances shifted by the mid-1980s. Military rule was established by a leader who struck out against Americo-Liberian ties from the past and consolidated government monitoring from Monrovia. There, in 1985, Won Ldy Paye met George Tabmen, a highly respected cultural affairs officer who had collaborated with researchers coming to study art during the last two decades. Paye and Tabmen worked together at the National Culture Center of Liberia, where they had to negotiate a new format for masquerading. Masks from home villages were brought to the capital to perform, representing long-established family and clan alliances and power. The Dan understanding of what a masquerade was meant to do could not be questioned, and the coordinators had to observe secrecy.

> Every performance was out of control.   —Won Ldy Paye, 1998[22]

Many masks would never do what you told them to do. If you say enter stage left, they come out the right. If they tell you they are coming one way, they will do something else. Once there was a huge Vai costumed performer on stage who wouldn't get up. The performer kept saying something was wrong. I assumed the costume was coming off. His attendant said a *dash*[23] was needed. The mask kept saying that what we offered was too little. Part of their need is to show power and project power. Like tipping things over, setting things on fire, demanding money, is all to increase the fear and to test the audience. If the audience is passive, then act loose. If aggressive, the mask will leap from the stage and throw fifty people down.[24]

Until 1989, the government encouraged masquerades to come perform in Monrovia. A delicate balance was struck between national leaders and village leaders who sent masqueraders to demonstrate their power. Their creative chaos was contained on stage in the city and maintained by leaders in villages. A Liberian National Dance Troupe drew the finest talents in drumming and performance from all over the nation to collaborate. Dan, Krahn, Vai, and Bassa cultures each contributed masks and young artists, who overcame differences to perform in an arena at once artistically competitive and spiritually charged. Won Ldy Paye and other coordinators had to negotiate the time each group spent on stage, who would speak about the performances, and how to establish the levels of secrecy needed to surround forest spirits. Museums devoted to collecting and displaying masks from the many regions of Liberia and Côte d'Ivoire were established in Monrovia and the college town of Cuttington.

They are the worst people in the world, and they are our children.

—Liberian elder, 1995[25]

Fig. 62. Village Drum and Masquerade, Seattle Art Museum, 2001, masks and costumes: left to right, Wo Puh Gle (Talking Entertainer), Yeh To Gle (Authority); overleaf, Gbinan Gle (One That Gets Tall).

Then in 1990, a coup toppled the Liberian government, and set off "long term degenerative disease."[26] War engulfed the entire country and led to a massive refugee movement. The authority usually invested in elders and the reliance on masked spirits to settle disputes were upended, overthrown by economic chaos and warlordism. News reports featured pictures of rebel leaders wearing plastic and rubber masks while carrying submachine guns. Children as young as nine have been handed AK-47s and forced to fight. This war has been prolonged by several factors: the massive influx of arms "more available than bread,"[27] numerous casualties, the anarchy of rival leaders who avoid direct confrontation, and the inability of the United States, the United Nations, or the Organization of African Unity to enforce a peaceful conclusion.

Liberian performers like Won Ldy Paye are finding ways to adapt masquerading far from home (fig. 62). As civic life in Liberia has been largely destroyed, nearly all Liberian families have suffered the loss of relatives or endured years in refugee camps in Côte d'Ivoire and Ghana. No trace exists of the museum collections once housed in Monrovia and Cuttington College. The National Cultural Center has not functioned for a decade, and members of the National Dance Troupe are adapting to life in cities such as Paris, Minneapolis, Oakland, and Seattle. Trying to sustain their skills and a once-thriving spirit, members of the troupe exchange tapes and periodically collaborate in performances around the United States. Won Ldy Paye performs as a storyteller, dancer, musician, and organizer of masquerades for audiences in the Pacific Northwest. He constantly expresses his hope that masquerading will not deteriorate, as it "seems to work for people."[28] In the course of the twentieth century, masks have worked to spawn artistic discoveries, judge misconduct, resolve disputes, and order societies in ways that leaders alone now seem unable to do.

Notes

1. Won Ldy Paye, interview by author, November 9, 1998.

2. Ibid.

3. André Salmon, *La Jeune Peinture française,* (Paris: Société des Trente, 1912).

4. Quoted in Edward Fry, *Cubism* (London: Thames & Hudson, 1966).

5. André Malraux, *Picasso's Mask,* trans. J. Guicharnaud (New York: Holt, Rinehart and Winston, 1976), 10–11.

6. Patricia Leighton, "The White Peril and L'Art Nègre: Picasso, Primitivism and Anticolonialism," *The Art Bulletin* 72, no. 4 (December 1990). Leighton cites the estimate of eight to twenty million people dying in the Congo during the "red rubber" period when the famine, depopulation, and atrocities committed by the Belgian policies were most devastating. In a typical region, the population dropped from two thousand to two hundred between 1898 and 1903. For a further discussion of this period, see the case history above, "The Fetish and the Imagination of Europe: Sacred Medicines of the Kongo" (p. 143).

7. Georges Braque is quoted by André Salmon as saying: "C'est comme si tu buvais du pétrole et mangeais de l'etoupe enflammée!" *L'Art vivant* (Paris, 1920), 123.

8. *African Negro Art* (New York: Museum of Modern Art, 1935).

9. *Alter Ego: Masks—Their Art and Use* (New York: Cooper Union Museum for the Arts of Decoration, 1950).

10. George Harley, *Masks as Agents of Social Control,* Papers of the Peabody Museum of American Archaeology and Ethnology (Cambridge: Harvard University, 1950).

11. Svend E. Holsoe and Bernard L. Herman, *A Land and Life Remembered: Americo-Liberian Folk Architecture* (Athens: University of Georgia Press, 1988).

12. Lutheran missionary John Day, quoted in ibid., 17.

13. Videotape interviews, 1991, Seattle Art Museum.

14. William Fagg, *African Tribal Images* (Cleveland: Cleveland Museum of Art, 1968), ill. no. 58.

15. Michael Kan, *African Sculpture* (Brooklyn: Brooklyn Museum, 1970), 49.

16. This passage is cited with slight modifications from Robert Farris Thompson, *African Art in Motion* (Berkeley: University of California Press, 1974), 161–63.

17. Eberhard Fischer and Hans Himmelheber, *The Arts of the Dan in West Africa* (Zurich: Museum Rietburg, 1984).

18. Eberhard Fischer, "Dan Forest Spirits: Masks in Dan Villages," *African Arts* 11, no. 2 (January 1978), 23.

19. B. Holas, interview, 1982, in Marie Noel Verger-Fevre, *Masks in the Dan Area of Côte d'Ivoire* (Geneva: Barbier-Mueller Museum, 1994), 155.

20. "Picasso," in William Rubin and Kirk Varnadoe, *Primitivism and Modern Art* (New York: Museum of Modern Art, 1984), 254. The strong objections to this publication's approach to non-Western art and its perpetuation of the devaluation of contextual research as "primitive" were recorded in reviews and heated exchanges in major journals such as *Artforum.*

21. Won Ldy Paye, interview, 1998.

22. Ibid.

23. *Dash* is a West African term for "tip" or "bribe."

24. Won Ldy Paye, interview, 1998.

25. Jeffrey Goldberg, "A War without Purpose in a Country without Identity," *New York Times,* January 22, 1995, 38.

26. William Zartman and Victor Kremenyuk, eds., *Cooperative Security; Reducing Third World Wars* (Syracuse: Syracuse University Press, 1995), 8.

27. Karl P. Magyar and Earl Conteh-Morgan, eds., *Peacekeeping in Liberia* (New York: St. Martin's Press, 1998), 4.

28. Won Ldy Paye in a 1998 interview recounts a performance before an unlikely audience as surprising his expectations. A Catholic group had rented the ballroom of a Sheraton Hotel in Tacoma and "filled it with people wearing black tuxes and gowns. We played music and they danced but they kept asking about our masks. 'We heard you do masks,' 'we've never seen masks,' they kept saying. We finally agreed to perform, and they all responded and got involved with the masks. It was funny to see how much they got out of it."

Beauty Stripped of Human Flaws: Sowei Masks

The Sande society made a strong impression on me when I was twelve. Living in a Liberian compound known as Sunken Heights, I had a friend named Sarah who would climb up the almond tree with me to survey the neighborhood.[1] We played together nearly once a week, but then one day she disappeared without saying goodbye. A few months later, she peered in my bedroom window. I ran outside to greet her but was disoriented when she turned away quickly and I saw that her body was covered in white chalk. Ignoring my yelling, she got away as fast as she could. I headed for the compound's central hub, a veranda overlooking the swamp where there were always people sitting and talking. Everyone was silent at first when I asked about Sarah's strange sudden appearance; then I was told that she had entered "bush school." They said her white coating was meant to make her invisible, but when I countered that I could see her, the subject closed tight for many days. I got used to Sarah's mysterious "invisible" visits, which continued through the year. By the end of that time she was no longer a girl who climbed trees. Her manner of talking, acting, and playing had changed—we were divided by a huge wall of differences in how our separate cultures taught a girl to leave childhood and become an adult. Despite my constant questions, she wouldn't say anything about where she had been, but she spoke freely with the adults on the veranda. She was secretive about some things and confident about others in a way that was extremely confounding for me as a thirteen-year-old. Sarah had been initiated into the Sande society, and I was still a preteen.

That was Liberia in the late 1960s, when Sande was an active women's society in parts of Liberia as well as Sierra Leone, Côte d'Ivoire, and Guinea. Sande provided a sanctuary and school for girls to be initiated into adulthood in seclusion. Among Mende women of Sierra Leone, the Sande society were also major patrons of the arts, sponsoring masquerades that made their presence quite visible (fig. 63). Masks worn by women are an extreme rarity in Africa, so their existence en masse in Mende country attracted many collectors and researchers. Collectors have endowed the Seattle Art Museum with a group of masks that have no direct field documentation attached to them; I rely here on the work of researchers whose accounts of Sande masquerades

Pl. 86 (detail)

Fig. 63. Sowei masqueraders with attendants, Liberia, 1987.

are primarily from the 1970s, when Sierra Leone was filled with "a bustle and optimism of the post-independence years."[2]

Sierra Leone in the 1990s disintegrated into a war zone. Growing up amid fearsome conditions, the fiercest fighters are said to be children, "confusing war and play" and remaining "heedless of danger."[3] As ten-year-olds are conscripted into armies, the future of an entire country is called into question. While the Sande masquerade presents a "beauty stripped of human flaws" (to borrow Donald Cosentino's phrase), human flaws are being writ large in Sierra Leone, as other nations seem indifferent to the needs of the children. This look at Sande masquerades pays tribute to the creative play and learning that helped generations of young women come of age in a more peaceful time.

> She goes through a sort of dumb show—as she never does any talking. Her dress is of long shaggy fibre, dyed black, and over her head she wears a grotesque wooden mask.   —T. J. Alldridge, 1901[4]

"The Bundu [Sande] Devil, Upper Mendi" is the first photograph of a Sande society masquerader to appear in an English publication (fig. 64). *The Sherbro and Its Hinterland* was written by T. J. Alldridge, a career colonial officer who arrived in Sierra Leone in 1871 and became a district commissioner when British protectorate status was declared in 1896. His reports contain extensive details of certain aspects of Mende life, but are tinged with an obvious bias derived from his position. When a fierce revolt known as the Mende Rising, or House Tax War, resulted out of frustration over British policies in 1898, Alldridge dismissed such irritation. Instead, he asserted the "rising may be traced to the enormous influence fetish or 'country medicine' has on people." Such medicines were the workings of the secret societies, Poro for men and Sande for women, which he deemed "an enormous force for good and evil." At the same time, he acknowledged that the societies maintained absolute secrecy, saying "I have never yet succeeded in penetrating the inner mysteries." His definitions of Sande masqueraders as a *bundu* devil, "a medicine woman … arrayed in all her barbaric grotesqueness," set a tone that prevailed in publications for many years.[5]

> Each new initiate in the secret societies takes an oath never to disclose what she learns, and from this there is no future release.
> —Kenneth Little, 1967[6]

Trained in social anthropology, Kenneth Little took a careful approach to the study of secret societies in the 1960s. He formulated an oath, vowing that "the anthropologist is bound to consider everything that comes within view as proper grist for the mill; but he has also an obligation to the people studied, if he is to deserve their confidence." In his research, Little maintained a distance that upheld the rights to privacy of Poro and Sande members. He declined invitations to join Poro and asked only for information available to nonmembers living among the Mende. After submitting his texts to the Mende for their censorship, he published this scrupulous research full of objective description and detail, particularly of the Poro. Of the Sande society for women, Little wrote far less and deflated its role by comparing their initiation school to a "European type of finishing school."

> Unlike Europeans, who seem to wish to universalize their style of life, Mende guard the deep core of their cultural values within the veil of secret societies.   —Darrell Reeck, 1976[7]

Secrecy is a defining factor in Mende life. No Mende write about secret society issues, though many publish on other subjects. Communication preferably takes place face to face, from one person to another. Initiates in particular are committed to the notion that information about Mende societies should not be given out to those not subject to its laws. However, as masquerades attest, the societies do have a semipublic side. Women conducting fieldwork in Sierra Leone in the 1970s were the ones to begin sorting out what of Sande could be written about and what could not.

> It seems far more consonant with Mende practices of art making and reception to view *sowei* headpieces as constituting a system of visual representation whose significations are not fixed but rather shifting and variable.   —Ruth B. Phillips, 1995[8]

Female researchers offer new waves of scholarship about the Sande society and its masks. Three women taking different approaches illustrate the range of this study. Carol P. MacCormack emphasizes the extent of training that Sande provides—

Fig. 64. "The Bundu Devil, Upper Mendi," from T. J. Alldridge, *The Sherbro and Its Hinterland* (1901).

covering practical skills, problem solving, and moral principles. She sees Sande as raising girls with strong, positive images of their role as leaders. Sande teachings are said to "stress that the girls observe everything: farming, spinning, child-care, diagnosing illnesses, compounding and administering medicines, singing and dancing." In her appraisal, Sande officials use "executive strategies" when serving as community leaders and encourage storytelling in the Sande bush, where a moral or dilemma can be "debated long into the night, encouraging a more mature exploration of the human condition."[9] Sylvia Boone offers the definition of Sande as a "university of the forest" with an advanced curriculum of graded instruction in myth, history, ethics, and herbalism.[10] Focusing attention on the masks of Sande as "good made visible," she devotes her text to a poetic exploration of how the masks present ideals of feminine physical perfection and sexuality. Ruth Phillips combines a wide repertoire of approaches to set many new observations in place. She looks at the interactions between other society masquerades and Sande, the full range of other Sande masks, the names of the masks, the kinds of personalities they project, and how they are received by a Mende audience. Despite her warning against the "persistent academic delusion that definitive monographs are possible," she comes very close to writing one.[11]

This era of study enriches our examination of a Sowei mask. Each feature has the potential to send a different message to different audiences. A Sande official may see and speak of a mask in one way, and a male observer in another. This review combines comments from the authors mentioned to create a composite portrait of Mende mask aesthetics.

A [Sowei mask] must be shiny black.

"Black" and "wet" are both designated by the Mende word *teli*. Masks are called "the beautiful black thing" when they acquire a desirable dark hue, obtained by rubbing the surface with palm oil or shoe polish until it is sleek and shiny (pl. 85). Blackness and wetness refer to the ultimate origin of Sande knowledge—the nature spirits who dwell in rivers in the bush, embodying the medicines to be found there. The highest ideals are said to arise from the depths of their underwater home, where miraculous delicate beings are the norm. When Sande girls emerge from initiation in their perfected physical state, their skin is oiled to emulate the appearance of underwater spirits. In addition, Sowei masks are most frequently seen at night, in the darkness (fig. 65). When Sande dancing occurred at night, the black masks would blend into the darkness, until light was cast and a luminous face would emerge.

Yivi yivi.

No Sowei mask would display *yivi yivi*, untidy or messy hair, because "it signifies insanity." Those few who "buckle under the strains of everyday life, retreating into madness, signal their illness graphically by no longer grooming their hair, thus

Pl. 85
Sowei mask
Mende, Sierra Leone
20th century
Wood, metal, raffia, leather, fiber
W. 55.9 cm (22 in.)
Purchased with funds from the Mary Arrington Small
Estate Acquisition Fund, 89.68

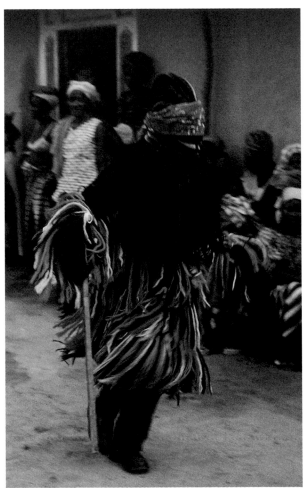

Fig. 65. Vai performer dancing as Zooba (Vai term for Sowei), Christmas celebration, Bulumi, Liberia, 1977.

Pl. 86
Sowei mask
Mende, Sierra Leone
19th century
Wood, metal
H. 37.4 cm (14¾ in.)
Gift of Katherine White and the Boeing Company,
81.17.185

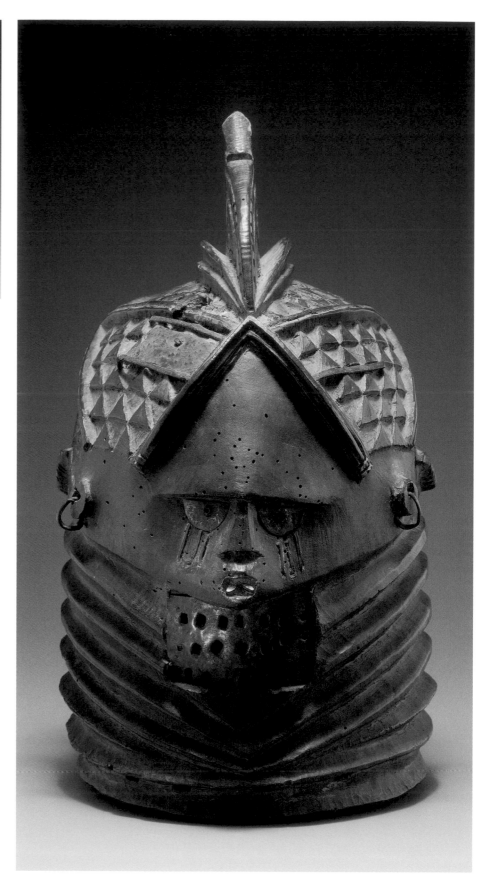

abandoning the community's standard of behavior."[12] A disciplined attention to hair is evident in masks where plaits, central ridges, and bands of decoration are all tightly defined and precisely rendered. Crisp rows of diamond patterning or lines with fine ridges illustrate a coiffure under control. Long abundant hair is seen as a sign of a productive, growing spirit, since all water people have spectacular hair. During initiation, girls reside with these spirits, who teach them new hairstyles that are more complicated than could ever be done by human hands.

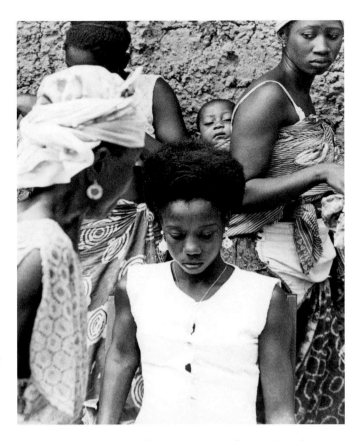

Fig. 66. Hawa Lansana, a new Sande graduate showing ideal composure with downcast eyes, Mattru, Tikonko, Bo, Sierra Leone, 1972–1973.

The brow is the parlor by which you enter into a relationship with another person.

In much of West Africa, when you want to reward performers, you "spray" coins or bills onto their foreheads. Mende say the forehead is the place where prosperity enters a person's life. Mask foreheads are broad and extended, compressing the facial features near the chin (pl. 86). In full view and free of wrinkles, the forehead announces a young woman poised and ready to meet challenges. By contrast, a woman who is feeling ill, grief-stricken, or sad may lower her head tie over her forehead to signal that she needs to be left alone for a while.

The slitted eye is a ritual screen.

The eyes on these masks are usually downcast, often diminished to the extent of being mere slits. The human masquerader's eyes are concealed, as the Mende consider eyes to be the most distinctive feature of a person. The screen also protects Sowo, the exalted spirit who dwells in the mask, and emphasizes that Sowo is endowed with extraordinary vision—the carved eyes and the eyes of the dancer allow her to become a "two-eyed creature with all the attendant mystical powers."[13] As a model for feminine behavior, half-closed eyes offer a reminder that direct eye-to-eye contact is considered disrespectful (fig. 66). Narrowed eyes can be seen as alluring, creating romantic privacy by literally blinding the Sowo in her focus on only one man. In other cases, slitted eyes may imply the demure qualities of a serious woman who is above playing amorous games.

Talk makes palaver.

The mouth of a Sowei, never open, is tightly shut and, again, often just a pursed slit (pl. 87). Silence is ideal for Sowo performers, who dance and interact with audiences but never utter a sound. An attendant speaks for Sowo to reinforce her serenity as a spirit who is not about to chat or laugh as a human would. Extending this lesson, elders offer observations about certain kinds of talking. Inconsiderate chattiness and malicious backbiting are common causes for human suffering. One example cited is the case of a child cursed by a mother. Elders speak of their understanding that a mother does this only when frustrated with her husband, but nonetheless the effect

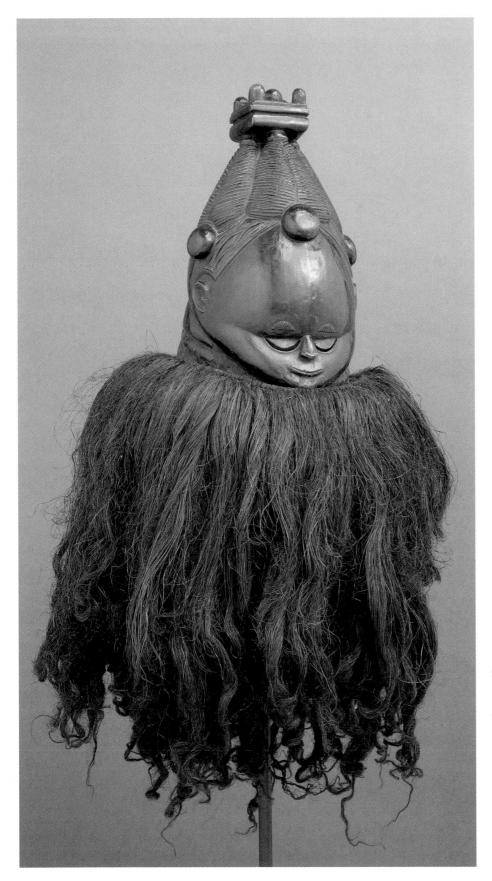

Pl. 87
Sowei mask
Mende, Sierra Leone
20th century
Wood, raffia, yarn, leather, tape
H. 86.4 cm (34 in.)
Gift of Mark Groudine and Cynthia Putnam, 98.56

Pl. 88
Sowei mask
Mende, Sierra Leone
20th century
Wood, raffia
H. 81.3 cm (32 in.)
Gift of Mark Groudine and Cynthia Putnam, 98.57

on the child can be ruinous. When a person becomes known as a drunk, a bully, or a thief, people conclude that he was once cursed by his mother and will suffer from a life without any hope of success. "Talk makes palaver" if not properly channeled, as Sowo demonstrates.

A ringed neck is god's *bonya* (gift).

The neck of a Sowei headpiece has to be as wide as the head since it is worn as a helmet. Necks on the masks are always endowed with rings, a convention that has spawned many readings. Rings of fat, signifying a well-fed and comfortable person, is one notion. But rather than viewing the rings as signs of corpulence, others think they suggest the new roundness and softening of body contours that occurs in adolescent girls. Rings may also be an exaggeration of natural lines referred to as "cut neck," considered a beautiful feature bestowed by God as a blessing. Mythology offers another possible reading based on the origins of Sande as a spirit living in heavenly towns under the water. When Sowo's head breaks the surface of the water, a pattern of concentric waves surrounds her. One analogy gives the rings a broader association: "Cut neck functions like a halo does in western painting, signifying what the eye sees is human in form but divine in essence."[14]

Small horns of a gray duiker antelope rim the hair of one mask (pl. 86, detail), while large bush cow horns swoop over the crown of another (pl. 85). The duiker horns, neatly carved in a row, could refer to an early twentieth-century manner of adding elements to the hair. Since large horns would be worn around the neck, the crowning bush cow horns are an artistic invention. Horns serve mainly as containers, recalling the debt Sowei owes to herbalists who prepare medicines and stuff them into horns for the masker to carry. Such horns are tied onto mask costumes or carried to activate a zone of protection around the masker, who often faces a competitive atmosphere.

Masks also carry protection in the form of amulets, consisting of pieces of paper with Koranic inscriptions encased in cloth or leather. Leather-covered amulets are mixed into the black raffia costume around the neck of one mask (pl. 87). At the top of another, a large rectangular amulet is carved at the top of the hair (pl. 88). Such amulets indicate that the Sowei has sought Allah's words to protect her and to increase her powers of attraction. In other Islamicized Sande societies, the Mori Jande, masking has been eliminated altogether.

Additions to one mask enhance its attraction. Cowry shells are carved into the hair border, while brass bands frame them, and a fragment of a star adorns the forehead (pl. 85). Cowry are a charged currency, "an ancient thing" passed down from ancestors who recognize it as the only form of exchange they will accept. Actual cowry shells are regarded as another connection with a watery domain and can be added to costumes in large numbers.

> The Mende think of *ndoli jowei* in the first instance as a dynamic personality and a talented performer and not as a static sculptural object.   —Ruth Phillips, 1995[15]

Mende endow the mask form with a name, a personality, a costume, and a volatile character. Names like Gbango (loud and troublesome), Hide and Seek (mysterious in coming and going), Quarrelsome (not having a clean heart), Pepper (wild in dancing) are called out by her attendant when Ndoli Jowei (dancing Sowei) first appears. From then on, she asserts a personality that strives for attention, often eccentrically, to remind viewers she is not subject to human rules. Her attitude adjusts to the circumstances that have called for her—somber movements lead a procession to the grave, frenzied activity is appropriate when a Sande school opens, and her dancing signals rejoicing when a new paramount chief is being installed. To maintain complete disguise, she wears capes of black dyed palm fiber around her neck and waist, and shoes conceal her feet. Women accompany her with dancing and singing, which inspire bursts of rapid steps or twirls that send her capes flying. Ndoli Jowei is not usually seen solo—Mende audiences prefer the variety of seeing three, four, or five performers at once—(fig. 67), and she has memorable counterparts who mock her dignity. One is called Gonde (funny Sowei), who wears broken masks and discarded clothes, and shamelessly approaches the audience for money. Another is Samawa, who wears no headpiece but dresses in rags, paints her face with large spots, adds a pouch to suggest a swollen scrotum, and interrupts the proceedings with loud, raucous laughter or satires of men.

> Without her, the town will not be lively.   —Saying of Mende women[16]

The ceremonial highlight of the year is introduced by Ndoli Jowei as she presides over the coming out of new initiates. All eyes focus on the initiates, who emerge in the morning from the bush, covered in white clay and flowers. In the afternoon, they come out again, dressed in modern clothes, and are led by masked officials to the town hall, where their newly refined femininity is put in a spotlight. They retire to

Fig. 68. Hannah Samba, 1973.

Fig. 69. Mariatu Sandi, 1973.

spend several days on their parents' verandas, receiving relatives and friends who award them with gifts and feasts. Afterward, they graduate into the next phase of life, either marrying or going on in school.

> **Domeisia are a major source of speculation in a society which thrives on the contest of opposing ideas.** —Donald Cosentino, 1982[17]

Sande society members might not write about their experience, but they do talk. In fact, Mende women are raised with a strong awareness of proficient, entertaining speech. Oral narrative is elevated to a lively performance art known as *kpua domeisia,* or "to pull stories." Throughout their lives, Mende listen to members of their family and neighbors pull stories. Those who excel at this art form become celebrities, entertaining large audiences who come to hear gifted storytellers. Intellectual precision is admired, as their narratives take on ideas circulating in the towns where the speakers perform. To study *domeisia,* Donald Cosentino spent a year listening to men and women of one community pull stories in the evening. There he and his wife "witnessed the arguments and rivalries of the day transformed into the competing domei performances of the night," and he concluded that the "women who argue with narrative are the intellectuals of Mende society."[18]

So we turn to them for a different view of Sande society and the issues that once surrounded the masks now silently housed in the museum. On one evening, after dinner, from about 8:30 to 9:00, three women gathered on their veranda to pull stories for themselves and a small audience of five people from their compound. They touch on aspects of Sande teachings that have a tremendous impact on their lives: how women are to negotiate their relationships with men; which aspects of their society can be questioned and which cannot; what constitutes beauty, manners, and etiquette; how a woman should handle disappointment and good fortune; and the way to show respect for the sacred—all are present in this evening performance. A major subplot to these stories also becomes clear—how women negotiate with each other. The three women who speak are rivals, "locked in a permanent state of mutual suspicion and harsh feelings" during the day, an animosity that is transformed into competitive performances at night. Donald Cosentino, in *Defiant Maids and Stubborn Farmers,* carefully recorded a sequence of such evenings, transcribing them in full. His thorough transcriptions offer the chance to hear three women spar with stories on a night in Sierra Leone. Their words can be found in the appendix. Who they are and what they offer as veiled comments about Sande are summarized here.

Hannah Samba pulls "A Defiant Maid Marries a Stranger."
–September 19, 1973, 8:30 P.M.

Hannah Samba was put in charge of the daily affairs of the compound after her husband died (fig. 68). She is about fifty years old, the mother of one child, and extremely dedicated to her work in rice farming. She introduces the evening with a common theme, the visiting gentleman who tests a woman he meets at a Sande society dance. The woman, Yombo, happens to be "a great fornicator" who is seduced not by a human but by a spirit named Kpana, who keeps telling her, "Our destination is not pleasant," but she insists on following him.

Samba's story features a promiscuous woman who is stubborn and willfully ignorant. She is seduced by Kpana, who takes her into the forest—a journey no woman should undertake without Sande support and guidance, because the forest is not a place where humans can live forever. She disregards Kpana's warnings, resulting in the death of her child and herself. Yombo pays the price for not aligning herself with Sande or other women, and for making decisions alone.

Mariatu Sandi pulls "A Defiant Maid Marries a Stranger."
–September 19, 1973, 8:45 P.M.

Mariatu Sandi is about thirty years old, a mother of three, known to abhor farming, preferring to live by her wits and handouts from her family (fig. 69). She takes the performer's seat and pushes her powers of invention and humor to the forefront. Sandi follows the basic structure of Samba's focus on the visiting gentleman but spins off from it, adding a flourish of details that fill it with exaggeration, scandal, and satire. In her version, there are twelve spirits in the forest who came to see two Sande dances. The spirits make love to twelve girls and then dance for ten months before they decide to leave.

Sandi's Yombo overturns the morality of Samba's version. She does everything she can to defy manners, etiquette, and decency. Despite all her bad behavior, Yombo is greeted as a cultural heroine when she returns home, revives her mother, and begins building new houses for everyone. Cosentino concludes, "Mariatu created a topsy turvy world of values, one in which 'bad' triumphed over 'good,' adultery over marriage, women over men, and most especially Mariatu Sandi over Hannah Samba.... The same faults of stubborness and sexual promiscuity account for female ruination in the first narrative and female salvation in the second."[19]

Manungo pulls "A Defiant Maid Marries a Stranger."

—September 19, 1973, 9:00 P.M.

The third storyteller, Manungo, is about seventy years old, widowed and childless, an herbalist/midwife and official of the Sande society (fig. 70). Her version of the story again relies on the initial staging of a girl named Yombo who meets Kpana at a Sande society dance. Instead of Kpana being a spirit, however, this time he is an ancestor. He admonishes Yombo not to follow him, but she does. Kpana leads her to a land of deformed people, and gives her guidance in how to treat them.

Manungo's heroine is not stubborn and unwilling to learn (like Samba's) nor expecting the impossible—to overturn the order between men and women (like Sandi's). In her version, Yombo learns lessons in humility. After absorbing these lessons of the bush, she is ready to return home and receives the most valuable array of gifts.

Fig. 70. Manungo, 1973.

Summaries of *kpua domeisia* can only hint at this lively art, which includes sound effects, gestures, facial expressions, and nuances of language and phrasing. Cosentino laments the fact that most translations give "no sense of the devastating irony which inspired them, or the awesome intellectual rigor, daredevil wit and dramatic skills which saw them through performance."[20] His careful transcriptions, however, do indicate the imaginative power unleashed when women speak about the choices they make—what men they choose, how they envision the worst in-laws, which rules for female behavior they accept readily and which they question. These are the kinds of issues facing a young girl at the age of initiation, before she leaves with a new husband to establish their own life. Just as Sande masks articulate lessons for flawless beauty, so these women articulate their ongoing life stories of what realistic beauty is.

You know who a person really is by the language they cry in.

—Mende proverb

Mende women's language has recently been credited with tying together Africa and African America. When people from Sierra Leone were forced across the Atlantic, many were sent to one region of the United States—Georgia and South Carolina. There people known as the Gullah evolved. While no Mende women were able to take along masks or other artifacts, they did bring their words, stories, songs, and reliance on invisible institutions such as Sande. In establishing an entirely compromised life

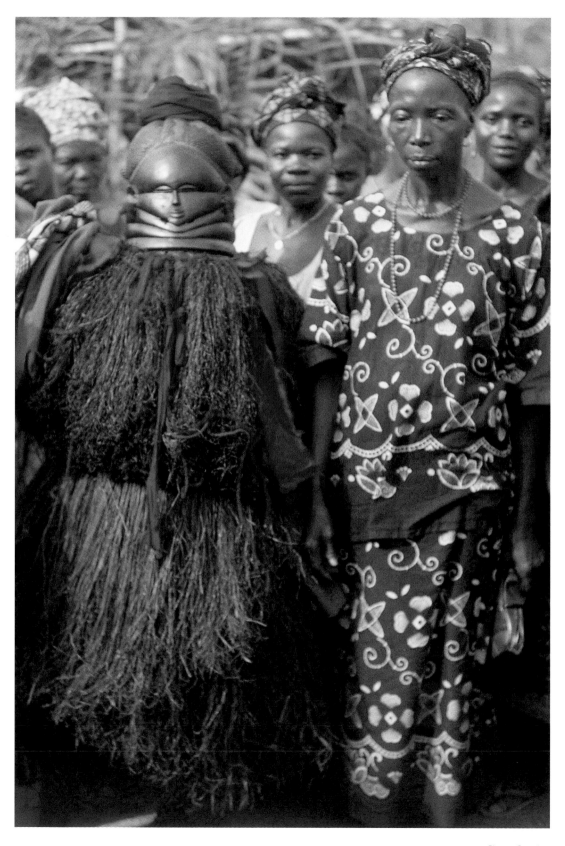

Fig. 71. Sowei masquerader with attendant, Jayama,
Sierra Leone, 1990.

as slaves, it is said that "rather than being converted to God they converted God to themselves."[21] Christianity took a new form in Gullah communities, as loyalty to the initiation experience was reconstituted in praise houses.[22] Elders of the praise house presided like a religious court overseeing the "just laws" and notions of morality that guided members. In a form of initiation, "raw souls" entered a long process of self-examination and solitary prayer in seclusion, guided by the advice of a spiritual parent who helped shape candidates for praise house membership. As research into these connections with African practices was unfolding in the 1980s, scholars also turned their attention to language. Researchers listened to work by a linguist who had recorded Gullah people in the 1930s. Among them was a Gullah woman from remote Georgia, Amelia Dawley, who sang one song that was clearly Mende. Dawley's daughter, Mary Moran, remembered the song as just a playful tune, but it inspired a determined search for a Mende source that led researchers into remote interior villages of Sierra Leone. Eventually one woman, Baindu Jabati, in the village of Senehum Ngola, recognized the song as one her grandmother had taught her for a graveside ceremony. This one song had lasted more than two hundred years to indelibly link a Sierra Leonian woman to a Georgian woman.

A film narrating this research process, *The Language You Cry In,* accompanies Mary Moran on her 1997 trip to meet Baindu Jabati in Sierra Leone.[23] Despite the destruction surrounding the women of Sierra Leone, they rise to greet the American with full ceremony. In the midst of the greetings, Ndoli Jowei enters the picture in a flurry of motion and dancing that stamps the occasion with the presence of the Sande society. This record of a joyous occasion has been replaced with reports from Sierra Leone of lives filled with terror, affecting children especially. The men's Poro society underwent a renaissance in the 1990s, but the Sande society's attempts to reestablish initiation have not succeeded. In former eras, the Mende would speak of the uninitiated as madmen, children without sense, dangerous beings, or animals. News from Sierra Leone evokes the consequences of an entire country run without initiation, without any sense of flawless beauty (fig. 71).

Notes

1. "Sunken Heights" was the name given to the compound built by American engineers who, the local story goes, had not stayed long enough to witness a full rainy season. They began building during the six dry months and then were surprised when the torrents of rain came and many foundations sank into the saturated soil. What had looked like a valley nearby became a swamp; our house bordered on it and noticeably sloped in that direction.

2. Ruth B. Phillips, *Representing Women: Sande Masquerades of the Mende of Sierra Leone* (Los Angeles: UCLA Fowler Museum of Cultural History, 1995), 10.

3. Krijn Peters and Paul Richards, "Why We Fight: Voices of Youth Combatants in Sierra Leone," *Africa* 68, no. 2 (1998), 182.

4. T. J. Alldridge, *The Sherbro and Its Hinterland* (London: MacMillan, 1901), 141.

5. Ibid.

6. Kenneth Little, *The Mende of Sierra Leone: A West African People in Transition* (London: Routledge and Kegan Paul, 1967), 9.

7. Darrell Reeck, *Deep Mande: Religious Interactions in a Changing African Rural Society* (Leiden: Brill, 1976), 65. See also Beryl L. Bellman, *The Language of Secrecy: Symbols and Metaphors in Poro Ritual* (New Brunswick, N.J.: Rutgers University Press, 1984).

8. Phillips, *Representing Women,* 114.

9. Carol MacCormack, "Sande: The Public Face of a Secret Society," in *The New Religions of Africa,* ed. Bennetta Jules-Rosette (Norwood, N.J.: Ablex Publishing Company, 1979), 34.

10. Sylvia Ardyn Boone, *Radiance from the Waters: Ideals of Feminine Beauty in Mende Art* (New Haven, Conn.: Yale University Press, 1986).

11. Phillips, *Representing Women.*

12. Boone, *Radiance from the Waters,* 186.

13. Ibid., 177.

14. Ibid.

15. Phillips, *Representing Women,* 100.

16. Ibid., 104.

17. Donald Cosentino, *Defiant Maids and Stubborn Farmers: Tradition and Invention in Mende Story Performance* (Cambridge: Cambridge University Press, 1982), 11.

18. Ibid.

19. Ibid., 157.

20. Ibid., 12.

21. Paul Radin, "Status, Phantasy, and the Christian Dogma," in *God Struck Me Dead: Religious Conversion Experience and Autobiographies* (Nashville: Fisk University, 1945), i–ix.

22. See Margaret Washington Creel, *"A Peculiar People": Slave Religion and Community–Culture among the Gullahs* (New York: New York University Press, 1988); see also Margaret Washington Creel, "Gullah Attitudes toward Life and Death," in *Africanisms in American Culture,* ed. Joseph Holloway (Bloomington: Indiana University Press, 1990), 69–118.

23. *The Language You Cry In,* Alvaro Toepke, producer/director, and Angel Serrano (1998), California Newsreel.

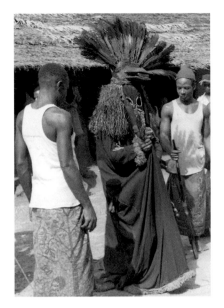

"God's Medicine" against Witchcraft: Costume for Basinjom

In recent years, witches have entered the mainstream of Western culture with surprising force. Harry Potter, a literary young English boy, flourishes at the Hogwarts School of Witchcraft and Wizardry and keeps parents and children reading about his exploits. *The Blair Witch Project,* a film about the stalking of contemporary witches in America, proves that the role of the practicing witch is not fading away. From Shakespeare to Disney, J. R. R. Tolkien to Anne Rice, the witch slips in and out of fictional typecasting, and modern Western incarnations keep a growing belief alive. Witches can be boys on broomsticks, goddess worshipers, and secretive shamans.

Bloodhounds who have no friends. —Emma Agu, 1987

Ideas about witches circulate in both African and Western minds, but comparisons spread thin when they reach across continents. In a museum label or book caption, the term can misdirect viewers who already have their own idea of what witches are up to. Reports about witches abound in the African popular press and continue to give meaning to discomforting traits that threaten community life. In a Nigerian *Sunday Statesman* article, they are characterized as "predators, bloodhounds who have no friends.... Greed is their hallmark; an abiding zest for destroying the successful, the healthy, and the 'lucky' in the community."[1] How to confront witches and rehabilitate them is the concern of a masquerade whose costume came into the Seattle Art Museum's collection with unique documentation gathered firsthand.

One glides backward through the ages to a land full of mystery and terror, to the childhood of the world, where the terror of witchcraft stalks abroad. —P. Amaury Talbot, 1912[2]

The first photograph of Basinjom (literally "God's Medicine"), appeared in a 1912 publication entitled *In the Shadow of the Bush* (fig. 72).[3] A tall character concealed in a gown and a headdress crowned with a corona of feathers appears stiffly posed between two men. The trio look straight toward the camera at the author, P. Amaury

Pl. 89 (detail)

Fig. 72. "Juju Akpambe," from P. Amaury Talbot, *In the Shadow of the Bush* (1912).

Talbot, a British colonial officer of the Nigerian Political Service who was stationed in the Cross River region of western Cameroon. He spent his spare time gathering data and trying to "record the story of a people most of whom were untouched by white influence on my arrival among them in 1907." His words about the masquerader he photographed are spare. He calls it Juju Akpambe and writes that it is "supposed to be the strongest Juju for smelling out witchcraft."[4]

Talbot often laces his observations with statements about what he perceives as the deficiencies of the Ekoi (Ejagham). He states: "Like most primitive peoples, the Ekoi have the haziest ideas as to the causes of their being.... In the interior the old vague myths still hold their ground."[5] Vagueness prevails again as he writes, "Juju is so elusive as to defy definition, but as far as may be gathered from the vague conception of the Ekoi, it includes all the uncomprehended, mysterious forces of Nature."[6] Despite his doubts, Talbot describes what he calls "articles of belief" about how those forces of nature interact with humans. Drawing on cases brought before the native courts of the district, he records the belief that a man can leave his human form and take on that of a wild creature. When a man wants to transform, he drinks a potion that enables his soul to float invisibly through town until it reaches the forest, where it begins to swell. Once safely hidden in the shadows of the trees, the soul is able to take on the body of an elephant, leopard, buffalo, wild boar, and crocodile. As a crocodile, a man might drag a woman to an underwater house and devour part of her.

A philosophy of misfortune. —Malcolm Ruel, 1965[7]

In Talbot's descriptions, Basinjom remains a hazy presence. The fieldwork of another generation of anthropologists enables a closer look at who Basinjom is and what he does. Malcolm Ruel spent several years in the 1950s working among a neighboring group, the Banyang of western Cameroon. His writing carefully introduces a web of circumstances and a "philosophy of misfortune" that lead to witchcraft's domination of Banyang thoughts. He identifies one major influence that stimulated witchcraft at the beginning of the century—the attempts by Europeans to overpower small-scale community politics. By 1904, the Ejagham and their neighbors were rebelling against German colonial dictates, which later forced the population to resettle in larger villages.[8] It was during this tumultuous era that witches proliferated and demand for Basinjom's services spread. Soon thereafter, when the British established their version of government, they sidestepped traditional leaders to build roads, set up law courts, and erect schools and clinics. Local associations began asking Basinjom to offset British intrusions and relied on his help behind the scenes of the foreign administration. As colonial efforts expanded, so did the role of witchcraft.

A person alone is an animal. —Banyang saying

Banyang witchcraft addresses a central tension facing individuals—one becomes a person through unity with one's lineage, but one can also excel beyond what that lineage considers appropriate. Personal achievement can ignite doubt or uncertainty about how much status should accrue to a single person. When someone begins separating from others and indulging in deceit, it is a sign that an animal soul has overtaken the human and is causing misfortune. Two classes of animals (or animal familiars) exist—those of a destructive nature like the python, which slithers into the body and, residing in the intestines, inflicts injury on others. The second class includes creatures like the mudfish, which causes the carrier to sweat profusely and endows him with the ability to slip out of any opponent's grasp.

Witchcraft is a person's thoughts. —Malcolm Ruel, 1965[9]

Animal souls taking over a human were not the sole cause of concern to Ruel's Banyang informants. How people acted with their animal associates could change abilities from assets into destructive forces. A person could take on the strength and power of a leopard or harness the command of lightning and use the powers well. But when such special abilities were employed to promote oneself and trample on others, the community agreed that the animal counterpart had to be detected and exposed.

> The power of Basinjom to see and speak the truth is always emphasized. —Malcolm Ruel, 1968[10]

When circumstances require his presence, Basinjom comes to earth and manifests himself as a detective masquerade. Kept separate and hidden from the colonial government, Basinjom was most active in the years when communities were disrupted. British rewards for individual achievement threw the public-lineage order into question, and accusations of witchcraft escalated. Malcolm Ruel briefly describes the performance of Basinjom as a gowned figure with an entourage of musicians and gun carriers who sing along with his appearance (fig. 73). He glides into view and searches for places where misfortune and medicines might be located. As an endnote to his description, Ruel reveals that he did become a junior grade of Basinjom. Because initiates agree not to disclose secrets of the association, Ruel hints at many elements of Basinjom but doesn't discuss them openly.

> It won't be the usual mask hung on a wall with a label beside it.
> —George Ellis, 1974[11]

Katherine White aligned herself with a curator in a project that was to place Basinjom in an exceptional spotlight (pl. 89). In July 1970, she moved herself, her three sons, and her collection to Los Angeles. Soon after her arrival, Frederick Wright, the Director of the Dickson Art Galleries and an Art Council officer at the University of California, Los Angeles, asked if her collection could be featured in the university's galleries. She agreed and suggested Robert Farris Thompson, a Yale graduate and professor, as the curator and author of the catalogue. White funded two visits to Africa for Thompson to obtain materials and documentation. At the end of 1971, in western Cameroon, Thompson began hearing from people on the coast about an extremely impressive figure known as Basinjom. Traveling inland to pursue this lead, he accepted an invitation to be initiated into Basinjom teachings. Thompson's experience in a blue costume with a headdress and all its instruments resulted in a significant addition to the exhibition *African Art in Motion,* a context-rich display of White's collection.

> Obasinjom means "God's Medicine."... Medicine is God's gift to mankind. —Ejagham informants, 1984[12]

One concept that stands outside Western usage is essential to the following account of Basinjom's initiation and appearance. Medicine, in Ejagham terms, is a knowledge of plants and herbs that God provided to fight witches and criminals. Medicine can be manifested in the form of a mask or be located in a container or even a person. In a story recorded in the 1980s, medicine emerges as a gift from God, who showed a man which herbs would protect him from witches and crush their

Fig. 73. "Basinjom Association," from Malcolm Ruel, *Leopards and Leaders* (1968).

influence. After providing this gift, God left man and "closed the door."[13] Basinjom is said to be the strongest of the medicines available. A Basinjom association holds meetings (*ocha njom,* "assembly of medicine") at which members eat and drink and have the mask perform. Knowledge of potent plants is a cornerstone of the association, as are the methods of contacting the ancestors to alert them that the medicines need to be activated.

> The essential power of Basinjom lies within his eyes "to see pictures of the place of witchcraft—that is the force of the Basinjom image."
> —Robert Farris Thompson, 1974[14]

When Thompson brought a Basinjom costume back to the United States for exhibition, his experiences as an initiate and performer uniquely equipped him to install it. Forming a backdrop to the actual costume, a large photomural and videos of an initiate show him preparing the mask and performing in it. The exhibition catalogue provided a detailed account of the masquerade as described by elders of the Basinjom society, who explain what materials are assembled to create the costume and how it is called upon to perform:

When a man is initiated, in a ceremony called The-Pouring-Of-The-Medicine-Within-The-Eyes (*bajewobabe*), the initiating priest and an assistant prepare a mixture of material taken from the African Tulip Tree and palm wine. . . . The medicine is dropped in the eyes of the initiate. . . . The medicine stuns the initiate. It is believed to "wash his eyes magically, so that he can see the place of the witchcraft." The medicine also aids him to gain the possession state without which he cannot wear the gown.

After this sequence, the initiate is taken to a grove where the Basinjom mask and gown are displayed next to an *ekponen* owl. A priest then narrates the essential ingredients of the medicine incorporated into the costume and their associations:

A knife (*isome*), an iron instrument whose blade has been perforated with eyes to enable Basinjom to see the place of the witches.

A rattle made of wicker to hear the sound that evil makes.

Blue feathers of a very strong "war bird," or *touraco*, that cannot easily be shot by a gun.

Porcupine quills, which prevent intrusion from strong elements, even thunder and lightning.

Eyes that act as mirrors to see into other worlds, especially at night.

A snout like the mouth of the crocodile, which can speak for the people about controversial things. Eggs are broken over this snout to feed Basinjom.

Inside the mouth, a piece of the King Stick, the most powerful tree in the forest, used to protect bodies.

On the back of the head, many herbs that have been collected and pounded together with liquids to serve as a medicinal protection. On top, a mirror enables Basinjom to "see behind," and a small upright peg with an amulet serves as a bodyguard.

Deep black and blue cloth, a color that will "not hold death," because in darkness no human or witch can perceive you.

Raffia used for hair and a hem as an element from the forest, a dangerous realm that weak men should avoid.

A genet cat skin, invoking the spirit of an animal familiar who snatches fowls and shields Basinjom from harm.

Next to Basinjom, eyes of the owl, alluding to enhanced vision in the deep forest and the bird's long, strange legs.[15]

Having mixed parts of dangerous animals and natural powers from the herbal and mineral realms, Basinjom's costume sits awaiting an assignment. In spring 1973, a sudden outbreak of dry rot in crops calls for a trial of two women suspected of

Pl. 89
Basinjom mask and gown
Ejagham, Nigeria and Cameroon
Collected 1972
Cloth, wood, feathers, porcupine quills, mirrors, herbs,
raffia, cowry shells, rattle, eggshell, metal, genet cat skin
H. 216 cm (85 in.)
Gift of Katherine White and the Boeing Company,
81.17.1977

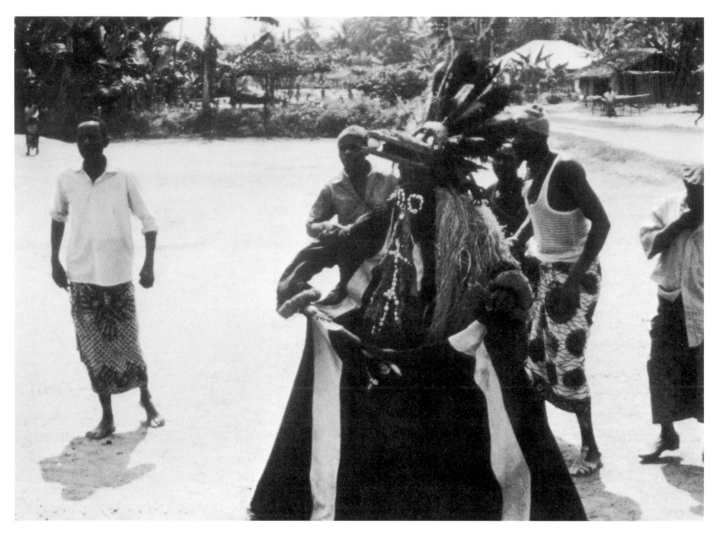

Fig. 74. Basinjom performing, Cameroon, 1973.

witchcraft. A priest invokes a ranking mask carrier, who is prepared with eye drops, an orchestra, and accompanying guardians. Basinjom holds his knife and rattle, shakes his head to listen for witches, and begins to direct an ever-growing crowd like a "mystic hovercraft" whose gliding search builds suspense (fig. 74).

Suddenly, as Thompson recounts:

He loomed over the two women accused of witchcraft. He put down the gown. The followers stopped. He knelt, bending slowly down. The followers knelt simultaneously, in perfect unison with their lord, lowering their weapons. A person explained, "He is bending down to read, to read with his knife; he wants to see things, the *bad things.*"

He turned his back on the two women, flew through the village common, and there followed more gliding and listening, more wheeling and scrutiny, with a counterpoint of head-shaking miming supernatural listening. This created gradually, but overpoweringly, an image of complex detection of all evil steps, from the vantage point of a circling owl moving over the surface of the earth.

Basinjom lifted his knife of vision above the level of his head. This silenced percussion. He began to speak, facing the women and the crowd behind them. He related intimate things, divinatory insights, thoughts, dreams. He specified certain selfish acts, breaches of cooperative contract, lapses of generosity, unkind words, and then he said, "With this evil familiar did you go out, when the planting was under way, and sow your filth into the earth. You planted it. You! And You! You are the ones responsible. All our crops have been affected."

He called their names. He asked, "Have you done this?" They answered, "Yes." They apologized and said they did not know that their powers had been so destructive. They begged forgiveness. They offered material amends and these were accepted. They were purified by Basinjom, who said, "From today I do not want to see any further trouble from your house." The women were purified by Basinjom and forgiven. The case was closed.

Basinjom had spectacularly satisfied the village. He had humiliated a source of evil, specifying, under the metaphor of the "place of witchcraft," sources of anxiety and discontent. The accused women were conscious actresses in a public drama meant to inculcate deep decorum, meant to warn the world of the dangers of polluting social landscapes by dark and hidden thoughts. The ritual humiliation was, in a sense, more performance than trauma, an artistically phrased combat between real or imaginary sources of evil (the witches) and metaphoric opposition to this action (Basinjom). The trial was an artistically perceived act, a model of confronted evil, with basis in fact and basis in myth, not so real as to leave the women socially destroyed, and not so abstract as to have no binding force. The women were rewarded with reconciliation. All had participated in a moral drama that was meant to show the consequences of resentment and bad thinking.[16]

> **The one with graceful movements, the one who speaks, the one who never tells lies.** —Ejagham informants, 1984[17]

Basinjom still appears, in a form remarkably similar to the first photograph of 1912. While examining medicines and rituals in the town of Kembong, Cameroon, in 1980, Hans Koloss found that Basinjom remained an important presence, able "to see well, hear well, speak nothing but the truth, and act in time."[18] He does state that many medicines were disappearing from use, most likely because their judicial actions had been overtaken by public courts and government agencies. Looking for evidence of such changes in nearby Calabar, Nigeria, Rosalind Hackett saw Basinjom perform in 1982 at the coronation of a new *obong*, or paramount ruler (fig. 75), of the Efik.[19] In her 1988 study of the religious life of Calabar, she evaluates the effect of Christianity and modernity on indigenous beliefs. While shrines to local deities

Fig. 75. Basinjom masquerade, at the installation of the new king of Calabar, Nigeria, 1982.

are largely gone, the destructive powers of witches continue unabated. "Mysterious deaths, nightmares, sickness, barrenness, impotence, persistent sores and the mysterious appropriation of people's money" are still counted as evidence of witchcraft.[20] Conflicts surrounding such difficulties are now litigated in law courts, but concern continues over witchcraft as a cause of misfortune.

> **Witchcraft is a metaphor for selfish individualism.**
>
> —Robert Farris Thompson, 1974[21]

Robert Farris Thompson translates Basinjom's powers by saying, "Here is the one who can smell out the Lee Harvey Oswalds and figure out what to do with them."[22] Basinjom puts such individuals on trial and extracts their confessions, then their pleas for forgiveness. His performances lead to promises of rehabilitation, thereby demonstrating the healing force of a masquerade that is also medicine.

Notes

1. See Misty L. Bastian, "Bloodhounds Who Have No Friends: Witchcraft and Locality in the Nigerian Popular Press," in *Modernity and Its Malcontents: Ritual and Power in Post-colonial Africa,* ed. Jean Comaroff and John Comaroff (University of Chicago Press, 1993), 133.

2. P. Amaury Talbot, *In the Shadow of the Bush* (London: William Heinemann, 1912), 22.

3. Basinjom is a masquerade that spread through the Cross River region of Cameroon and Nigeria. The Seattle Art Museum's mask and gown were collected among the Upper Banyang people, in the territory known as Kenyang, and among the people living in Defang. The community in 1974 numbered over eighteen thousand people. The Ejagham are their eastern and northern neighbors and have also been referred to as the Ekoi.

4. Talbot, *In the Shadow,* p. 22, describes the "Juju Akpambe": "It is a very old Ekoi juju, but was renamed a few years ago when the axe was placed between its jaws in addition to the other insignia. The image was robed in a long gown of dark blue cloth, daubed with mud from the river bed. Over the robes of the image dark-spotted juju leaves were fastened here and there. On its head it bore a crocodile mask, carved in wood. . . . It was attended by two hunters armed with flint-lock guns, a third bore a fishing net, and a fourth a curious earthen trumpet covered with leopard skin."

5. Ibid., 120.

6. Ibid., 49.

7. Malcolm Ruel, "Witchcraft, Morality and Doubt," *ODU* 2, no. 1 (July 1965), 3.

8. Hans-Joachim Koloss, "Obasinjom among the Ejagham," *African Arts* 19, no. 2 (1984), 63.

9. Ruel, "Witchcraft, Morality and Doubt," 22.

10. Malcolm Ruel, *Leopards and Leaders: Constitutional Politics among a Cross River People* (London: Tavistock Publications, 1968), 213.

11. Quoted in Judy Awyang, "UCLA Presents 'African Art in Motion,'" *Evening Outlook,* January 26, 1974.

12. Koloss, "Obasinjom among the Ejagham," 63.

13. Koloss recorded the following story (ibid.):

    At first God and man lived together in peace and mutual trust. One day this harmony was disrupted when a well-to-do man was attacked, his wives and animals killed, and his children bewitched by a less successful, greedy man. The victim appealed for help to God, who showed him herbs with which to protect himself: "I will give you these medicines, which will fight all evil powers. From the leaves Mfam, Amok, and Okeboho you can form medicines." The man then went into the bush, collected the herbs God had named, prepared the medicines, and was able thereby to crush the witch and its cohorts. In addition, God taught man the art of divination, enabling him not only to discover witches before they could do any harm, but also to find truth and righteous-ness in all walks of life. After God had revealed these secrets to his people, he closed the door. God and man were separate.

14. Robert Farris Thompson, *African Art in Motion* (Berkeley: University of California Press, 1974), 210.

15. Ibid.

16. Ibid., 215–16; cited with slight variations.

17. Koloss, "Obasinjom among the Ejagham," 99.

18. Ibid.

19. Rosalind Hackett, *Art and Religion in Africa* (London: Cassel, 1996), figs. 5.9a, 5.9b.

20. Rosalind Hackett, *Religion in Calabar: The Religious Life and History of a Nigerian Town* (Berlin: Mouton de Gruyter, 1989), 37.

21. Thompson, *African Art in Motion,* 209.

22. Robert Farris Thompson, lecture/demonstration, Seattle Art Museum, 1997.

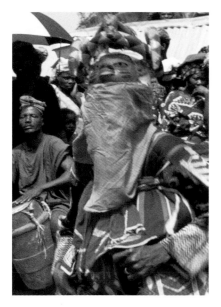

The Ultimate Spectacle for Powerful Mothers: Gelede Masks

In August 1990 on the road south to Oshogbo, Nigeria, the taxi driver made a short rest stop and I ran into a local bar to get a Coke. Rushing to the counter, I looked up at the television and saw a scene from *Dynasty,* a cat fight between Crystal and Alexis. They were pulling on each other's evening gowns and throwing lame punches into thin air, screeching all the while. I laughed at their absurd antics before realizing all eyes in the bar were on me. Here I was, an American woman watching American women in a bar surrounded by men who might think that this was my life too. Should I take on all the ways that this soap opera deviated from my reality? Explain that most American women did not live in mansions; wear furs, diamonds, and designer gowns; and have hairdressers and servants in constant attendance while they staged elaborate parties, kept track of what men were where, and gossiped? That most Americans were not simultaneously rich, good looking, and psychologically screwed up? I ran out as the Carringtons continued to flaunt their blatantly bad behavior.

Crystal Carrington, James Bond, Bruce Lee, and numerous soaps are exported around the world. Created for an American audience, their exaggerations and exploits are comic. At the same time, James Bond does exemplify an obsession with machines and gadgets to save the planet from secretive enemies, Crystal Carrington reflects the opulent decadence of the 1980s in Texas, and Bruce Lee offers a reminder of how prevalent violence can be. Each character rings hollow but stands for aspects of an American state of mind. When those characters are exported, it isn't always obvious to another audience to what extent they are valid or false reflections of American life. The episode in Oshogbo comes to mind when I approach African masks. Which masks are worn by characters who are honorable, flamboyant, or controversial is often not obvious. Which masks would evoke awe and mystery, laughter or fear? Were some worn for complete transformation and others not? Did some make sense only to a local audience, or address universal concerns, or do both at the same time? In the Seattle Art Museum's set of Gelede masks, a range of associations are explored (pls. 90–96). When worn in performance, these masks contribute to a masquerade not easily

Pl. 94 (detail)

Pl. 90
Gelede mask
Attributed to Arobatan (active 1920–1940)
Yoruba, Benin
Early 20th century
Wood, pigment
H. 63.5 cm (25 in.)
Gift of Katherine White and the Boeing Company,
81.17.587

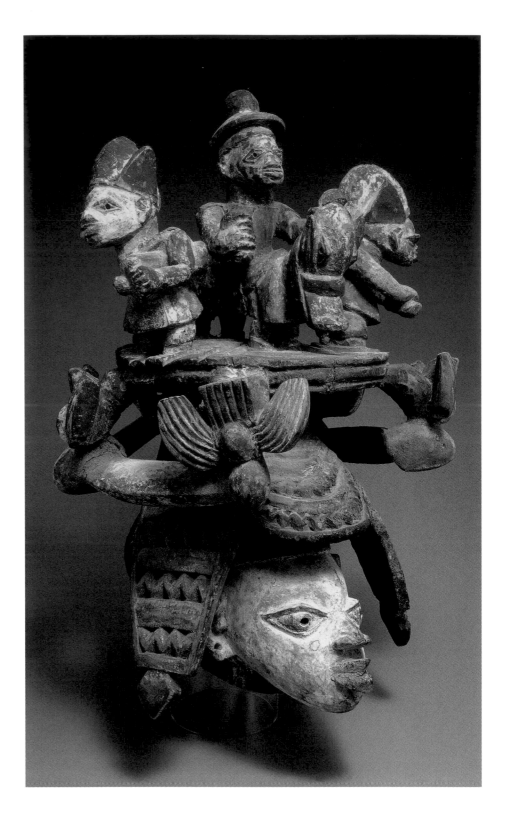

explained to an outside audience, although Yoruba scholarship is presenting a rigorous review. With Gelede, their words are directed toward a unique vision that men construct in tribute to women, especially "the powerful mothers."

Yoruba scholars have set the agenda.   —John Picton, 1998[1]

Yoruba masquerades come from an area of southwestern Nigeria that has been home to towns and cities for at least a millennium. From the sixteenth to nineteenth centuries, the slave trade exacted a heavy toll, as hundreds of thousands of Yoruba were forcibly shipped to the New World. Early in the nineteenth century, a dispute set off nearly a century of civil wars. During the unrest, the British moved in, set up a mission at Abeokuta in 1843, and occupied part of the port city of Lagos in 1851. When the British declared a protectorate in Lagos ten years later, the Ijebu-Yoruba closed their roads. It was not until spring 1892, when a British force armed with powerful weaponry toppled the Ijebu king, that the wars officially ended. Other Yoruba kingdoms entered the British protectorate up to 1914, and the British ruled over Nigeria until 1960.

While colonial rule began early, so did the efforts of Yoruba scholars working on behalf of their culture. The first primer of the Yoruba language was completed in 1849 by Samuel Ajayi Crowther, a Yoruba taken as a slave in 1821 from his home in the Oyo empire who became a bishop in the Anglican Church of England. A history of the Yoruba people written in 1897 by Reverend Samuel Johnson was published in 1921. Christian scholars and their Muslim counterparts joined forces to challenge British assumptions that only the English language and European history were to be taught in the schools. Such interactions helped to forge the way for a Yoruba identity with a flexible religious agenda.

More scholars see the need to allow the culture to speak for itself.
—Roland Abiodun, 1994[2]

More than written sources, a vibrant oral tradition sustains Yoruba inquiry. Speaking, singing, reciting, and debating create dynamic daily exchanges in Yoruba cities. Olabiyi Babalola Yai sees this pattern as a strong undercurrent that unifies Yoruba people regardless of the comings and goings of kings, dynasties, and the divisive effects of slavery or colonialism. Yoruba cities thrive on the intellectual heat of interaction among religious leaders, herbalists, poets, and artists. Inside Yoruba households, male elders keep history alive with their recitations of lineage memories. This kind of narrative is known as *pa itan,* which can be translated "to tell a story." Yai's translation takes it further: "*Pa itan* is to de-riddle history, to shed light on human existence through time and space."[3] While the male elder untangles aspects of the past, the wives and daughters of the family step in to sing *oriki,* a song to "cite one's origin" or "to provoke" (*ki*). They learn lineage songs to chant during family gatherings, extolling the triumphs (and embarrassments) of family character. And they sing showers of praise on individuals. Famed *oriki* singers go beyond the family to gain acclaim—for their skill at entertaining, but also for their ability to provoke a deep awareness among listeners. Akin Euba says, "A knowledgeable Yoruba would

listen attentively to *oriki* in the same way that a European listens to a string quartet."[4]
The tonal nature of the Yoruba language encourages drummers to coordinate complementary rhythmic patterns with the words of *oriki* songs.

> It will not be spoiled in our own time
> It will not be spoiled in our own time
> The world will not be spoiled in our own time
> Ifa will mend it.   —Ifa verse

One person who sets the highest standard for intellectual commitment to the oral tradition of Yoruba life is the *babalawo*, "father of secrets" or priest of a divination complex known as Ifa. His command of the full Ifa oracle with all its poetry requires him to retain in memory 256 sets of text and keep countless verses at hand for immediate reference. The verses, chants, and incantations of Ifa divination preserve the knowledge of medicinal plants, myths, and ritual processes in a volume of texts that guide Yoruba thought. People consult *babalawo* when facing difficulties and find their readings open up a lifelong dialogue between oral recitations and personal experience. These texts are not frozen into a single meaning but are open to continual experimental interpretations. For an audience that values a rich command of language and innovation, the Gelede mask emerges.

Since the first article about Gelede in 1958, many researchers have watched, recorded, and added to a corpus of materials about the tradition.[5] Openly performed in the centers of towns in the western and coastal regions, Gelede has been an unusually accessible masquerade to experience and study. In a recent publication on Gelede, Babatunde Lawal states, "Among the Yoruba, art and oral tradition are so interrelated that the one is like a pictorial abstraction of the other."[6] Reviewing Gelede today, we can start with the oral tradition and allow it to dictate the direction our inquiry should take.

> The world is a market, the otherworld is home.   —Yoruba saying

Gelede masquerades take over the market as a stage. Already outdoor gathering points, markets are alive with cavalcades of sound, movement, and unknown forces. They shape the interactions between men and women and between visible and invisible beings who may come to do business or watch people's activities. Women traders manage the selling on a daily basis and must face conflicts, complete transactions, and respond continually to the demands of others. Markets are a natural place to enact a festival intended to soothe women. All community members interrupt business and welcome a performance by men who appeal to women by showing respect for mothers as the guardians of society.

> The Great Mother, the powerful mothers.

The ultimate audience for Gelede performance is Iya Nla, the Great Mother, and her disciples on earth, the powerful mothers. The Great Mother is best pictured in her rambling palace at the bottom of the ocean, where she entertains visitors all day and night. She dances through her reception hall dressed in white cloth with white coral beads around her neck. For Yoruba living near the coast, the pounding of the surf is set off by the drumming, feasting, and dancing surrounding the Great Mother in her underwater home. She likes the music and dance so much that she conveys her love of performances to the powerful mothers. They are instructed to grant favors to all those who honor them with music and dance. But, like the Great Mother, they are not easily pleased and must be treated with care.

> If the mothers are annoyed, they can turn the world upside down.
> —Priestess Edun, 1975[7]

Powerful mothers can and do turn against humanity when they are provoked, especially by men who insult or show disrespect. In such cases, they might not strike out physically but will activate special powers to undermine people in the community. They might form an alliance with the *ajogun* (warriors against humanity), who unleash destructive diseases, droughts, and other troublesome forces. Or a mother could enter the soul of a bird and fly off to attend meetings and attack unsuspecting victims while they sleep. Gelede is designed to eradicate annoyances that provoke the mothers' wrath and turn women back into guardians of life: "It is believed that from the beginning, the creator-God put women in charge of all the good things on earth. Without their sanction, no healing can take place, rain cannot fall, plants cannot bear fruits and children cannot come into the world."[8]

> *Ge:* to soothe, placate, pet, indulge
> *Ele:* women's private essence
> *De:* to relax, soften with care

The name "Gelede" is explained in several ways. One meaning traced to the mid-seventeenth century relates to a performer named Gbarada (One Who Stole the Show). He won the prize as best entertainer with his pair of spectacular masks—a male and female who sang, danced, cracked jokes, and performed all kinds of wonders during the competition. Gbarada was taken by a grandson of the king to entertain others in Yorubaland; "Gelede" may be a distortion of "Gbarada." Another explanation of the term translates the components as "to soothe the female with care" or "using art to dissolve tension."[9]

> Who sent for the king of secrets to appear? Please mind how you call me, the humorist.   —Efe narration recorded by Babatunde Lawal, 1996[10]

Poetic humor is one of the first strategies to please the Great Mother. It comes with food in a night devoted to Efe (joking, buffoonery)—the night of fun. Meals of redemptive food are distributed to friends, neighbors, and relatives to begin the festival. As the crowd settles down, all lights are extinguished. Iya Nla herself makes a swift, discreet appearance; barely seen, she is heard. Soon afterward, a "Path Clearer" masquerader appears with a brightly colored mask featuring a human head on a tray (pl. 91). A cloth veil is attached to the brim but doesn't completely conceal the man wearing the mask. Singing and wandering through the audience, the Path Clearer opens the way for the courageous critic to follow. Around 10 P.M., as if in a darkened theater, a flickering light focuses all attention on an entrance framed by palm fronds.

Oro Efe, the King of the Night, appears with a microphone and asks, "Who sent for the king of secrets to appear?" Then begins a program that lasts until dawn. For hours, he blesses the audience and the powers of the universe, and does his best to dissolve tension with satire, ridicule, jokes, and jests, "so they can laugh off their grievances." His performance is said to be like a blazing fire with the power of a leopard and a voice as sweet as honey.[11] His songs and poems target current events without fear of reprisal. All thefts, sex scandals, corruption, political disputes, and abuses of power are ripe for commentary. Scandals are especially relished.

World Does Not Love a Slanderer. —Efe performer

Efe performers are poets and social critics at the same time (fig. 76). As their bold words attack everyone from misbehaving women to politicians in high office, they must assure their audience that they speak with the voice of an unquestionable source, that of Iya Nla, the Great Mother. Sanctioned to say what no one else dares to, they are known to launch critical songs against swindlers, playboys, prostitutes, and corrupt officials. In one performance, a mask called World Does Not Love a Slanderer sang about an official who wanted to steal property rights and sell a shoreline to foreigners who would put local fishermen out of business.[12] Akin to the editorial column of a newspaper or radio, Efe songs don't just report on events but also comment on their effect on the community. In another song, Oro Efe serves notice to a young man whose behavior is annoying and even criminal:

Fig. 76. An Efe mask in full regalia, Ijio, Nigeria, 1991.

> The conceited man with all his money is teasing his elder
> Did Ogunsola marry his wife for you?
> Wicked person who pulls on the snake's neck
> If the viper bites you should I be concerned?[13]

In this song, a man is accused of committing adultery with an elder's wife and using his money to justify acting superior. His foolishness is compared to that of a man who pulls on a snake's neck and doesn't care what happens. While Efe songs are critical of individuals, they also berate politicans:

> This world is harsh for you politicians
> Anyone who wants to live in this world must be very careful
> Watch what you say, for the world is heavy
> You politicians, the world requires caution
> Those who were doing it whom we were told were not doing it properly
> "The world" cut them away as bananas are cut from the stem
> Those who were doing it whom we were told were not doing it properly
> "The world" blew them away like shafts from wheat.[14]

In the 1940s, one Efe performer was arrested for ridiculing colonial policies, but was later released on the argument that the words were not his own. Throughout the colonial era, physical revolt was discouraged because of the brutal retaliation it could unleash. People would rely upon the Efe singer to air their distress over colonial policies and to direct a dose of ridicule at the foreign officers.

Pl. 91
Efe mask: Path Clearer
Yoruba, Nigeria
20th century
Wood, enamel paint
Diam. 54.6 cm (21½ in.)
Gift of Mark Groudine and Cynthia Putnam, 95.130

Pl. 92

Efe mask: bird holding snake

Attributed to Alaiye Adesia Etuobe of Ketu

Yoruba, Benin

Early 20th century

Wood, pigment

H. 37.8 cm (14⅞ in.)

Gift of Katherine White and the Boeing Company,
81.17.584

A fowl perches on a rope. The rope feels uneasy. The fowl also feels
uneasy.   —Yoruba saying

The Efe singer's flair for taking risks is evident in the headdress he wears. A tense
situation is enacted atop the singer's head (pl. 92). A bird is holding onto a swirling
snake, while the human face below is a study in composure. Bathed in white chalk,
the Efe face would stand out in the darkness of the night and evoke the need for the
cool, covert patience of the mothers to deal with this kind of violent encounter. Birds
and snakes approach confrontation differently. Powerful mothers are known to turn
into birds at night and attack sleeping victims, while snakes are thought to rarely
attack unless they are provoked, and then not to let go. Interlacing this duel is a belt

with sheathed knives on either side, adding the
potential of a human attack. Knives refer to
Ogun, an *orisa* (deity) whose special skills with
iron were first employed when all the *orisa*s
arrived on earth and found themselves trapped
in the thickness of the primeval forest. Ogun
used his iron cutlass to cut a path, thereby
opening the world for humans to inhabit. He
offers tools and weapons to be used when necessary, but he fiercely opposes those who use
the inventions unwisely. Careless violence is
subject to Ogun's wrath, just as the wrath of Efe
is expressed with ridicule and satire. Wearing
a mask to advocate balance and reason, the Efe
performer paces back and forth in a slow tempo
all through the dark night.

For the moment, life feels like a paradise.   —Babatunde Lawal, 1996

Fig. 77. Pair of Gelede masqueraders dancing, Imeko,
Nigeria, 1970.

After hours of singing and offering prayers, jokes, and riddles, the Efe masquerader retires at dawn. Everyone rests until the next afternoon, when families attend
the larger Gelede spectacle—three to seven days of extensive performances. Pairs
of masqueraders dance into view and mirror each other's movements, matching the
drum phrasing of songs, proverbs, and slogans (fig. 77). As the afternoon progresses,
the rhythms intensify, testing the precision of the dancers. Each duo must move in
tight unison as their leg rattles keep time with the drumming. Their bodies become
instruments themselves, somewhat akin to tap dancers, whose legs accent every
move with sound. The Gelede headdresses they wear offer a moving parade of diverse subjects—a promiscuous woman, a dignified priest, a banana stalk, and two
snakes swallowing a porcupine. The afternoon performances are an occasion when
"everybody is in a joyous, celebratory mood as the music takes over the body; even
the aged, the sick, the bereaved, the poor, and the distressed temporarily forget their
problems. For the moment, life feels like a paradise."[15]

Character is the essence of beauty.   —Yoruba saying

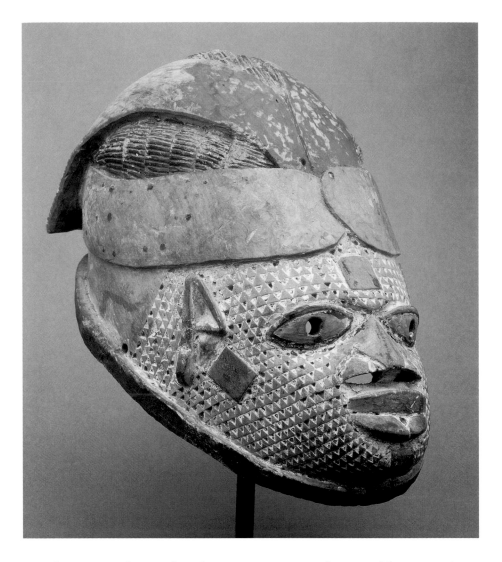

The virtues and vices of Yoruba women are portrayed in two of the museum's
Gelede headdresses, one neat and controlled, the other an obvious parody of grace-
lessness. Precisely incised triangles adorn a face with balanced, carefully outlined
features (pl. 93). A broad head tie sweeps around her hair, revealing tight linear rows
of braids. No details are out of place, suggesting that this is a woman of balanced
character. *Iwa,* or "ideal character," is cultivated by the Gelede festival and encouraged
as the source of beauty and joy in life. Positive, ethical behavior makes one attractive
not only to Iya Nla, the Great Mother, but also to Olu Iwa (Lord of Character and
Existence), and finally to all those who live in the community. The performer likely
emphasized the grace and control of this mask with the gestures of a sociable and
virtuous woman.

Just as this woman is tightly composed, her opposite is not (pl. 94). A rather
plain face supports a leering woman who bends at the waist, exposing her private
parts. The mask wearer's movements would depict a promiscuous woman who walks
provocatively and makes suggestive gestures to her admirers. Such parody could be
pushed to an extreme by the male dancer, who would interact with the audience.

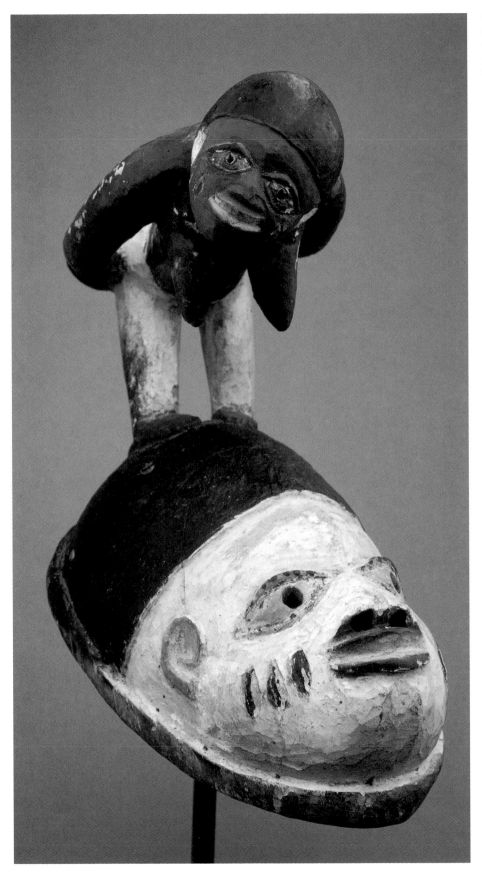

Pl. 94
Gelede mask: female exposing herself
Yoruba, Nigeria
20th century
Wood, pigment
H. 35 cm (13¾ in.)
Gift of Katherine White and the Boeing Company,
81.17.590

Pl. 95
Gelede mask: male with skull cap
Attributed to Amusa Akapo of Igbesa
Yoruba, Nigeria
Early 20th century
Wood, pigment, leather
H. 20.2 cm (8 in.)
Gift of Katherine White and the Boeing Company,
81.17.585

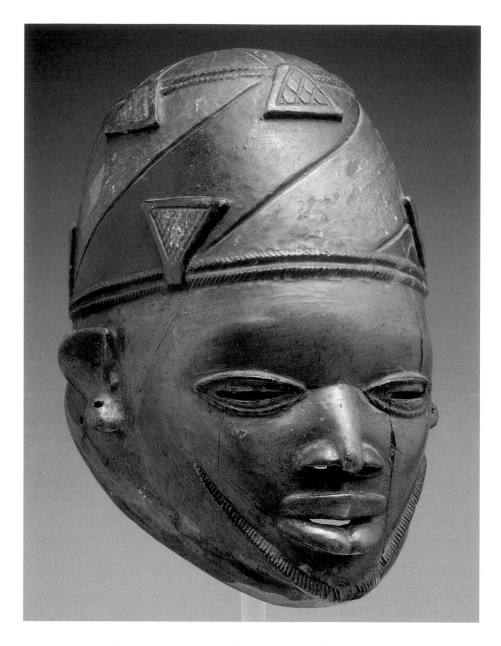

My mother, the nursing mother with the rolling buttocks.

—Yoruba saying

Men use Gelede costumes to transform their bodies into visions of mothers. Most almost double their size by adding layers of costuming to exaggerate the wide buttocks and hips that allow a safe and easy delivery of children. Sashes used for carrying a baby and head wraps borrowed from women are tied on to create a truly plump mother, whose dancing is considered far more alluring than a slim woman's. A hoop is suspended over the hips to allow them to rotate in a smooth, suspended motion, while wooden breasts are positioned to draw attention to the female form. Some performers mimic specific characters by imitating their walk or carry implements to suggest their role.

Some masks chant in Arabic. Some say amen and quote the Bible.

—Babatunde Lawal, 1999[16]

A Muslim cleric is commemorated in a headdress whose mouth seems about to speak or chant (pl. 95). To complete the impression of a devout Muslim, a performer wearing it might carry prayer beads and prayer mat and a teapot used to wash his face and feet before reciting verses from the Koran. The key to this man's identity is suggested by the amulets on his cap. In former centuries, Muslim clerics in Yoruba courts supplied protective amulets to leaders and holy persons. Christians and Muslims participate in Gelede, and Muslim support for Gelede has remained constant, despite disapproval of other masquerade forms. In turn, Gelede is circumspect in its criticism. Islam, a religion that sixty percent of all Nigerians now follow, would not become a target. Instead, Gelede focuses attention on certain kinds of individuals whose eccentricities invite satire.

> **Anything handled with care becomes easier**
> **Anything handled with force becomes harder.**   —Yoruba saying

A liquor barrel, dark glasses, fine-toothed comb, and cigarette over one ear are elements of a headdress that jokes about a certain elite (pl. 96). Two groups of repatriates with Europeanized attitudes have not been entirely well received. In the late nineteenth and early twentieth centuries, a group of Brazilian residents of African ancestry returned to Nigeria. They spoke Portuguese, were Catholic, and tended to segregate themselves. Following them were repatriates from Sierra Leone, more British oriented and Protestant. Both groups tended to part their hair as on this mask, drink Western liquor imported in barrels, and smoke. It is also possible that the mask simply refers to European colonialists who overindulged in drink, wore sunglasses, and smoked imported cigarettes. In assembling these clues, the mask jests as Gelede is best known to do: "In jesting, you approach someone in an intimate way—it is an aspect of friendship and it creates trust. It can promote well-being and purify a relationship."[17]

> **The Yoruba possess and practice a most effective system of naming**
> **everyone in their society.**   —Roland Abiodun, 1994[18]

Arobatan of Pobe, Dahomey, a master carver of the 1920s to 1940s, created a Gelede mask depicting a king on horseback with praise drummers saluting his ride (see pl. 90). In its original performance, the mask was likely greeted by a praise name and reflections of the personal histories that guide Gelede. Without knowing who this king is, we can only read the mask literally as a confident leader whose procession is supported (or about to be disrupted?) by birds waiting beneath.

Yoruba sculptors continue to be identified by distinct stylistic traits. In the effort to name artists, however, Yoruba authors provide a note of caution. Names are closely tied to a person's essence, which determines success or failure in this world. Reciting someone's name can act as a summons to the person's spiritual essence, causing it to act. Some situations call for reciting full names, but the person can then become

a target for those with evil intent. Because artists are especially vulnerable, they rarely reveal their full names to strangers, and many are known by nicknames or bynames from their place of origin.

> Even today to sell a commonly owned mask requires consensus.
> —Babatunde Lawal, 1999[19]

Single masks are usually all that museums have of the Gelede performance. Pairs are expected to establish equilibrium and balance, but are often separated over time. One might be damaged while the other continues to perform or appear in children's rehearsals. Typically owned by families, the masks are commissioned by the heads of households and kept until the Gelede society decides to sponsor a ceremony. To sell an ordinary Gelede mask of a general nature requires an agreement by the entire family, and a special character mask must be deactivated by a priest and a council of elders before it can be sold. All but one of the museum's masks were acquired through American dealers; the Arobatan mask came from an African source.[20]

> Art is an aspect of what the Yoruba call *ifogbontaayṣe*, "using wisdom to remake/improve the world." —Babatunde Lawal[21]

Yoruba infuse Gelede with an ambitious agenda—to improve the human condition. Masquerades illustrate what ideal character is and how the warriors against humanity operate. Ultimately, it is the women in the audience who receive and evaluate the success of a Gelede performance. They may be moved to praise or embrace a masquerader who demonstrates accomplished dancing and moving mimicry, aptly honoring the mothers. Gelede continues to honor the powerful mothers in Yorubaland and beyond. Yoruba took the masquerade to Sierra Leone in the late nineteenth century and created a society that sponsored annual festivals. Although masks were left behind in the violent passage across the Atlantic, the mothers were not forgotten by Yoruba in Brazil, Cuba, the Caribbean, and the United States, who continue to pay tribute to them. Gelede is reported to have been reshaped in Brazil in the nineteenth century and performed until the 1940s, when elements of it may have fed into the vibrant public performance arena of Carnival. On Caribbean islands with large Yoruba populations, like Trinidad and Tobago, headdresses with superstructures became a feature of Carnival. Looking and listening carefully, Robert Farris Thompson has posed a connection to the Geledesque headdress of Carmen Miranda, the Brazilian star, who performed as a market woman with a massive scarf around her hair and tray of fruit atop her head. Her performance popularized elements of Yoruba identity that would have been seen on the streets of Bahia—beads and head ties, and female control of the market.

> Kingly mother, I thank you
> Kingly mother, I thank you
> Powerful king, fearful indigo depth within the river,
> Make way for her,
> Kingly mother, I thank you, mother of the world.
> —Chano Pozo, 1947[22]

Pl. 96
Gelede mask: male wearing glasses
Yoruba, Nigeria
20th century
Wood, pigment
H: 24.2 cm (9½ in.)
Gift of Katherine White and the Boeing Company,
81.17.583

In continuing the indelible reliance on a rich oral tradition, the Yoruba in Cuba offer just one of many tributes to a close relative of the Gelede complex—devotion to Yemaya. "Yemaya" in Cuba, "Yemanja" in Brazil, "Yemoja" in Nigeria, is "the ultimate symbol of motherhood."[23] She resides as a queen in the depths of the Ogun River in Nigeria and in the Atlantic Ocean—all waters are at her command. She makes an appearance at the conclusion of certain Gelede performances in Nigeria, but in the New World she receives tribute as the goddess who gives birth to fish in the sea and people on earth. Altars recall the images of Iya Nla, the Great Mother, who lives in a world of radiant white beads, shells, and clay. Yemoja favors beads of blue and white, recalling the depths of the ocean from which she comes and the froth of the waves that she sends to lick the shores. At the seaside festivals for her that take place on countless beaches, she is ready to hear requests for protection and healthy children, and to receive thanks for all that mothers have to offer.

Notes

1. John Picton, "Islam, Artifact and Identity in Southwest Nigeria," in *Islamic Art and Culture in Sub-Saharan Africa,* ed. Karin Adahl and Berit Sahlström (Uppsala: Almquist and Wiksell International, 1995), 79.

2. Roland Abiodun, "Introduction: An African (?) Art History: Promising Theoretical Approaches in Yoruba Art Studies," in *The Yoruba Artist* (Washington, D.C.: Smithsonian Institution Press, 1994), 41.

3. Olabiyi Babalola Yai, "In Praise of Metonymy: The Concepts of 'Tradition' and 'Creativity' in the Transmission of Yoruba Artistry over Time and Space," in ibid., 109.

4. Akin Euba, "Drumming for the Egungun: The Poet-Musician in Yoruba Masquerade Theater," in ibid., 165.

5. See Ulli Beier, "Gelede Masks," *Odu,* June 6, 1958.

6. Babatunde Lawal, *The Gelede Spectacle: Art, Gender, and Social Harmony in an African Culture* (Seattle: University of Washington Press, 1996).

7. Quoted in Henry John Drewal and Margaret Thompson Drewal, *Gelede: Art and Female Power among the Yoruba* (Bloomington: Indiana University Press, 1983), 8.

8. Roland Abiodun, "The Concept of Women in Traditional Yoruba Religion and Art" (paper presented at the Conference on Nigerian Women and Development in Relation to Changing Family Structure, University of Ibadan, April 26–30, 1976), 1.

9. Lawal, *The Gelede Spectacle,* 74–75.

10. Ibid., 106.

11. Drewal and Drewal, *Gelede,* chap. 3.

12. Ibid.

13. Ibid., 53, revised from 1971 text, which doubled each line.

14. Ibid., 55.

15. Lawal, *The Gelede Spectacle,* 152.

16. Babatunde Lawal, interview by the author, March 26, 1999.

17. Ibid.

18. Abiodun, "Introduction," 42.

19. Lawal, interview.

20. The dealers were Ed Primus, Gallery K, Kahane, Merton Simpson, Ed Storrer, the May Company, and Abdullah Alhassone.

21. Lawal, *The Gelede Spectacle,* xvii.

22. Song by Chano Pozo, Afro-Cuban drummer and follower of the *orisha* and of the Abakua faith. Recorded on *Dizzier and Dizzier,* Dizzy Gillespie Orchestra, Victor LP IJM-1009, side 2, band 2.

23. John Mason, *Orin Orisa* (New York: Yoruba Theological Seminary, 1992).

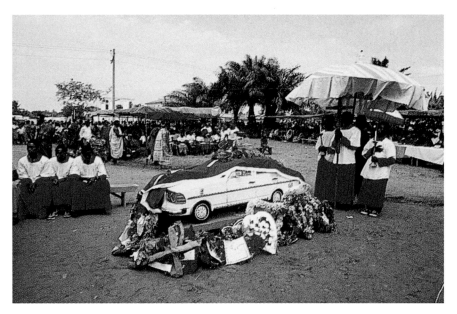

Riding into the Next Life: A Mercedes-Benz Coffin

A realistic Mercedes-Benz in a gallery of African art elicits many reactions (pl. 97). "What is this doing here?" is usually the first question. Children are often quite vocal about wanting to know, now. Adult viewers, particularly teachers, look for the label. When they read that the car is a coffin, they notice that it's cut in two horizontally and is just big enough to hold a recumbent body. The next question hangs in the air: "Why is an empty, fully functional coffin considered art?"

> **In the everyday life of the Ga, the dead are everpresent.**
>
> —M. J. Field, 1937[1]
>
> **And when men die, we do not mention them.**
>
> —Ralph Waldo Emerson, 1903[2]

For southern Ghanaian observers, it isn't art. Coffins are a necessity, provided to honor the deceased and assist them in their transition into the next life. Coffins are ordered from a workshop when a member of a wealthy family is nearing death. One

Pl. 97
Mercedes-Benz coffin
Kane Quaye, 1922–1992
Teshi, Ghana
1991
Wood and paint
L. 256.5 cm (101 in.)
Gift of Oliver and Pamela Cobb and Mark Groudine and
Cynthia Putnam in honor of Pamela McClusky, 93.163

Fig. 78. Shoe coffin at Paa Joe's carpentry shop, Teshi, Ghana, 2001.

of several shops is called Six-Foot Enterprises, where the coffin carver Paa Joe keeps photographs of the coffins ordered by other families. The number of selections grows each year. The deceased person's profession or role in the community often determines the image.

> **Now we average ten a month.** —Paa Joe, 1995[3]

Some coffin forms are inflated versions of everyday items:

a shoe for a man who owned a shoe shop (fig. 78),
a large pink object (fallopian tubes and womb) for a gynecologist,
a chicken and chicks for a woman with many children,
a beer bottle for a serious drinker,
an economy pack of sweetened whole milk for a storekeeper,
a saw for a carpenter,
an oil can for a garage owner,
a parrot with a pen in its beak for a university lecturer,
a cocoa pod for a farmer,
a trowel for a builder.

Others are miniature versions of larger elements:

an airplane for a Ghana Airways employee,
a lorry (truck) with headlights or a cassette player for a lorry driver,
a canoe for a fisherman.

Ghanaians order coffins not for display but to hold the body of the deceased and convey it through a lavish burial ceremony. Such custom-made coffins are a fifty-year-old tradition whose inspiration can be traced to the special role the dead have among the Ga people.

When doing fieldwork among the Ga, M. J. Field documented how the influence of the dead was felt. Every time people ate or drank, they offered a portion to the ground for their forefathers. Whenever an oath was sworn, it was uttered in the name of the dead. When asked about their personal history, people were guarded in speaking of their predecessors. Field cited the word *gblamo* as an underlying explanation for this sense of the dead. *Gblamo* means "reincarnation," and is the name of a vine that twines around a post. The most visible expression of this belief in life's recurring cycle came during funerals, when the dead were treated to as much opulence as the family could afford. Their bodies were laid out in fancy imported bed linens and adorned with gold ornaments. The house was open for a week, and wine and rum were provided for visitors. After friends and relatives had paid their respects, the deceased would be placed in a basket or wood coffin and carried around town for a goodbye. Once buried, the dead were believed to wander many days before crossing a river to a place from which they could observe the living and intervene on occasion.

> **The dead are always watching to see that the living preserve what their forefathers established.** —M. J. Field, 1937[4]

The innovator of the custom coffin was raised with the notion of the watchful dead. His history has been traced by Thierry Secretan, whose 1994 book and 1988 film are the sources for the following details of the artist's life.[5] Kane Quaye was born in 1922 to a father who worked as a linesman on the Gold Coast railway and made oil lamps in his spare time—hence the name Kane, which means "light." Taught carpentry by a brother, he went away to cut wood in the forests and then returned to his home on the coast in 1947. During his absence, American forces had transformed Quaye's home by building vast military camps to serve as a supply base for troops destined for North Africa. Quaye remembered hearing jazz playing wherever he went, and planes landing daily. He began working for a master carpenter whose workshop was known for an innovative palanquin made in the shape of an eagle for the chief of the village of Teshi. Another chief requested a palanquin resembling a cocoa pod, a source of great wealth in Ghana at the time. When the chief died before the pod was finished, it was used as his coffin instead. While part of this workshop, Quaye made a coffin in the form of an airplane for his grandmother, who had dreamed of riding in one of the planes she saw flying into Teshi. He opened his own carpentry business in 1951 and offered custom-made coffins as one among many items. They became his sole product as Ghana's world profile changed.

Ghana became independent in 1957 and launched an era of industrial growth. A massive dam being constructed on the Volta River gave new work to Ghanaians. Kane Quaye established a workshop on the road from the capital of Accra to a new port, Tema. Suddenly, the lavish burials that had once been the privilege of chiefs alone were now much more commonplace. Coffins were so much in demand that Paa Joe, Quaye's apprentice, remembers, "We worked night and day! We made Chevrolets, cocoa pods, whales, canoes."[6] This boom had been in effect for more than ten years when an American art dealer commissioned seven coffins for display in her gallery

Fig. 79. Green Leaf Barber Shop sign, Kumasi, Ghana, 2001.

in 1973. In a 1974 article, she called them "fantasy coffins" and remarked how they resembled "oversized toys," but marked a "somber occasion with a gesture that is cheerfully confident and personally expressive."[7]

In modern societies, the dead person is simply a zero, a non-value.

—Linda Nochlin, 1971[8]

Construing a coffin as a "fantasy" sculpture speaks more to an American dilemma than to Kane Quaye's motivations for carving a coffin. By the 1970s, death in America was increasingly removed from sight. One study concluded, "The dead world is disappearing."[9] Victorian funeral practices such as defined periods of mourning, dress codes, and churchyard cemeteries had long since faded away. More Americans were dying in hospitals than in family homes; the bodies were transferred to a funeral industry; and grief was purged more in private than in public. Cemeteries began eliminating individually designed headstones, mounds, and plantings in favor of a drive-through park with uniform hills. Elderly people moved into nursing homes, which removed families even further from the handling of death and illness. Corpses were often not even touched, having been reduced to ashes by cremation. Notions of the afterlife faded. Into this perplexing phase of American life comes a colorful coffin, which presents a definite location for the dead. Kane Quaye is discovered and proclaimed an artist, and his work is soon shown internationally.

Magicians of the Earth.   —Centre Georges Pompidou, Paris, 1989

Kane Quaye was dubbed a "magician of the earth" in an exhibition and publication produced in Paris in 1989.[10] A selection of coffins including a full-size Mercedes-Benz, half-size fish, lobster, elephant, eagle, and onion were sent for an installation of his work. That same year, Thierry Secretan's film about Kane Quaye was shown in the United States under the title *Leaving in Style*. A 1991 exhibition in New York, *Africa Explores*, featured Quaye's Mercedes coffin and advised viewers to view the car not as a critique of success, but rather as an embracing of the wealth, status, and respect that it would command. In the catalogue, Susan Vogel emphasizes that the coffins are not

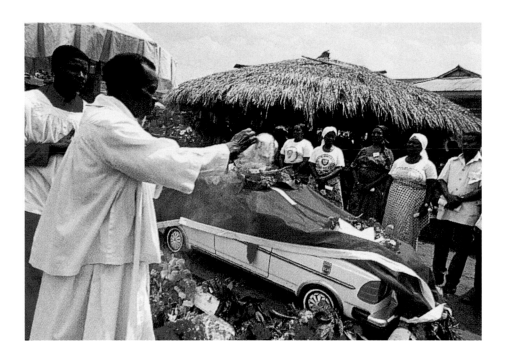

distant from the real world, but express connection with plants, birds, cars, airplanes, and all manner of things in the clients' daily lives.[11]

Indeed, Quaye's innovation is partly indebted to the streets of West Africa. On a daily walk through any market area, direct display is ever present. Unlike a supermarket, where packaging disguises the potato chip, cereal, or toothpaste within, the outdoor market relies on open display and pictorial communication. Traders walk along or sit by the street with trays full of oranges, cigarettes, candies, boiled eggs, or tomatoes. Outside a bar, there will be a picture of a man drinking beer. Heads with various hairstyles tell you where a barber shop is (fig. 79). A large alarm clock signals a watch repair shop. Printed cloth, worn everywhere, is loaded with pictures of everything from bottles of beer to enamel pans to birds in flight. Paying homage to the commonplace, the coffins have an immediacy and lack of pretense that brought them clients with unexpected purposes in mind. In a 1995 catalogue for Neiman Marcus, the lead line asks, "How about a chili pepper for the living room or a fish for the garden?" Instead of emphasizing what they are for, the catalogue calls the coffins "more fun than any little decorative figurine."

A Mercedes-Benz is for wealthy motorists.   —Kane Quaye, 1992[12]

Choosing a proper coffin in Ghana requires matching the image with the status of the deceased. The Mercedes is ordered for few people, as it remains a symbol of great success, reserved for someone with enough money to buy Western imports. Funerals with a Mercedes coffin are said to be unusually somber and aligned with Christian services conducted outside the dead person's house (fig. 80). Sometimes the family's actual Mercedes is parked beside the coffin. When the time comes for the burial, the coffin travels directly to the cemetery in a serious procession; it doesn't detour to all the places the deceased liked to go in life.

Fig. 80. Funeral services with Mercedes-Benz, Ghana, 1992.

The Seattle Art Museum's coffin was commissioned to serve as a sculpture for display, not as a vehicle for the dead. It replaced a Mercedes coffin that toured in the exhibition *Africa Explores* in 1991 and had been damaged by being packed and moved frequently in a manner completely unforeseen by its makers.

> **Burial ... is the single most important community activity taking place every Friday and Saturday of the year. In these funerals tradition finds the main frame of its evolution.**
>
> —Thierry Secretan, 1995[13]

Ghanaians are still the main clients for the custom-made coffins used to honor their dead. Life is conditioned by funerals, which require families to attend and sometimes travel around the country from Friday to Sunday. The coffins in Ghanaian funerals are not seen in the quiet restraint of a Western funeral home (fig. 81). The November 1997 funeral of a taxi driver, Holala Nortey, is a point of reference.[14] For most of his career, Nortey drove an old Mercedes-Benz sedan for a hotel in Accra. When he died at sixty-three, a Mercedes coffin was purchased by his family. Three days of celebration brought together nearly four hundred people—his four children, ten grandchildren, coworkers, neighbors, friends, and relatives. "Sponge ladies" prepared the body, and then columns of mourners walked around his funeral bed to praise him, sob, vent anger, or ask him for help once he was established in the next life. Outside the house, crowds of friends and family visited, danced and helped themselves to food. On Sunday, eight pall-bearers lifted Nortey's body in the Mercedes coffin above the sea of mourners. Crowds followed the coffin as the dead proceeded around town to say goodbye. An older woman led the way, offering libations of palm wine on the ground as the procession moved. They moved past the Victory Spot Bar, the Congo Cafe, and the Step by Step restaurant and finally began the descent down a rugged road to the public cemetery. The crowd watched as the coffin was placed six feet down and covered with soil.

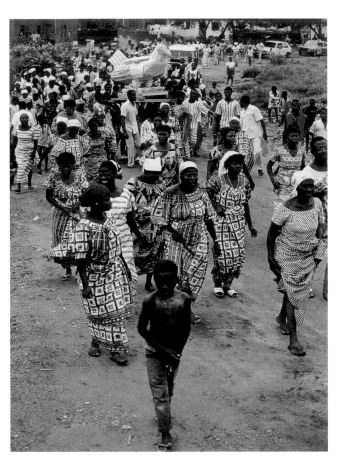

Fig. 81. Chicken coffin with crowd escort, Dansoman, Ghana, 1992.

> **All a dead person owns is his coffin.**
>
> —Kane Quaye, 1992[15]

When the coffin goes underground, it concludes a collective mourning process. The emotional catharsis and public acknowledgment of the accomplishments of the deceased are both valued ways of honoring the dead. A funeral object transformed into sculpture is seen as an odd choice for contemporary art by some African observers. Made by carpenters for clients who expect the coffin to be seen only for a short time, it has an awkward air of unfulfilled purpose when not put to its intended use. In America, it serves quite another purpose. When the coffin stays above ground at the museum, it suggests that other cultures openly face what here has become a hidden conclusion to life.

Notes

1. M. J. Field, *Religion and Medicine of the Ga People* (Oxford: Oxford University Press, 1937), 196.

2. *The Complete Works of Ralph Waldo Emerson,* Concord Edition (Boston: Houghton Mifflin, 1903), 143.

3. *New York Times,* December 18, 1995.

4. Field, *Religion and Medicine,* 196.

5. Thierry Secretan revealed the lineage of the coffin tradition in *Il fait sombre va t'en* (Paris: Hazan, 1994), translated as *Going into Darkness* (London: Thames and Hudson, Ltd., 1995). He notes that originally palanquins were baskets used to carry chiefs during ceremonial processions. Kane Quaye's tutor, Ata Owoo (1904–76), carved the first version of a wooden eagle for the Teschi chief Nii Ashitey Akomfra (1902–77) in 1947.

6. Quoted in Thierry Secretan, *Going into Darkness: Fantastic Coffins from Africa* (London: Thames and Hudson, 1995), 18.

7. Vivian Burns, "Travel to Heaven: Fantasy Coffins," *African Arts* 7, no. 2 (winter 1974).

8. Linda Nochlin, *Realism* (London: Penguin, 1971), 60.

9. See Charles O. Jackson, *Passing: The Vision of Death in America* (Westport, Conn.: Greenwood Press, 1977), a compilation of essays that trace the changes from colonial America to the twentieth century.

10. *Magicians de la terre* (Paris: Centre Georges Pompidou, 1989). The National Geographic Society broadcast the film *Leaving in Style* in 1989, and the BBC aired it in forty-two countries. Directed by Thierry Secretan, the film was released in 1988 with the title *Les Cercueils de monsieur Kane Kwei.*

11. Susan Vogel, *Africa Explores: Twentieth Century African Art* (New York: Center for African Art, 1991).

12. Quoted in Secretan, *Going into Darkness,* 9.

13. Ibid., 7.

14. Stephen Buckley, "In Africa, Funerals Use Rituals of Joy to Ease Sorrow," *Washington Post Foreign Service,* December 22, 1997.

15. Secretan, *Going into Darkness,* 20.

"Negatives That Breathe Like You and Me": Photographs from Bamako

Visitors to the Seattle Art Museum in 1997 were invited to spend $10,000 on African art. The funds were derived from a lengthy deaccessioning process, and one gallery was turned into a polling booth. Eight choices were displayed—some rooted in time-tested aesthetics, such as the fortress-like face of a black monkey mask from the Dogon of Mali, and a selection of beadwork including a rickshaw outfit from South Africa. Others were more process oriented, such as a proposal for an artistic collaboration with Fred Wilson, and an effort to purchase a portion of the Schneider archives (see "Assembling a Royal Stage: Art from the Kom Kingdom"). As thousands of votes and supporting comments were posted, a set of six photographs by Seydou Keita and Malick Sidibe inspired a wealth of statements, of which a selected few appear here:

I'm interested in how people, regardless of race or ethnicity view themselves. I want to know and see what they think is important, not what I think *I* should know about them.

It is important to get a culture's view of itself.

These photographs have a terrific sense of honesty about them.

The best way to understand others is to look through their own eyes.

Unquestionably powerful images—combines art with documentation.

African art, for/by/about Africans.

Need to reflect multifaceted and evolving African cultures rather than what is expected.

The U.S. needs to open its eyes to the interpretation of other cultures through the eyes of its own people. Exterior interpretation is often innocently biased.

Africa is not only yesterday, it is today also.

It gives a view of people, not just disembodied artifacts.

Pl. 98 (detail)

Pl. 98
Untitled (Family with Car no. 266)
Seydou Keita (b. ca. 1921)
Mali
1951–1952
Gelatin silver print
W. 61 cm (24 in.)
General Acquisitions Fund, 97.35

As a contrast to the symbolism of the art in African exhibits, photos are clear, startling, intimate, and realistic.

Images of prosperous Africans are rare.

Like a war story from a soldier, not an outsider who didn't fight.

After forty weeks, the six photographs did not receive the most votes, but their evident attraction for the audience (as well as the curators) led to the purchase of two from a gallery in San Francisco.[1] Just as the visitors' comments stated over and over, the photographs counteract images of famine, conflict, and odd, exotic Africans; instead, they present people dressing up for a wedding, taking children to visit relatives, having a good time at a picnic, and walking down the streets of cities like Bamako, Mali. The photographs of Seydou Keita and Malick Sidibe are perhaps so startling because they are so unsensational. It's apparent that their subjects asked to have their pictures taken, which is often not the case with photographs by outsiders. Both responded to clients who wanted to record their families, friends, and events for their own use. Keita's and Sidibe's candid work records life in Bamako from the late 1940s through the 1970s. In the 1990s, both were caught in an unexpected wave of international recognition and sudden renown for the visual milestones they had created.

> **I started by taking pictures of my family.** —Seydou Keita[2]

Seydou Keita began as a carpenter. He was given a camera by his uncle in 1935, and took a decade to learn how to use it. He says, "In 1948, I set up my studio in our house in Bamako-Koura, in what was then 'New Bamako' and which was a lively neighbourhood. That's where I took all the photos that you've seen. And today, I'm still there."

> Bamako … was a major crossroads then and had a really good atmosphere. … The whole central section was very bustling because of the cathedral, the railway station, the post office, the big Marche Rose, the Soudan Club, and a very busy zoo. My studio was in a good place. … There was always a crowd around my studio, and I was working all the time. All the elite in Bamako came to be photographed by me: government workers, shop owners, politicians. Everyone passed through my studio at one time or another. Some days, especially Sundays, there were hundreds of people. Even our first president, Modibo Keita, came by. Everyone knew about me. I had a rubber stamp "Photo KEITA SEYDOU" that everyone wanted on their prints.
>
> To have your photo taken was an important event. The person had to be made to look his or her best. Often they became serious, and I think they were also intimidated by the camera. It was a new sensation for them. I always told them to relax more: "OK, look over here, try to smile a little, not too much." In the end they liked it. It took only about ten minutes.[3]

> **A lot of people getting off the train came to me to have their photograph taken on their way to visit the zoo.** —Seydou Keita[4]

Seydou Keita did not record the names of his clients; hence the number in the title *Untitled (Family with Car no. 266)* (pl. 98). Some asked to be photographed in front of the two cars Keita owned in the 1950s, as this family did. Or, rather, most of them did. A sliver of a male presence is evident in the man's hand on the hood of the car. The hint is just enough to let us know he is wearing a light suit, while the women at the center are dressed in a lineup of patterns—polka dots on all three, and wax prints on the two older women. Their faces offer a study in ways to respond to a camera: knit your eyebrows with a slightly wary reserve, stare it down with confidence, or offer youthful eagerness. Buffed and shiny, the car reflects the photographer with his camera, and its slick surface contrasts with the gritty dirt road. Seeing just the hand of a well-dressed gentleman, we can't help wondering who he is and why he set himself apart from the women in the center frame.

> **Close your studio, the government needs a photographer.**
> —Issa Traore, 1962[5]

Seydou Keita was asked to be the official photographer for the Malian government in 1962, a position he held until his retirement in 1977. Tens of thousands of negatives from his independent years of 1948 to 1962 were stored in a large padlocked chest for the better part of three decades. They remained there, largely untouched except for occasional requests—for instance, an American curator, Susan Vogel, picked up three negatives in 1974. After holding them for almost twenty years, in 1991 she placed them in an exhibition in New York entitled *Africa Explores: Twentieth Century African Art*. Displayed as the work of an unknown photographer, they inspired André Magnin, a French curator, to fly to Mali in search of the artist who had taken them. His search was brief because "the Elder Keita" was a well-known photographer. On a third visit, Magnin obtained two hundred negatives from Keita and had them printed for sale to galleries in Paris, London, and San Francisco.[6] This arrangement continues.

Working as a mechanic.   —Seydou Keita, 1995

Acclaim came quickly for Seydou Keita in the 1990s, as his work was featured in exhibitions in Africa, Europe, Japan, and the United States. But he says, "I can see that a lot of people really like my pictures. Ever since my work has been known in your country, I've had a lot of visitors, but I prefer to leave everything up to one person. That way I can live a more peaceful retirement, going regularly to the mosque, looking after the houses I've built and spending some time working as a mechanic, which I really like to do."[7]

Woodstock-in-Bamako.   — Manthia Diawara, 1998

Malick Sidibe was trained in jewelry making at the National School of Arts in Bamako. After graduating, he apprenticed to a photographer in Bamako and by 1962 opened Studio Malick. Venturing from the studio, he became a reporter, following the activities of young people in photographs that gave Bamako a reputation as a center for a world youth culture. Manthia Diawara, one of his subjects, has written about his re-creation of a "Woodstock-in-Bamako," renting a building in the center of the city and dressing right:

> I wore a red cotton-and-polyester shortsleeved shirt with "Keep on Truckin" written on the back of it. Over the shirt I put on my embroidered blue-satin jacket, combining these with my blue bell-bottom trousers and my red clogs from Denmark. When I had added my Venetian-glass necklace, my cowrie-shell juju bracelets, and my dark glasses, not only did I look like Jimi Hendrix—I felt like his reincarnation.... When we arrived the amplifiers were blaring "With a Little Help from My Friends," by Joe Cocker. There were many people who had copied our style—that is, they were dressed like Jimi Hendrix, George Harrison, Richie Havens, Buddy Miles, Sly Stone, Frank Zappa, Alice Cooper and James Brown. . . . Soon Jimi Hendrix's "Voodoo Child" filled the air, and by then we were on top of the world.[8]

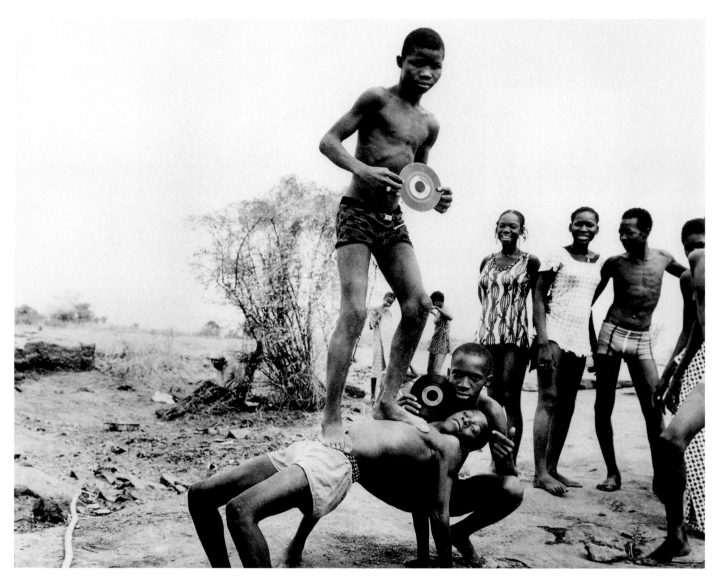

A group of teenagers have left Bamako on a hot summer day for a short drive to the nearby Niger River (pl. 99). Malick Sidibe takes pictures of their fun together: "The guys supply record players, stacks of records, they make tea, they swim and dance in the open air.... I like coming upon the young ones in good spirits, some are tired at the end of the party, some are play-boys or some perform bizarre antics I find interesting." Boys hold records as showpieces in the photograph. Sidibe says records from Europe and America, bought in shops in Bamako, led to fads like "The twist, the jerk, the cha cha cha, the hula-hoop, Cuban music, the first rock," and to "clubs which were named for their idols: the 'Sputnicks,' the 'Wild Cats,' the 'Beatles,' the 'Black Shoes.'"[9] Rock and roll records also promoted a confident defiance of authority. As the teenagers strike their jaunty poses and laugh at each other, they hint at a new rebellious independence that made its mark in the 1960s. Sidibe stopped this form of visual reporting in 1978, but continues to take black-and-white photographs around Bamako.

Pl. 99
Roadside Picnic
Malick Sidibe (b. 1936)
Mali
1976
Gelatin silver print
W. 61 cm (24 in.)
General Acquisitions Fund, 97.36

The advocacy and appreciation for these two Malian photographers voiced by the museum's visitors in 1997 were matched by a new international focus on them. Manthia Diawara contemplated his long association with both men in an article entitled "The 1960s in Bamako: Malick Sidibe and James Brown."[10] From a more distanced stance, Elizabeth Bingham discussed how Seydou Keita operated his studio in Bamako and the ways in which his photographs were received in new contexts, including a fashion shoot for *Harper's Bazaar* in 1997.[11] The study *You Look Beautiful Like That: The Portrait Photographs of Seydou Keita and Malick Sidibe* was recently published.[12]

These photographs entice partly by offering immediate recognition of something not seen enough. Families getting ready to ride the train, teenagers showing off at picnics—they remind us of lives that are hardly exotic, and of people who breathe like you and me.

Notes

1. *400 Men of African Descent,* 1997, by Marita Dingus received the most votes and was acquired in 1998 through the courtesy of the Francine Seders Gallery, Seattle. The display was entitled *Passion for Possession.* Paule Anglim was one of many tolerant dealers who extended loans for the length of the exhibition.

2. Quoted in André Magnin, ed., *Seydou Keita* (Zurich: Scalo Press, 1997). Title quote by Seydou Keita, interview by Alioune Ba, in *In/Sight: African Photographers, 1940 to the Present,* with essays by Okwui Enwezor, Octavio Zaya, Olu Ogube, and Clare Bell (New York: Harry N. Abrams, 1996), 268.

3. Quoted in Magnin, *Seydou Keita.*

4. Ibid.

5. Ibid.

6. The two photographs discussed here were purchased in 1997 from Paule Anglim Gallery in San Francisco.

7. Quoted in Magnin, *Seydou Keita.*

8. Manthia Diawara, *In Search of Africa* (Cambridge: Harvard University Press, 1998), 101–2.

9. Malick Sidibe, interview with André Magnin, in *Malick Sidibe: Bamako 1962–1976* (Paris: Fondation Cartier pour l'Art Contemporain, 1995).

10. Manthia Diawara, "The 1960s in Bamako: Malick Sidibe and James Brown," no. 11, Paper Series on the Arts, Culture and Society from the Andy Warhol Foundation for the Visual Arts, Pittsburgh, 2001.

11. Elizabeth Bingham, "Issues of Authorship in the Portrait Photographs of Seydou Keita," *African Arts,* spring 1999.

12. Michelle Lamuniere, *You Look Beautiful Like That: The Portrait Photographs of Seydou Keita and Malick Sidibe* (Cambridge: Harvard University Art Museums, 2001).

Collecting Beads and Wishes for the Future: Ornaments for a Maasai Bride

How museums collect, not what they collect, guided the last gathering of African art to enter the Seattle Art Museum's holdings in the twentieth century. The acquisition involved many adjustments, all suggested by an intern who helps redefine collecting to suit two cultural agendas.

This culture has to end.   —Kenyan government officials, 1999

The exchange began when I was invited to a meeting of archaeologists to hear a talk by Kakuta Ole Maimai Hamisi, a Maasai studying at a nearby college. It wasn't the usual student talk. Hamisi spoke as if he was two people at once—a warrior and an ethnographer, able to videotape his own initiation and critique its chance for survival at the same time. He described living in a country where government officials proclaim of the Maasai, "This culture has to end."[1] He outlined conflicts such as elders trying to keep children from going away to city schools, and of the need for Maasai to establish their own schools. When Hamisi decided a Western education was necessary, his father sold cattle to send him to college.

In preparing for his internship at the museum, I followed the standard plan of study and assembled a stack of publications about the Maasai and Maasai art. Hamisi's reviews of the publications were rarely positive. The survey revealed that the Maasai have been extensively photographed but not interviewed. Page after page of glossy photographs of even intimate aspects of Maasai life pushed Hamisi to the limit of his tolerance. We went through academic journals to seek more thorough texts, and Hamisi wondered out loud how many Maasai had ever known of such studies. He said though it might be hard to believe, he was one of the few. Out of a family of thirty-seven uncles and eight brothers, he was the only person to learn English and German, and travel to discover what outsiders said about his culture.

A stroll in the Serengeti   —Susan Minot, 1998

In contrast, the numbers of tourists who visit Maasailand are staggering. Millions have taken safaris to Kenya and Tanzania since the 1970s, and accounts of these   Pl. 107

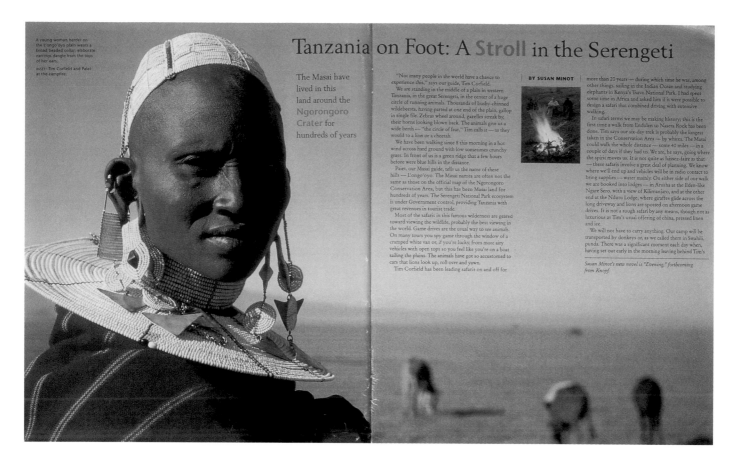

Fig. 82. "Tanzania on Foot: A Stroll in the Serengeti," *New York Times* (1998).

journeys often laud the experience. After working with Hamisi, however, articles like "Tanzania on Foot: A Stroll in the Serengeti," by a novelist writing for the *New York Times,* strike me differently.[2] It recounts the experience of walking across the Serengeti with two guides, one British who is quoted and a Maasai escort named Paiet— "a bony-shouldered beautiful man with a gap tooth"—who isn't. During the walk, they "pass women in wide collared beaded necklaces triangular earrings, aluminum coils, small shaved heads" (fig. 82), but the writer doesn't talk to them. After the walk is over, a "magnificent game drive" sums up the journey as they see "wildebeests, eland, ostriches, gazelles, jackals, zebras, hyenas, plovers, yellow-throated sand grouse, Egyptian geese, bateleur eagles, sacred ibises, larks." Despite the safari being a walk through Maasailand, it is striking how little part the Maasai play. They remain largely unknown, watching tourists pass by, while the Westerners focus their attention on carefully identified species of animals—a pattern of avoidance that has become a twentieth-century habit.

As the next step in the internship, a trip into the museum's storage revealed a collection that is documented in the same way: photographs of the people wearing or carrying the objects are available, but their names and comments are not recorded. Determining the origin of this evasion became my concern. How did the safari system begin and why are Maasai so silent about it? The search for an answer led me to accounts of the first European to record his journey across Maasailand, and the first Maasai to travel to Europe and the United States.

Sixty thousand strings had to be made up.   —Joseph Thomson, 1883

Joseph Thomson, a twenty-nine-year-old Scotsman, rode into Maasai lands on a donkey at the head of a small regiment under the auspices of the British Royal Geographic Society. In March 1883, he set off with 113 porters carrying nearly four tons of wire coils, beads, bolts of cloth, ammunition, food, instruments, and supplies. By the end of March, he had reached Taveta, near Mount Kilamanjaro, the stopping place for caravans to Maasailand. Hearing about Maasai preferences, Thomson realized, "The whole of my beads had to be restrung into the regulation lengths of the Masai country. Unless in this form, they would not be accepted.... 60,000 strings had to be made up."[3] Thomson spent over two weeks stringing beads, and finished just as two thousand Maasai were headed straight toward his regiment. "[We] set our eyes on the dreaded warriors that had so long been the subject of my waking dreams, and I could not but involuntarily exclaim, 'What splendid fellows!'" As one warrior began speaking, Thomson recorded the effect: "With profound astonishment I watched this son of the desert as he stood before me, speaking with a natural fluency and grace, a certain sense of the gravity and importance of his position, and a dignity of attitude beyond all praise."[4]

On May 3, Thomson finally entered a vast treeless plain at six thousand feet to confront lines of cattle, smoke from kraals, and a group of Maasai *moran* (warrior) demanding entry fees. The *moran*s laid aside their swords and shields while porters threw beads and cloth near the Maasai before sprinting out of the way. Thomson realized he was in trouble as load after load of his carefully strung beads disappeared and the *moran*s became "overly inquisitive." The next day, a report that the Maasai were planning a dreaded dawn attack prompted his hasty retreat to the coast. Walking more than thirty miles a day, Thomson regrouped after learning that one of his interpreters had invented the threat of attack. Allying himself with a Swahili trader named Juma Kimameta, Thomson was back in Maasailand by August 11.

Early on, Thomson nearly set off a riot when several Maasai women complained that he used a camera to bewitch them. Trying to find new ways to interact and avoid conflict, Thomson began to cultivate an impression that he was a white *laibon* (spiritual leader) by experimenting with odd behavior. He used intricate instruments with exaggerated drama; he prescribed Eno's salts (an effervescent foaming drink); he danced a Scottish jig; and he let out screams of convulsive laughter. *Moran*s continued to visit him, invading his privacy ever more boldly.

Thomson pushed on to reach Mount Kenya, but learned that his presence wouldn't be tolerated much longer. In the dogged seven-month journey back to Mombasa, he was gored by a wounded buffalo, battled dysentery, slipped into comas, and traveled through famine-stricken territories. Overall, he had walked three thousand miles in fourteen months. Thomson's book, *Through Masailand,* testifies to his tenacity and infatuation with exploration. Thomson hiked for the next seven years through other parts of Africa, until he died at age thirty-seven in 1895. His final words were said to be, "If I were strong enough to put my clothes on and walk a hundred yards, I would go to Africa yet!"

Thomson's walking expedition is remembered in many forms. His books and speeches to the Royal Geographic Society in London are well-known sources on the history of East Africa. One of the animals most often seen on safari bears his name: the Thomson gazelle. In naming the Aberderes mountain range, he marked the Kenyan map with a Scottish term. Above all, he is known for his assessment of the Maasai: "A more remarkable and unique race does not exist on the continent of Africa. Indeed I might safely say in the two hemispheres.... They are the most magnificently modeled savages I have ever seen or read of."[5]

The greatest menace of East Africa.   –Colonel Hall, 1893

In the aftermath of Thomson's portrayal of their mythic stance (and his own heroism), the Maasai were hit by "The Disaster." Humans fell to epidemics of small pox, while rinderpest and pleuropneumonia severely depleted their herds of cattle. Ruinous droughts weakened them all. Incursions by raiders from neighboring Kamba, Kikuyu, and Kalenjin worsened the disorder. In 1891, a mortality rate as high as ninety percent crippled the herds, and while the Maasai were adapting to this loss, British officers moved in to "introduce order into blank, uninteresting, brutal barbarism."[6] Within just a few years, the mythic Maasai who had so entranced Joseph Thomson were recast as "the greatest menace of East Africa."[7]

The primary agents of this change in perception were British settlers who wanted to transform the immense rolling hills of the highlands into an agricultural heartland. When Sir Charles Eliot became governor of the East Africa protectorate in 1900, he initiated the first wave of change. A railroad opened in 1901 and began transporting settlers. Eliot argued that the Maasai inhabited more land than they needed and should be moved aside so that "superior races" could develop it. In 1902, a Land Acquisition Order cleared the way for the most fertile lands in Kenya to be turned over to immigrants from Britain, Canada, Australia, and South Africa. Their highlands property is situated in an area shaped like a fist in the center of Kenya. A treaty gave the Maasai two areas that were to remain theirs so long as they "shall exist as a race." In 1904, Maasai were removed from their grazing grounds in the central Rift valley and relegated to two areas: the Laikpia plateau and the Southern Rift near the border of the German colonial holdings.

The highlands of East Africa . . . a winter home for aristocrats.

–Advertising campaign, 1910

The Maasai moved as white settlers took over the "white highlands." One of the best-known settlers was Lord Delamere, who arrived from Cheshire, England, to establish a 100,000-acre ranch. At first, he encouraged a few Maasai to stay on the ranch and assist him in experiments with livestock. Relying on their knowledge of cattle breeding, he became their advocate in the land battles with the British. Once the success of his ranch was assured, however, his loyalties switched. Lord Delamere became the settlers' advocate, and the Uganda railway commenced advertising trips to "the highlands of East Africa as a winter home for aristocrats."[8]

The low culture of many of the savage tribes.
—Theodore Roosevelt, 1910

Lured not by settlement but by safari, an ex-president of the United States arrived in Kenya to lead an expedition for the Smithsonian Institution in 1909. Theodore Roosevelt set a high standard for flamboyant travel and bolstered the idea of the safari when he marched for ten months through Kenya with five hundred porters, his son Kermit, and a team of scientists (fig. 83). Their weapons were said to never stop smoking, as 512 animals were killed. Roosevelt himself shot more than 296, including nine lions, eight elephants, thirteen rhinoceros, and six buffalo. One critic said the volume of killing bordered on slaughter and deplored "the devastation that is done in the name of or on behalf of museums. Do those nine white rhinoceros ever cause ex-President Roosevelt a pang of conscience or a restless night? I venture to hope so."[9]

Despite such objections, Roosevelt's visit spotlighted the safari and the museum expedition as a manner of collecting. Within the year, an expedition from the American Museum of Natural History in New York was gathering specimens, including the enormous elephant family that still greets visitors in the central lobby. Roosevelt's *African Game Trails,* which became a best-seller in 1910, established wild animals as the central attraction for a visit to East Africa—a place to experience nature but not culture. "The teeming multitudes of wild creatures, . . . and the low culture of many of the savage tribes, especially of the hunting tribes, substantially reproduces the conditions of life in Europe as it was led by our ancestors ages before the dawn of anything that could be called civilization."[10]

While the earliest Europeans and Americans to visit Maasailand are quite well documented, their counterparts are largely unknown. The first Maasai to visit Europe is only briefly mentioned in texts. One Maasai was taken to Germany by Carl Hagenbeck, an entrepreneur who originally displayed wild animals and later presented ethnographic shows called *Volkerschau,* which proliferated after 1874.[11] Classified as *Naturvolker* (natural peoples), his ethnographic natives were exhibited behind bars or wire fences in zoos, fairgrounds, and public parks. No specific accounts of this Maasai in Europe are known. The first Maasai to come to the United States was Molonket Olokorinya ole Sempele, who sold cattle to purchase his fare with the intent of gaining a higher education. In 1909, he arrived and was placed in an African American Bible institute in the South.[12] After learning about lynchings and feeling the effects of intense racial prejudice, he returned to Kenya and spoke of white Americans' treatment of black people. "He would tell how white children took hold of a black doll, painted it up with thick white lips and white eyes to look like a golly wog, and then threw sticks and stones until it was broken."[13] For the next forty years, friends said he

Fig. 83. "Mr. Roosevelt and One of His Big Lions," from Theodore Roosevelt, *African Game Trails: An Account of the African Wanderings of an American Hunter-Naturalist* (1909).

would recall such memories, especially when British missionaries seemed to trivialize what an African had been saying.

Maasai artifacts entered museums during this era. The initial illustration of African objects in the British Museum's *Handbook to the Ethnographical Collections* of 1910 is a lineup of shields and spears from all over the continent (fig. 84).[14] A Maasai spear leads the lineup. Spears fanning around a central shield became a classic format, repeating the heraldic displays of the European past. This arrangement of shields and spears underlined what separated the foreign from the native warrior: their choice of weapons. Spears were no match for the new class of arms that the European and American soldier and sportsman carried. Theodore Roosevelt spoke of the beauty of his weapon, a double-barreled elephant rifle, one of many specialized rifles he carried with him on safari. The British became nearly invincible in battle when the automatic rifle was invented. A Maasai spear on display in 1910 was an outdated weapon of the past, overwhelmed by the superior new technology of the colonial enterprise.

Fig. 84. "Types of African Spears," from British Museum, *Handbook to the Ethnographical Collections* (1910).

Maasai soon faced pressure to move even farther from their homelands. White highland settlers stirred up dissent over the lands allocated to them in the 1904 treaty. By 1911, a new treaty was being drawn up. The majority of Maasai felt that armed resistance would be hopeless; instead, many decided to fight the move in the courts. This initial attempt by people in East Africa to protect their rights through the political process failed. The colonial authorities moved the Maasai farther south into a new reserve and then avoided them as much as possible from that time on. An armed uprising by *morans* in 1918 prompted the British to ban their activities in 1921. The next year was the last active rebellion before the Maasai cut off contact with British authorities. Decades of indirect rule allowed the highlands to be dedicated to the experience of the 1920s and 1930s described in Karen Blixen's *Out of Africa*. The Maasai were relegated to the role of exotic "smocked yokel":

> Again the enchanting contradictions of Kenya life; a baronial hall straight from Queen Victoria's Scottish Highlands—an open fire of logs and peat with carved-stone chimney piece, heads of game, the portraits of prize cattle, guns, golf-clubs, fishing-tackle, and folded newspapers—sherry is brought in, but instead of a waist-coated British footman, a bare-footed Kikuyu boy in white gown and jacket. A typical English meadow of deep grass; model cow-sheds in the background; a pedigree Ayrshire bull scratching his back on the gatepost; but, instead of rabbits, a company of monkeys scatter away at our approach; and, instead of a smocked yokel, a Masai herdsman draped in a blanket, his hair plaited into a dozen dyed pigtails.[15]

Spartan, Aristocratic warriors, scornful of civilization.

—*National Geographic Magazine*, 1954

Fig. 85. "Hunt Council: Masai Spearmen Plot a Lion's Death," from *National Geographic Magazine* (1954).

The Maasai became known as idealized warriors who defied civilization. An expedition from the American Museum of Natural History contributed a report to *National Geographic Magazine* in October 1954 with this portrayal of the Maasai role:

Masai, once terrors of East Africa, live today on a vast reserve....

These spartan, Aristocratic warriors, scornful of civilization, fearlessly hunt big game with spears and swords [fig. 85]....

Virile warriors in earrings and hair braids kindle a fire with iron age tools....

Nor has the white man offered much in a material way that attracts them. The only concessions I observed were occasional incongruous aluminum pots; woolen blankets...calicos....

They are a temperamental, sullen, difficult, and diffident people. The haughty moran eyes the visitor and his entourage with disdain. Beneath the forbidding surface of the Masai, however, lie substrata of warmth, humor, fidelity and integrity. This deeper character is discovered only through prolonged and rather intimate association. The casual visitor never sees it.[16]

Still alive is Blixen's romantic vision of a "pith helmet and lace" lifestyle that flourishes amid safely restricted aristocratic warriors.[17] The fantasy of a thrilling safari adventure is evoked in tourist brochures and travel writing. So compelling is the lure of seeing the "wild kingdom" in relative luxury that an entire industry has sprung up. Kilaguni was the site of the first game-park lodge to provide safari service in 1962. Airlines began transporting visitors in the 1960s, and tourism exploded in the 1970s. Big game hunting was accommodated until a government decree banned it in 1977. Safaris quickly switched to a photographic hunt, as the number of tourists rose to a million yearly by 1990. Tourists often see Maasai as photogenic subjects and sellers of souvenirs, but lack avenues for any further association. This suits the Kenyan and Tanzanian governments; they enforce laws against Maasai practices and want access to their lands, but thrive off permits sold to tourists who come to photograph the natives.

> **I looked as carefully as I could, without making them nervous, to see what I might want to bargain for.** —Katherine White, 1978[18]

Katherine White took her three sons on a photographic safari in 1978 on what was to be her last trip to Africa. Her journal entries for the trip begin with an inventory of the 120 objects she brought back, and then follow with a daily account of her search for the right object to purchase. White made note of every belt, calabash, and staff that caught her eye. As her accounts underline, the art was extremely personal, often literally attached to its owner. Many whom she approached wouldn't sell what they were wearing, but a few did:

> Yesterday afternoon, as we were entering the Masai Mara Reserve, some old highly decorated Masai ladies approached the car with things to sell. New necklaces of gaudy beads, trinkets, calabashes. I bought two silver wound-wire earrings on an old cord. I thought they had some wear. Then a marvelous old lady had some unique earrings standing from the tops of her ears. I couldn't figure them out. Slim, dark, some kind of wood, from a thorn tree perhaps. She was reluctant to sell them, but she finally did, for only 5 shillings.
>
> Among others was a young *moran* who wanted money for posing. He was not quite beautiful enough. All his jewelry was new, and not enough. He kept standing about, leaning on his spear, and looking superb. Those long legs, those easy swaying lines, that Egyptian-like head.
>
> We drove downtown to look. A marvelous old man with a white feather headdress, ostrich plumes and one of those woven brass wire lip plugs [fig. 86]. I was fascinated to see how they were worn. I asked for a photograph, the lip plug and a large ring he had on a thumb. We struck a bargain for 20 shillings [$2.25]. And then he tried to remove the plug. It got so heart-rending, I couldn't watch. It was grown in. Quite a crowd collected. We waited and waited. We even got 10 shillings back. The poor old man was frantic. Finally it was delivered to me, and I wasn't sure I could touch it. I felt I had part of that old man's anatomy in my hand. It was extremely worn.
>
> We got a soft drink in town at one of the bars. We were the odd ones, but it seemed peculiar to be shoulder to shoulder with one of these "authentic" natives in full regalia. The fatted hair, the sprouting earrings, the jewelry, the loincloth, knife, and cloak. The dirty feet in dusty sandals. The ankle rings.[19]

A collection of art from East Africa was waiting in storage when Kakuta Ole Maimai Hamisi arrived at the museum. The limits of the story it told were clear: Katherine White had roughly noted where she bought items, but hadn't asked the owners about the art. It wasn't common to do so, given the invisible wall between tourists and the people they saw while on safari. Although tourists observe this wall, anthropologists have undertaken studies of Maasai culture; the first in-depth study of Maasai art appeared in 1987.[20] And yet the pages written about, and the photographs taken of, the Maasai by European and Americans still far outweigh those written by Maasai.[21] Similarly, the number of Maasai who visit or study in the United States remains low in comparison to the million Americans who visit Maasailand each year.

What if Maasai were to decide what Maasai art belongs in the museum? —Kakuta Hamisi, 1999

At the end of his internship, Hamisi presented a proposal to the museum's Committee on Collections asking for funds to acquire Maasai art. It was the first time the committee considered an abstract proposal—there was nothing to evaluate but a possibility, and Hamisi could not state a price for the art. In his home community, far from the major tourist pathways, the idea of selling art is not common. Neither is a cash economy prevalent in a region where cattle are still the primary measure of wealth and exchange. Even the idea of a museum is not familiar. Hamisi's account of the formation of the Maasai collection reveals how the museum's request turned into a community project that amazed everyone involved:

When the money from the museum came, it was a surprise in my bank account. I called a meeting of the community to talk. I started by asking, "What have we been talking about that can benefit us all?" I talked about how medical services, schools, and water projects have all been promised by the government and missionaries, but the promises haven't been fulfilled.

Part of what the community was remembering was this past of forgotten projects and how hard a time I had in getting my education. When I wanted to come to the United States to study, a member of parliament who knew the Hamisi name and knew of my father's disagreement with politics (he burns his voting cards) had sent a letter to the U.S. Embassy telling them not to issue me a visa. He said that sending a Maasai man was not a good idea because they would develop diseases when they left the country, or they would disappear. I had to go to the U.S. Ambassador myself and ask her to issue one. She went against the wishes of this man of parliament and gave me the visa.

So, when I talked with the community, I said, "Remember when I was finding the passport and visa? The MP said I would disappear or bring back disease. Here I am and this is the disease I will bring—a school that has been promised but never appears." This was well received with much respect and welcome.

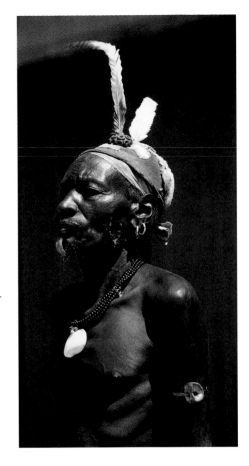

Fig. 86. Elder, Lodwar, Kenya, 1978.

I told them that in return there was a museum that would like some Maasai things. I read a list I had made up, and some of the women were shocked that I knew about their ornaments. And with the *mankala* board and donkey bags—people had forgotten about some of these things. I told them I didn't want to collect them myself or collect them from any particular person, but wanted to do something that would benefit them all. That every child from any family would be able to go to the school. We just need to have things ready when I go back in January. While you are collecting, Samuel [the school-teacher] and I will go to buy materials for the school. I didn't want them to see me as the collector, but left it up to them to decide what would come. We did have problems. Forty or so women who are now Christian said they didn't want to give anyone devil objects, related to devil worship, but they did want

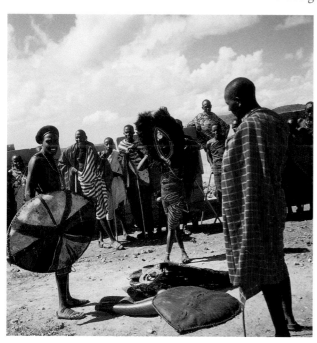

Fig. 87. Maasai collection being presented to Kakuta Hamisi by members of the Kaputiei section, 1999.

their children to go to school. Others pressured them to contribute and they did bring a calabash. All along, Samuel and I talked about how to keep this from being an issue that created individualism or became destructive for the community. During this time, the *laibon* [spiritual leader, prophet and healer] came to visit. This doesn't happen often. While he visited, women sang Christian songs to protest his visit. He said he wouldn't confront them, that "those are little things."

The community was pleased with the efforts. We didn't pay ourselves, only the architecture guy. He gave me a list of materials to make the school and we went to get them in a Kamba [neighboring peoples] town. The whole way was very powerful and emotional. We had to go to Loitokitok during rainy season. The Kamba store was surprised to see Maasai buying things for building. It hasn't ever happened before. They gave us a truck to carry things back, but it was going over a poor road and it took five days to return. We had to get the community to help by collecting rocks to make a bridge across a river that covered the road. Then they collected rocks to make the floor level. The *moran*s made bricks and joked about how "we look like Kamba people now." All the generations were there helping. It was a big group process to lift the roof. The school got built. We went and got blackboards, textbooks, pens, and pencils. There are sixty kids now, three teachers, and more kids coming. Since I left, Samuel has written that people have heard about the school and are sending children to live nearby. We did what the church and government haven't done.

For the collecting part, I did have to explain what the museum was. I called it a place where *wazungu* [white people] keep things from all over the world. That I had been to this place in Seattle where they already had some Maasai things. "In America? What Maasai would take them there?" they wanted to know. This is a place where tourists don't stop, so no one knows how that happens. I told them about how an American woman had come and gotten some things.

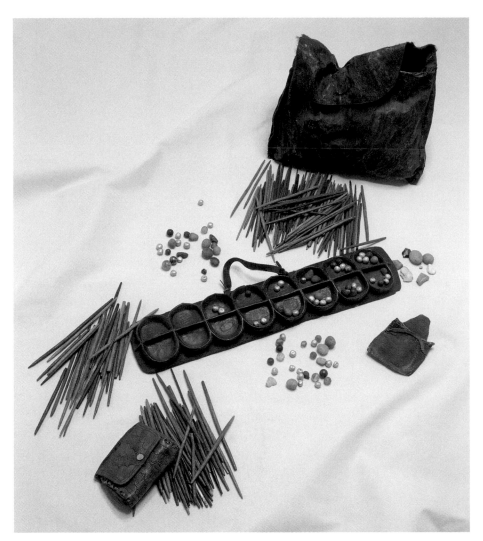

Pl. 100
Gameboard *(enkeshui)*, **with leather bags**
(olbene loo-inkeek), counters *(isoito le enkeshui)*,
and counting sticks *(inkeek e-nkeshui)*
Merrueshi community, Maasai, Kenya
Collected 1999
Wood, rubber, leather, calfskin, rock, aluminum, glass
L. (gameboard) 61 cm (24 in.)
General Acquisitions Fund, 2000.2.1–.5

When people brought things for the museum, we did a ceremony. We cooked tea, rice, and goats and talked about how everything had been given with open hearts. My father helped to bless the whole project. This little sum did so much. But it seems like it was matched many times by people bringing their effort to it. It's a matter of trust. I think my community was shocked, confused, and amazed by what we did.

The Maasai collection now housed in the museum contains a range of art that a community chose to send to Seattle. For each object, the owner's name is noted and his or her words about the transaction are recorded on videotape (fig. 87). This thorough documentation is largely the result of Hamisi's coordination. Some of the items have seen so much use that they immediately convey a sense of the owner's long possession of them. A gameboard, worn smooth, is accompanied by two leather bags: one filled with round counters made of aluminum and glass was given to a Maasai man by a colonial officer (pl. 100); the second bag is filled with myriad small sticks used to count hundreds of game animals over many years. A donkey bag, calabashes, and a length of fence are reminders of the once completely portable, pastoral

Fig. 88. Nasha ene Sipoi modeling bridal costume now in the collection of the Seattle Art Museum, 1999.

nature of Maasai life. Most of the objects illustrate that Maasai art reaches its peak of expression in ornaments. Personal adornment is worn as ensembles—that of a young warrior includes a spear, shield, ostrich feather headdress, necklaces, shoulder strap, armband, wristband, thighband, and ankleband. An elder's flywhisk, authority staff, and snuff bottle are the basic ornaments that hold importance in later life.

You know from whence you come but not where you are going.

—Maasai saying

Artistic brilliance is reserved for the person who is the most vulnerable. A bride as she prepares to leave home is adorned in jewelry of an exacting order. Twenty different women of the Merrueshi community of the Irkaputiei section of Maasai territory contributed twenty pieces to complete a vision of the bride as she sets out on the long journey to her bridegroom's homestead (fig. 88). Their selections show the color preferences, patterns, material choices, and specific sequence that a Maasai bride is required to wear. This is the showcase for the women's talents as beadwork-ers and their sense of collaboration. A bride's costume is a collection of beadwork, stories, and wishes for the future.

A young girl between ten and sixteen is told she is leaving childhood by her father on the night before her departure. He blesses her and advises her in the duties of a good wife. The next day her female relatives dress her with careful attention to each and every item of clothing. One by one, layers of her costume are added and fitted. She carries little with her—a collection of beads and a milk calabash tied onto her back. The calabash expresses a symbolic wish that her new family will provide her with milk for the rest of her life. As a new bride, she faces an unknown future. She may cry and walk very slowly, or be dragged away from her mother's house in a dramatic separation from her family.

Wearing her full bridal apparel, she walks all the way to her new home with her husband and his best man. She is expected to be reluctant, and to stop suddenly and refuse to budge when the final destination is in view. The bridegroom's female relatives rush out to greet her, first with teasing and mocking comments, but then with enticements and a feast when she finally enters her husband's homestead. The milk calabash is taken from her back, and the milk inside becomes her gift to the children of her new family. She sits all day while children and relatives come to meet her and examine her layers of ornaments.

There is so much to explain that we don't even know how to begin.

—Kakuta Hamisi, 1999

Hamisi affirms that women do the beadwork. Men devote all their efforts to tending cattle, sent from heaven to allow a perfect life for the Maasai. Chosen to care for these divine creatures, Maasai men are not to pollute themselves with other efforts. The grass that cattle eat is produced by God-given rain and is a holy sign. But anyone who practices agriculture, kills and eats wild animals, or works metal is tainted by handling the products of the earth. Men are not to form anything, but women form children, build homes, and create ornaments.

Maasai women in the twentieth century seized upon the artistic potential of beads provided by outsiders. In the nineteenth century, ornaments were largely made of iron, copper, and brass wire shaped by blacksmiths. Ornaments woven of fresh leaves and grasses added a layer of perfume. By 1902, massive quantities of small, durable, multicolored beads were being traded along the East African coast. As Maasai women gained access to beads through inland trade, they began to create patterns with them. Eventually, women made all Maasai ornaments, rendering obsolete the iron ornaments forged by blacksmiths of the past. What had been heavy wire spirals became light supports for colorful beads applied much like paint on canvas.

Color preferences are clear: white, blue, red, green, and orange. Yellow and black are secondary and mediate the primary colors. Patterns are built of main colors and carefully aligned accents that keep ornaments lively. Hamisi points out examples such as a necklace of primary blues and red, which "would be boring" without the two white strands that separate the primaries (pl. 101). Certain layers are compulsory, like the small blue necklace that is always worn on top; it has red and white beads on the inside and orange on the outside (pl. 102). High contrast is achieved by setting strong colors (red, blue, black) against weak (orange, green, yellow, white). Some patterns have symbolic importance. In a medallion-style necklace, the round shape signifies the universe, and the button in the middle represents the moon (pl. 103). According to Hamisi, young girls say this ornament is "like the moon that will light up the night when I need to find my warrior."

Women work closely together to create an assembly like the group of twenty ornaments for the bride, choosing pattern after pattern that declares which of the sixteen sections of Maasai territory is her home. Just a glance at an earflap can indicate where a women is from, and a trained eye can perhaps detect precisely who

Pl. 101
Bull necklace *(norkiteng)*
Nalepo ene Matinti
Kaputiei section, Merrueshi community, Maasai, Kenya
Collected 1999
Wire, glass beads, plastic
Diam. 34.3 cm (13½ in.)
General Acquisitions Fund, 2000.12.2

Pl. 102
Necklace *(emankeki kiti pus)*
Noolarami ene Solonka
Kaputiei section, Merrueshi community, Maasai, Kenya
Collected 1999
Wire, glass beads, plastic
Diam. 18.4 cm (7¼ in.)
General Acquisitions Fund, 2000.12.7

Pl. 103
Medallion-style necklace *(orkamishina)*
Kumolasho ene Kenedi
Kaputiei section, Merrueshi community, Maasai, Kenya
Collected 1999
Leather, glass beads, button
Diam. (medallion) 8.9 cm (3½ in.)
General Acquisitions Fund, 2000.12.12

Pl. 104
Earflap *(inchonito oo nkiyaa)*
Ngoto Saitoti ene Moipei
Kaputiei section, Merrueshi community, Maasai, Kenya
Collected 1999
Cowhide, glass beads, sisal twine, metal
L. 17.78 cm (7 in.)
General Acquisitions Fund, 2000.12.9.1–.2

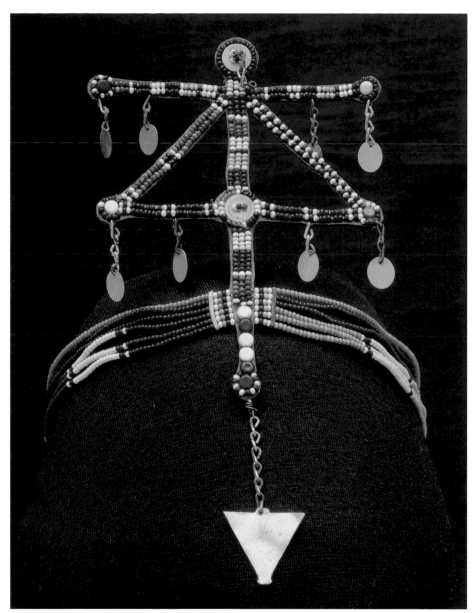

Pl. 105

Bride's headdress *(enkishili)*
Ngoto Moris
Kaputiei section, Merrueshi community, Maasai, Kenya
Collected 1999
Glass beads, wire, plastic, metal
H. 14.8 cm (5⅞ in.)
General Acquisitions Fund, 2000.12.13

made it for her (pl. 104). Each section maintains its repertoire of patterns, and each generation is challenged to invent a distinctive new ornament. In this group, the triangle pattern representing an antennae is the latest design, reflecting the fact that many Maasai are beginning to use radios on a regular basis (pl. 105). Its presentation was accompanied by sung words from the youngest of the women: "I have antennae to call the warriors from far distances."

> Wives, children, and livestock bring visual returns every day.
>
> —Maasai saying

Considerable cost and effort go into a bride's ornaments. One necklace in this group is named the bull, because the family must sell a "bull" to purchase enough beads to complete it. When preparations for a wedding are underway, a mother and father will usually travel together to Nairobi to purchase beads. Wealth put in the

Pl. 106
Wristlets *(inkipilat oo nkaik)*
Noolarami ene Solonka
Kaputiei section, Merrueshi community, Maasai, Kenya
Collected 1999
Glass beads, plastic
Each: H. 10.8 cm (4¼ in.)
General Acquisitions Fund, 2000.12.15.1–.2

Pl. 107
Assembly of necklaces
Kaputiei section, Merrueshi community, Maasai, Kenya
Collected 1999
Glass beads, plastic, metal
Diam. (largest): 34.3 cm (13½ in.)
From bottom: Bull necklace *(norkiteng)*; Bull necklace
(emankeki pus); Pattern necklace *(emankeki oo muatat)*;
Blue and red necklace *(enkado arass)*; Small pattern
necklace *(emankeki kiti oo muatat)*; Small blue necklace
(emankeki kiti pus)
General Acquisition Fund, 2000.12.2–.7

bank is not seen, whereas an investment in ornaments yields daily visual rewards. Upon returning from the shopping trip, the family is approached by women of the community who offer their beading services. Maasai women show varying enthusiasm for beading—some are tight perfectionists (pl. 106) and others are less so, but the push to exchange beading talents is constant. The bride herself creates nothing for her ensemble, but waits to receive layers from women in the community who decide among themselves which ornament will be made by which woman. Men are also given ornaments by women who favor them, and the layers of ornaments a young *moran* wears show how popular he is with the women around him. In this way, women's art has the potential to identify not only your origin but your standing. As Hamisi says, "The more jewelry you have, the more it shows how special you are and how differently you need to be treated." A collection of ornaments is also a collection of compliments from other people (pl. 107).

Maasai culture hasn't ended, despite a full century of insistence that it must. After a century of little exchange, there is now a start with the Merrueshi community and their new notion of what collecting entails. Kakuta Hamisi is fulfilling the role of an ethographer-writer who intends to make sure that children are not "taught to see the world of the Maasai as a simple mind culture. This is the common argument. There are two different worlds—either school or Maasai, either hold a pen or hold a spear. They are two different worlds and they can't be combined because one is outdated and the other is updated." As places where people and their collections do meet and combine, museums provide a forum for reviewing notions of value and wishes for the future.

Notes

1. Kakuta Ole Maimai Hamisi, conversations with author, 1999. Subsequent quotations from conversations with author, partially videotaped and all transcribed, June 1999 to May 2000, and from collection notes prepared by Hamisi and entered in the object files.

2. Susan Minot, "The Sophisticated Traveler," *New York Times,* September 1998.

3. Joseph Thomson, *Through Maisailand* (London: Cass, 1885).

4. Ibid.

5. Ibid.

6. Quoted from a British officer's letter, 1890, cited in Richard Waller, "The Maasai and the British 1895–1905: The Origins of an Alliance," *Journal of African History* 17, no. 4 (1976), 538. Waller provides the estimated mortality rate (p. 530).

7. Ibid.

8. Mohamed Amin, James Eames, and Deborah Appleton, eds., *Insight Guides: Kenya* (Boston: Houghton Mifflin Co., 1993), 56.

9. Report by Cransworth in Charles Miller, *Lunatic Express* (New York: Macmillan, 1971).

10. Theodore Roosevelt, *African Game Trails: An Account of the Wanderings of an American Hunter-Naturalist* (New York: Syndicate Publishing, 1909–10), 2.

11. Hilde Thode-Arora, *Pfenning um die Welt: Die hagenbeckschen Voelkerschauen* (Frankfurt: Campus, 1989).

12. The school was the Boydton Academic and Bible Institute, Virginia.

13. J. T. Mpaayei, personal communication to Kenneth King, cited in "The Kenya Maasai and the Protest Phenomenon, 1900–1960," *Journal of African History* 12, no. 1 (1971), 117–37.

14. British Museum, *Handbook to the Ethnographical Collections* (London, 1910), 187.

15. Isak Dinesen [Karen Blixen], *Out of Africa* (New York: Random House, 1937).

16. Edgar Monsanto Queeny, "Spearing Lions with Africa's Masai," *National Geographic Magazine,* October 1954, 487–95.

17. Phrase from lecture by Angela Gilliam, Seattle Art Museum, 1995.

18. Katherine White Journals, Seattle Art Museum.

19. Ibid. This encounter was with a Turkana elder, but the episode reveals the degree of personal involvement with this art form so well that it is included here.

20. Donna Rey Klumpp, "Maasai Art and Society: Age and Sex, Time and Space, Cash and Cattle" (Ph.D. diss., Columbia University, 1987).

21. Tepilit Ole Saitoti, *Maasai* (New York: Harry N. Abrams, 1980).

Appendix: Sande Society Stories

The following transcribed narratives are reprinted from Donald Cosentino, *De°ant Maids and Stubborn Farmers: Tradition and Invention in Mende Story Performance* (Cambridge: Cambridge University Press, 1982), 164–79. See above, "Beauty Stripped of Human Flaws: Sowei Masks."

1. A Defiant Maid Marries a Stranger

Date: September 19, 1973
Time: About 8:30 P.M.
Place: Verandah of the Samba compound, Njɛi Woma quarter of Mattru,
                 Tikonko Chiefdom, Southern Province, Sierra Leone
Performer: Hannah Samba, a widow about 50 years old, a farmer
Audience: Three adult women, one young man and three children

HANNAH: *Dɔmɛi ɔɔ Dɔmɛisia.*
AUDIENCE: *Sa Kɔndɛ.*
HANNAH: Behold this girl from long ago, she was a great fornicator. She continued fornicating for a long time, then they initiated the Sande society in the town. Spirits came from the big forest; they came to this dancing place. One of the spirits was named Kpana. When that spirit came, he spoke words of love to her. She accepted these words of love spoken to her, but she said nothing of it to her parents. The spirits slept the night, then at daybreak they begged leave to go. They said, 'we are going tomorrow.'

She and her companions (they were five) went with these fellows; they accompanied them. Now they went accompanying them. Then their lovers said to them, "My dears, go back. Our destination is not pleasant." For that reason they said, "Go back!" Then they returned, those four, and she alone remained. Then her lover said to her, "Yombo go back!"

She replied, 'Let's go there.'

He said, 'My destination is not pleasant, for that reason, go back!'

'*Koo*,' she said, 'Kpana, your dying place is my dwelling place. No matter where you go, I must go!'

She begged him a long time. He gave her a hundred pounds. 'Oh,' she said, "I'll go for sure now.' She said, 'Even if you gave me three hundred pounds, I'd follow you wherever you go.'

So he said, 'All right.'

As they were going, this Kpana … all these things he had, these handsome features … behold, he was a Big Thing! His human features, all those features he had borrowed, they were finished. As they reached a place, he would go to visit that person and return his own handsome feature. As they reached another place, he would visit that person and return his own handsome feature. So he changed back into a spirit. Then they reached deep into his own forest.

Before they arrived at his own place, while that fellow was changing himself, a great fear came over her, but there was nothing to be done about it because they had gone so very far. There was nothing to be done now for her return. So she showed her womanness, her heart was strengthened now. They traveled far now to that Big Thing's own place.

At daybreak this Thing would go to the bush, the hunting place. He'd go there and catch this person, then he'd go back and catch an animal, a bush animal, and he'd come with it.

He would say, '*Hɛ hɛ,*' he would say, 'Yombo, Yombo, the smooth one or the hairy one, which do you prefer?'

'*Koo,*' she said, 'Father, we have always eaten the hairy one over there.'

He said, 'Then here it is.'

Then she took the hairy one and the Big Thing took the smooth one and ate it. He ate it all.

They stayed there. They sat together, and so they knew each other now. She stayed there and then she bore a child.

That Big Thing, long ago he'd sleep for a year. When he was sleepy he would lie down and he would sleep for one full year, and then he would wake up. (Ah, this stubbornness she had, she would show it again in the same way.) So this Big Thing packed up plenty of things, plenty of food, enough for her for one year; he gathered it all, and he came with it. He packed it all in one house till it was full, because he slept one year before he would wake. Then that Big Thing informed her about that.

'*Kwo,*' she said, 'I don't agree to stay out alone. We two, let's go into that house together.'

'*Ee,*' the Big Thing said to her, 'Yombo, this thing I said to you, listen to me.' He said, 'I will sleep for one year.'

She said, 'Let's go into that house together, I'll make that sleep too.' She thought it was a joke he was playing on her.

So they entered that house. She and that Big Thing, they entered that big story-house. It was all made of iron, even the window sills. So that Big Thing entered: *gbugbuŋ gbugbuŋ gbugbuŋ.*

Then all that house was locked, it was finished *seŋ.* Then he went and lay on his bed. When he went and lay on his bed, the Big Thing made this snore: I WILL SLEEP A YEAR, I WILL SLEEP A YEAR, I WILL SLEEP A YEAR.[1] He made that snoring sound. He stayed making this snoring sound a long time. He did so for two months, then for three months. In the fourth month the child in Yombo's hands became sick. Even though the child was sick in her hands, oh friends, the whole house was locked with iron! Thus, she could do nothing at all to open it. When this child was sick now in her hands, she thought it was a joke this Big Thing was playing on her. Oh *yaa.* She sang a song to this Big Thing lying there in sleep. She said:

> Don't sleep *lekemɔ,* don't sleep *lekemɔ.*
> You deceiving in-laws, you deceiving in-laws,
> Your child, look at him dying in my hands.
> Look at me dying like this.
> I WILL SLEEP A YEAR, I WILL SLEEP A YEAR.

She stayed singing that song. She stayed singing that song. Then that child died in her hands. When that child died in her hands, she herself fell down. She too fell and died.

For a long time that Big Thing was lying down. The year completely passed and he awoke. When he awoke, he discovered their bones there. He discovered them scattered there, she and her child. When the Big Thing got up, he took a straw broom and an empty dustpan and he gathered those bones *we we we*. He went and threw them away.

Therefore stubbornness isn't good. Whatever you do, whenever a person says, 'Don't do this,' listen to him.

My story passes to...

2. A Defiant Maid Marries a Stranger

Date: September 19, 1973
Time: About 9:00 P.M.
Place: Verandah of the Samba compound, Njɛi Woma quarter of Mattru,
                 Tikonko Chiefdom, Southern Province, Sierra Leone
Performer: Mariatu Sandi, a women about 30 years old, mother of three children,
                 a cook, a gin-seller, a nursemaid
Audience: Three adult women, one young man and three children

MARIATU: *Dɔmɛi ɔɔ Dɔmɛisia.*
AUDIENCE: *Sa Kɔndɛ.*
MARIATU: Behold these spirits long ago, there were twelve of them in their forest. Then a dance was held in the town; it was a big Sande initiation dance, a dance for getting married. There were two dances being held in one town. Then all these spirits, they all changed into young men. Oh! the beauty of these young men! When all the women saw them, they wanted them, without even getting a present! So they were all dressed up and coming to the dance; then they came and they all made love in the town—these twelve, all of them. They got twelve girls at this dance, and they danced for ten months—there remained only two months for completing one year.

Then they begged leave, they said, 'We are leaving tomorrow.'

All those small things which they had, they gave to their lovers. Then at daybreak they caught the road. Their pals went along as guides. There was one girl among them who was very stubborn; moreover, she was really seeking a man. (This story I'm telling, I'm telling it for us fornicators, I'm telling it for none other than we who truly commit adultery; it's our story I'm telling. We whose ears are closed to every warning, we stubborn people and we insatiable fornicators, this our story.) Then these companions of hers, the eleven girls, they went back. So of these twelve spirits also, eleven spirits all came out from their places one by one. They came to their meeting place on the big road; then those eleven went back.

So he remained alone, he and his girlfriend. So he said to her (this spirit is named Kpana, the girl's name is Yombo), he said to her, 'Yombo—return! There where we're going, there it is bad.' He said, 'You see all your comrades have returned; you too, I beg you, go back.'

On his finger there is a beautiful gold ring. When he went like this [*turning gesture*], it glittered. Really, long ago white people took it and turned it into electricity which shines so today...

AUDIENCE: *Kwo!*
MARIATU: Then he gave it to her and said, 'Go back!'

She said, 'I won't go back,' She said, 'Wherever you go, I will reach there. Your dying place is my sleeping place.'

This spirit then took out a kola from his trousers (from the small place where we put something—we call it *bɔi,* the white people call it pocket—it was on his trousers); then he took out the kola from the inside of the *bɔi* and he split it and gave part of it to her. So this girl took it in her hand, and the spirit also took part of it in his hand.

They went far, they passed one bush; then he said to her, 'Yombo, wait for me.' He said, 'Let me go into the bush.' (It is a shit place in Mende. You people, when you're out walking a Mende man might say, 'Let me go to the bush,' it's the wish to shit which is on his mind.) He entered the bush but it wasn't shit he was shooting. The first person he reached was the hairy person. (As you white people there, your hair is now, so too was his hair which he had lent to the spirit.) The spirit's own hair was really only one strand on his head. Then he took this hair and he went with it.

He said, '*Ee,* Hairy Fetingo my dear, I have your hair. Give me my one hair back.'

So Hairy Fetingo then grabbed his own hair and returned the spirit's one hair to his hand.

AUDIENCE: *Kwo!*
MARIATU: As he was coming out then this Yombo said, 'What the hell?' She said, 'What's coming?'

He said, 'Don't fear me, it's me Kpana.' He said, '*Hɛ hɛ hɛ* . . . Yombo, Yombo, your own kola, my own kola—isn't this it?'

Then he pulled this kola from his *bɔi,* his pocket; it's really the one. He said, 'Your own kola, my own kola, isn't this it?' He said, 'Let's go!'

This now caused a great fright. They went on and they reached Hakawama. Then he entered with two legs. He went and he returned them. Only one leg is under the spirit. He had returned them to him. I say it was like elephantiasis. Then he returned and Yombo feared him.

She said, 'Why is it as we traveled today my father's legs were two, but now he has one leg?'

He said, '*Hɛ hɛ hɛ* . . . your own kola, my own kola, isn't this it?'

She said, 'Father, let's go then!'

This created a great fear in Yombo. All those things God made for mortal men—his fingers, his hair, his neck, everything—this Kpana returned them.

Then they went and they reached a river. At this water-crossing place long ago there sat this fellow at the water's edge. He crossed the river with people in his boat. His name was Sherbro Man. As they were going then, this spirit told the Sherbro Man that he should cross the water with them. Yombo herself, as she walks beside men she is happy; she sucked her teeth at this fellow, Sherbro Man. Then she sang this song:

Sherbro Man—Sherbro Man—Sher . . .

You all say it.

AUDIENCE: Sherbro Man—Sherbro Man—Sher....

MARIATU: Cross the river with me-o
            I can't cross the river with you,
            You big fat lip.
            You go about eating dirty broom straws.

They continued like that, then they went and they reached his hometown. So this Sherbro Man remained sitting at the riverside.

Thus they reached this spirit's cement-block houses which long ago this spirit had built. It's only in America that there is this type of house. In the whole of Free-town, all Freetown, there isn't a block house of this kind. (If you tell lies, it's like this you should do it, you should arrange it so): the mirrors of these block houses, it is those which long ago the white people worked over and fastened to their car fronts which go about today on the roads helping people.

At daybreak this spirit would go to the hunting place. He'd go hunting and catch animals; sometimes he'd catch nine hundred animals. Of living people, sometimes he'd catch seven people. Then he'd come with them and pile them *bushu*, he'd pile them *bushu*, then he'd fall down. He lay there, he was exhausted. He remained lying a long time; the sun would set over there in the sea.

Now hunger wasn't troubling Yombo, simply because as soon as they arrived, he gave food to her which would suffice for two days. So Yombo was experiencing fullness.

He said, '*Hɛhɛ*, Yombo, Yombo, the smooth or the hairy one, which do you prefer?' (It's the devil's voice which is heavy like this.)

Yombo replied, 'As for us, Father, we usually eat the hairy one.'

Then he said, 'Take whatever you like.' (The spirit spoke like that.)

So Yombo remained taking care of this meat. While she was preparing this one, that one would be spoiling; that one would be drying; that one would be frying; that one would be steaming; that one would be salted. This fellow also put those human beings, all those seven people he had caught, in a place where he could eat them for seven months.

They stayed like this for a long time, then Yombo became pregnant. She bore a child. The child's name is Bobo (his father's name is Kpana, his name is Bobo Kpana). That child stayed there long, then he grew and he became truly handsome. He reached the age of a grown man, this Bobo Kpana.

So one year passed. Then Kpana went again to the animal-hunting place. When Kpana went to this hunting place, he would stay there for up to nine years hunting for these animals. He stayed in this hunting place because Yombo hadn't done anything to these nine hundred animals; some had maggots in them.

Then one man came and said, 'I've come, let's stay together in this place.'

She said, "Hm-m-m, I agree to this proposal to stay together which you've brought, because I'm here alone, the only living person, I and this my small child.' She said, "This person who long ago came with me is a spirit. Any kind of food I want, he hunts for it; he puts it in this house; he fills it *koobɔŋ*. When it's there we'll be eating it, we'll be playing in it, whatever we want with it, we do. But as you've come here, whether from Jericho or from in back of Freetown or from the stone-growing place, from wherever, father's nose will discover your smell. He'll come and when he comes, he will eat you yourself!'

He asked, 'Why?'

She said, 'He eats people. The only people he doesn't eat are me and my child. He doesn't eat only us two. Despite all that,' she said, 'we'll stay here.'

Then this girl cooked food quickly and she gave it to this fellow, to this guest. The guest's name is Majia. Then she gave it to Majia and he ate it. Oh ya. Then this spirit's coming-back time arrived.

A big storm was brewing. It was that very storm that God shared out between the land and the sea. When you are sitting by the sea and you hear it *daa daa*, it was such a storm; it does that in the sea. That storm would do that long ago, whenever the spirit returned. That very storm by the seaside which you hear *daa daa*. Oh ya. It started from over there and it reached nearly to the end of the world.

She said, '*Koo*, young man, this living together we've been doing, my husband's arrival time [*wati*] is now approaching.' (White people, you call it *taimi*, we call it *wati*.)

She said, 'The time is now approaching. This is what he said he'd do, and he's coming.'

Then shit came out of the girl. That very shit, it was none other than pig shit; it came out of her. Oo!

Then he came. So she picked up the youth and carried him there, to the tenth story of this skyscraper, this many-storied house that he'd laid—so far, *poloŋ!*

Actually, when this spirit would come, he'd drop down for seven years before he woke up. Just as he arrived, the spirit came and assembled those things. He said, '*Hɛhɛhɛ*, Yombo, Yombo, the hairy one or the smooth one, which do you prefer?'

She said, 'Father, it's the hairy one we eat, we in our own country.'

He said, 'Well then, take it.'

This spirit then lay down. His nostrils started doing this, so he said, 'Hm-hm, a fresh-fresh person is smelling.' (That one was a spirit.) He wanted to know what the girl had done for those seven years he had been to the flesh-hunting place.

'*Ee*,' she said, 'I say Father, you know Kpana Bobo is a human being; myself, I'm a human being. You say a fresh-fresh person is smelling; what about these people you came with, aren't they fresh-fresh people?'

He said, '*Hɛhɛhɛhɛhɛ*, Yombo, Yombo, I don't know what you're thinking of. Don't make a fool of me. I say a fresh-fresh person is smelling.'

They kept on [arguing] like that for a long time. Then that spirit forgot [about it]. So he arranged all those affairs.

So this person who had come today, whom Yombo had lifted to the sky, he had a *kpafei*. This *kpafei* was the kind twins also have. It was long and thin and small like this; it was inside his hair. All this wealth passing in the world, you white people, that wealth (of yours), it is Yombo who long ago came with that wealth which you white people came with. You who are giving us money, who are partial to our affairs, it is

Yombo who brought it. Well, then Yombo gathered up all that wealth and the lover brought out his *kpafei* for the sake of that one meal she had given him.

He said, 'I have struck the *kpafei gba!*'

The spirit was lying asleep because he used to sleep for even more than seven years. He was lying in this sleep.

He said, 'I have struck the *kpafei* here *gba!*'

He said, 'The block house, the skyscraper, the zinc roof, anything whatsoever a person needs, bags of rice, a thousand bags of hard rice,' he said they should all enter in his *kpafei*. He said that a thousand goats should enter into this *kpafei*. He said a thousand sheep; he said anything whatsoever, a thousand of them—cows, ducks, chickens, all—should enter (the *kpafei*).

Then this lover said he would strike his *kpafei* here and Kpana Bobo should then enter this *kpafei*. He said his mother also should enter and she entered in. So one year passed *tuŋ*. This spirit was in sleep; he slept, he slept, he slept *pu*. This fellow hit the road with them. As they were going *taki taki taki*, they slipped *tele* and they fell. Ah, then this spirit who had slept for five years awoke from his sleep and he hit the road. There he is hitting the road. Oh, the town is far. When you would be returning, you'd forget the road you had gone on, you would take another road. But this fellow, he knew the road which went to town.

They continued going, then this spirit said, 'Aa, great God, if you took a person and you came with her to your town, and you gave (gifts) to her, and you did everything for her, and then she went and she didn't even say goodbye to you—Oh, oh! it's me Kpana,' he said. 'Whatever she wanted I did for her. She stole all my wealth—my cows, my sheep, horses, chickens, ducks, pigs, everything—she went with them. She didn't even say goodbye to me! Oh Maker, that's the truth, I don't see her anymore, she's not here. Oh let me reach her now.'

I say, when this spirit arose the distance between them was from this verandah pillar here to the door of that house over there.

Then that fellow turned and from the inside of the *kpafei* Yombo said, '*Kpo!* Buddy, turn around, the spirit over there is coming up behind us.' Then she too said, 'Great God, suppose a person comes with somebody's child to his own town and doesn't return with her to her own sleeping place, doesn't return her to her own sleeping place? This spirit came long ago with me. He met me long ago on love business, he loved me; he said, "Come with me," but he wants to eat me! Maker, help me so that I might reach my own family.'

I say, a wind it is that set upon them. They remained going a long time, *haaŋ*, then that spirit slipped and fell. He was to remain four hundred hours in that fall. He was paralyzed, he couldn't get up.

They remained going *haaŋ*. At last they reached the outskirts of the town. The spirit had truly failed now, for when he saw the people in the town, then he became afraid. He didn't go on any further, but he returned. When he returned, there was nothing there, merely an empty farmhouse. He discovered that termites had eaten and finished off everything. All is broken and scattered *wojoŋ*. Food too he couldn't get; that spirit himself, he could get nothing.

So that fellow arrived beside that town with these people. Look at the house. Look at the town.

Then he set them down and said, 'We have reached there.'

Kpana Bobo and his mother Yombo got down then, and they greeted all the townspeople. All the people had missed them, but they didn't recognize them, for she had been just in her youth. She was a lovely, lovely youth when she got up long ago and followed that spirit.

Her real mother who had given birth to her, she had dried out. They had ground her up and put her in a jar. When her child came back, just then they turned it upside down and they shook her out. So that woman returned; she changed into a living person in God's chiefdom. Then she went and saw her child, and they went about greeting people.

The people agreed when she said, 'Hey, give me a place to build on.'

I say, no sooner was that said, then all of a sudden there was a town like Salɔŋ over there (like Freetown, where you were recently). So it was that town was like that. At once they were all joined together and cement was smoothed on there and tar was rubbed on and streets were laid everywhere reaching to all the forests, completely finished, *seŋ*.

Yombo it is who brought cement houses. She it is who long ago came with riches; she long ago brought cow stables and tame pigs. That stubbornness Yombo practiced long ago, her own suited her. Ah, Yombo has done this for us today. We who now stay in shiny places which they call 'zinc roofed,' we used to put elephant grass on top of our houses. Yombo it was whom that spirit enriched with his wealth. It is thanks to that food which she gave that young man, it is that which long ago brought wealth to the world, all that wealth of old.

I've heard that and I've said it.

3. A Defiant Maid Marries a Stranger

Date: September 19, 1973
Time: About 9:00 P.M.
Place: Verandah of the Samba compound, Njɛi Woma quarter of Mattru, Tikonko Chiefdom, Southern Province, Sierra Leone
Performer: Manungo, a woman about 70 years old, widowed and childless, an herbalist/midwife
Audience: Three adult women, one young man and three children

MANUNGO: *Dɔmɛi, ɔɔ Dɔmɛisia.*
AUDIENCE: *Sa Kɔndɛ.* (Don't tell a long story, Manungo.)
MANUNGO: It's the ending of jealousy I'm going to explain to you.
AUDIENCE: The *dɔmɛi* you told yesterday, don't tell it again!
MANUNGO: That's not what I'll tell you. I'll tell about jealousy; that's what I'll show to you.

There was a dance long ago; they initiated a great Sande society in a town. So a great dance took place. *Jeŋe jeŋe jeŋe* then the ancestors came out; ancestors, they were spirits, I'll call them ancestors. Then they came to that dance. They were two only.

A girl named Yombo. The bush person who came long ago is named Kpana. He proposed love to her. His mate, his name is Jinabemba, he proposed love to another. So they made love for three days at this dance; then they said, 'We're going.'

So they accompanied them. Then his mate told his own girl to go back. He said, 'Go back!' So she went back.

Yombo said, 'No matter what, you and I will go together.'

Her lover replied, 'Over there where we're going is far. Therefore, don't follow me!'

'*Koo,*' she said, 'my dear, since you've already loved me, I love you. Over there where you really stay, where you come from…'

He said, '*Ee?*'

She said, 'You and I are going there.'

Then they went. While they were going, they came to a small stream and they crossed it. He had a kola nut; he split it and gave part to her and kept part himself. So they went a while longer…

AUDIENCE: Don't tell lies.

MANUNGO: If I'm lying, when frogs make their croaking… I'll stop there, I'll say no more.

Then they crossed a small stream, and he split the kola *va,* and he gave his girl her own, and he kept his own. Then he said, 'Don't go back!'

She said, 'I won't go back.' So they went on. They went on a long way, then *va,* a chain came down from the sky. *Yoyoyoyo,* it came down.

He said, 'Girl…'

She said, '*Ee?*'

He said, 'With this chain, you and I will go to that town.'

She said, '*Ee.*'

He said, 'Hold this chain well.'

She said, '*Ee.*'

He said, 'Hold on to my waist tightly. I'll hold this chain, and you hold me tightly, hold on to my waist tightly. If one lets go of this chain, he'll fall and die.'

So he held that chain and said:

> *Jeŋ jeŋ jeŋ jeŋ jeŋ*
> *Ma jeŋ ki jeŋ*
> *Jeŋ jeŋ jeŋ jeŋ jeŋ*
> *Ma jeŋ ki jeŋ*
> Let's hold the rope well, let's go.
> I told you long ago
> My destination is Bugbalee.
> *Jeŋ jeŋ jeŋ*
> *Ma jeŋ ki jeŋ*
> Let's hold the rope well, let's go.

He would say, 'Let me say to you …'

She said, '*Ee?*'

He said, 'When you joined me, as we were going, I explained to you that when we reach that town, if you see a frog, or an earthworm, or a person with sores, or a sick person, or a leper, and if they come up to you with joy, you must greet them. You must not back away; do you understand?'

She said, '*Ee.*'

He said, 'You must not back away, do you understand?'

She said, '*Ee.*'

He said, 'Do you understand?'

She said, '*Ee.*'

> *Jeŋ jeŋ jeŋ*
> *Ma jeŋ ki jeŋ*
> Let's hold the rope well; let's go.

They continued going; they continued going; they continued going; they reached a town like Mattru is now. They reached there and he said, 'You see that town there?'

She said '*Ee.*'

He said, 'Love …'

She said, '*Ee.*'

He said, 'I told you we love each other. For three days I stayed in your town, you said you and I should come; I said "Don't come," I said, "my sleeping place is far": you came closer, *koniiŋ*. Now, as we're going [to the town], if you see a person with sores, or a frog, or a worm, if it comes to you *jogba jogba* [saying] "My wife has come! Mother has come! Something has come!", don't back away! If you back away from them, you'll be severely punished.'

> *Jeŋ jeŋ jeŋ*
> *Ma jeŋ ki jeŋ*
> Let's hold the rope well; let's go.

Kpuŋamɛ, they arrived in the town. People rushed to them: *kpi,* you'll see that one coming, *tiŋ,* big balls is coming *diŋde,* all sorts are coming (shouting): 'Our wife! Our brother has come with our wife. Our brother is coming …'

Then that one came and she hugged him *vigba,* they embraced. Then that one came, *vigba,* they embraced. Then that one came, vigba …

They entered the house, *kote.* He said to her, 'I said to you …'

She said, '*Ee?*'

He said, 'If my real mother who bore me, if you see her and if she has a sore, if she has a sore on her and there is nowhere that pus doesn't come out of her, and blood comes out of her, don't back away from her, okay? If she cooks food and gives it to you, don't back away from it, okay? Whatever sort of person comes, even a leper, remain seated. If she cooks food and gives it to you, don't back away from it, okay?'

She said, 'Yes.'

When she went, they all did (as he has said) with her. One month finished there, *kpoŋjoŋ.* Behold—all those people were good people!

So at daybreak her husband's mother said to her, 'Young lady, boil a little water so I might wash, okay?'

Then she boiled that water and she gave it to her. She washed with it. She showed her woman's strength for three days. Twice she brought the boiled water. On the third day she said, 'Girl...'

She replied, '*Ee?*'

She said, 'This water you've boiled for me so I could wash. Go in that forest now. You'll really see a wood which is very hard, like this *nikii* whip; it's really tough, *klekle.*'

She replied, '*Ee.*'

She said, 'You break it. Shake the leaves off, tie it tightly and come with it. Then you wash this sore, treat it *seŋ,* and then strike it *voli.* When you see something jump out at you, that will be yours.'

Then that girl left her washing and cut that thing—that *nikii* whip—quickly. She came with it. She cleaned the leaves off *poli;* she tied it like the *kɔɔgba* bundle which Wunde society people had long ago. When she came to that sore, she whipped it; she whipped it, *tɔnjɔŋ.* A gold ring which was the first on a chain jumped out. *Tɔnjɔŋ:* iron boxes, three iron boxes which were huge jumped out; all the iron boxes were her own. She went back and she whipped it again. She got that thing, that leopard's tooth, which if you had long ago, you were rich. So they lifted that big box, and the girl got up then, and she went with it to her house.

Then he said to her, 'Yombo...'

She said, '*Ee?*'

He said, 'When you take leave of me (your leaving-time is approaching), let me tell you: don't spoil things! When you take leave of me (your leave-time approaching), I'll report it to my family. When you go...'

She said, '*Ee?*'

He said, 'That box in that house, that iron box, if you see a very, very dirty one... are you listening?—don't pick out the shiny one! Okay?'

She said, '*Ee.*'

He said, 'Don't pick out the shiny one! Okay?'

(Co-wives' jealousy is what I'm getting to now.)

She said she agreed. They slept two nights. On the third she was going. So he went and arranged her leave-taking with his family.

He said, 'This girl who came accompanying me says she is leaving now.'

They said, '*Koo*—Kpana, let's sleep on this. At daybreak we'll discuss it.'

In the morning the girl washed herself completely. She brought her own mother-in-law's water and she washed. They said, 'Let's go there.'

Behold this they had built, a round house. It was a round house they had built. There is a center pole, one hundred people could sit on that seat. People of olden times used wood like that over there to circle a pillar with a seat.

So they crowded about *venjeŋ.* They said to her, 'Come and sit.' Then they gave her a chair. They said, 'My dear...'

She said, '*Ee?*'

'Our brother has come with you, but you say you are bidding us goodbye, you are going. Therefore, of those boxes standing there, which ones do you want to go back with?'

Then she pointed at one dirty one. So they took that one and set it over there. Then she pointed at another, and they took it and set it over there. Then she pointed at another, and they took it and set it over there. All three boxes, they are really boxes. Those who don't lie say that box—those three boxes—which that person pointed at stretched from here to that bridge over there. As for me, who *am* a liar... well, I'll stop there!

Then she went. The road they had gone on long ago was very far; her journey wasn't short. One mile—that second one—then *tjatjala* she jumped out there. Her family cried out; they were very happy; they were very happy; they were very happy.

Her co-wife and her own child are there. (This fornicating we're doing, we and these women are doing it... the ending of jealousy is what I'm getting at now...) That girl handed over those gifts to her family—goats... all sorts of things—my father, that family was now rich! That woman nagged her child all the time, 'Look at your mate. You're forever looking to get laid, but you get nothing for it. Look at your mate, she and you from one house! Those fellows came long ago, you hung around with them, but now she comes back with all that wealth for her family!'

God Almighty said, 'This [affair]—yes, I'll also see the end of this!'

After a short time, another dance was held again. *Wujugu,* a lot of people came again to that dance. When they came *feŋ,* her child hung around with that fellow. Her own now, he too slept for two nights, on the third...

AUDIENCE: Was it the same fellow?

MANUNGO: No, it was another. They slept for two nights. She said, 'Let's you and I go.'

'Let's you and I go.'

'*Koo,*' he said, 'girl, don't go!'

'Sweetie, my dear,' she said, 'let's you and I go there.'

He said, 'Don't go!'

'My dear,' she said, 'as I've said, let's go there!'

They went far. As they were going he said:

> Swing me gently *vio,* swing me gently-o.

A chain was entwined around her. I'll sing this song:

> Swing me gently *vio,* swing me gently-o.

It was a chain. You know how quick tricks are!

> Swing me gently *vio,* swing me gently-o.

Kunje, they jumped down and landed in the town. Behold the town over there.

He said, 'Girl...'

She said, '*Ee?*'

He said, 'When we go there, you and I, you will see sick people. You will see a worm, you will see a millipede, you will see all sorts of things. Don't back away from them! Do you understand?'

She said, '*Ee.*'

He said, 'Now that we're reaching the town, have you understood me?'

She said, '*Ee.*'

He said, 'You've seen the town, have you understood me?'

She said, '*Ee.*'

He said, 'This instruction I'm giving you, don't disregard it!'

> Swing me gently *vio,* swing me gently-o.
> Swing me gently *vio,* swing me gently-o.

Kunje, they landed in the town—'Our brother's come with our wife!'

'*Koo,*' she said, 'what the hell is this? Good heavens, my dear family, look at these nasty things—the filth I've entered into—ah, this screwing around will really throw someone's head off! God Almighty, don't let such filth get on me here.'

While she sits there then a person comes, his balls swinging *tiŋbeŋ.* '*Koo,*' she says, 'what kind of dangerous thing is coming?'

Since she came as a guest they cooked food that night. They cooked food and gave it to her. She ate it, '*haaaa*' (she was vomiting). On the third day she still hadn't eaten. The fellow said, 'This marriage is bothersome to me.'

'*Koo,*' she said, 'my dear, my dear, if it's like this here, since you brought me here, then try to help me for I'm going. I'm returning tomorrow.'

The fellow said, 'Is that right?'

She said, '*Ee!*'

He said, 'Let me report this tomorrow to my family since you're going back.'

That night he reported to his family, he did everything *seŋ.* He said, 'This girl I came with wants to return; therefore, I'm reporting to you.'

The people again said, 'We agree.'

At daybreak the following day, as the dawn was breaking, they filled their huge round house full to the top: *kpa.* Then they said to her, 'Girl, you came with our brother, you and he came and we loved you boundlessly, yet, nonetheless, you're going back. From among all these boxes …'

She said, '*Ee?*'

They said, '… take your heart's choice. The one you choose you may take and go with.'

Then her head went like this, she showed her choice like this: 'That's it. I want that very shiny one with gold rubbed all over it, the one with gold rubbed all over it!' (Really, if you didn't squint your eyes or when you open them, if you didn't squeeze them hard, you wouldn't be able to set your eyes on it.)

So he took that one and he set it aside. Then she looked at another and he set it aside. Her mate had taken three but she took four! They set them on her head …

> Swing me gently *vio,* swing me gently-o.
> Swing me gently *vio,* swing me gently-o.

She's gone. Behold—she's gone.

Kule: suddenly she reached the town. Her mother said, 'Oyaya, my child . . .'
That huge box, *ngwungwungwungwungwu* (they struggled to pick it up).

AUDIENCE: Will they be rich soon?

MANUNGO: Ah, my family, those boxes, none of the people could set their eyes on them unless they hung a cloth before their eyes. Then they could set their eyes on them.

AUDIENCE 1: Manungo, why didn't he, her husband or lover, explain about those boxes to her?

AUDIENCE 2: She didn't listen to his words so he didn't explain to her . . . don't make her go backwards!

MANUNGO: They went and spent the day; then they slept the night *gbu*. At dawn then she assembled her family like a wife who has returned from her husband's place laden with gifts her man had given her.

AUDIENCE: Just her family?

MANUNGO: Mm-m. Just her family. Then that girl said, 'My family, let's lock our house up tightly.' So they locked up the house tightly. They closed their bedroom doors tightly *kpaŋ kpaŋ kpaŋ*. Like our house is right now closed *kpaŋ*, so it was the same with their own. Then that person opened the big box and all those Things' teeth were like this. They killed them all! They cut their heads off!

Ah, therefore, to have your eyes set on a thing is not good. I've heard that little story and I've told it. My story now reaches to you . . .

Note

1. The Mende words *nga yii foo* also simulate the sound of a person snoring.

Index

Bamako, 75
    photographs from, 253–59
        Roadside Picnic, 253, 257, 257
        Untitled (Family with Car no. 266), 254, 255
Bamana, 44, 66, 74
    farming-animal crest mask, 52, 52
    hunter's shirt, 67, 69, 70
    twin statuette, 26, 26
Bamenda, 50
Bamgboye (Alaga of Odo-Owa), 42, 42
banganga (nganga), 156–57
Bangwa, 51
Bantu, 38, 55
Banyang, 23, 217
barurum sebe (armlet), 109, 109
Basinjom (God's Medicine), 19, 19, 222, 224
    association, 219
    mask and gown, 215, 218, 220
Bassa, 193
batakari (war shirt), 73, 73
Baule, 36, 37, 52
beads
    gold, 109, 110
    Maasai bride ornaments (*see* Maasai bride
        ornaments)
Belgium, 151–52
Benin, 19, 23, 57, 228, 234
bibaaku, 156
Bingham, Elizabeth, 258
Bird, Charles, 69
Bird (Man na Gle) mask, 179, 189, 190–191
bird holding snake (Efe mask), 234, 235
bird ring, 80, 80
birds-on-tree weight, 82, 82
bird weight, 81, 82
Blixen, Karen, 266, 267
Bo, 203, 206
Boaten, Okyeame Yaw, 88
Bonsu, Osei, 24, 24, 86, 88, 89
Bonwire, weavers of, 99–100, 105
    See also cloth
Boone, Sylvia, 57, 201
Bowdich, Thomas, 85–88, 87, 89
bracelets (*babadua*), 108, 109, 109
Brazil, 31, 241, 242
bridal ornaments, Maasai. *See* Maasai bride
        ornaments
British, 229, 266
    Asante and, 85, 86, 87–93, 95

Basinjom and, 217, 218
Maasai and, 264
Urhobo and, 170
British Museum, 122, 266, 266
bull necklace (*norkiteng*), 273
Bulumi, 201
"Bundu Devil, Upper Mendi, The" (Alldridge), 199
Bunseki, Fu Kiau, 154, 157, 160, 160, 162, 163, 166
burial ceremonies. *See* funerals
Burkina Faso, 64, 64, 66
Burroughs, Edgar Rice, 14
Busia, Abena P. A., 100
Butuakwa, Okyeame Kwame, 88
Buytendijk, F. J. J., 31

Calabar, 223, 224
Camara, Seydou, 66, 67, 71, 73, 74–75, 76
Cameroon, 14, 23, 136
    Basinjom in, 19, 216, 217, 218, 220, 222, 223
    Grassfields, 49–51, 131
    hat, 131, 134
    man's garment, 131, 134
    ndop cloth, 131, 132, 133, 136
    reliquary guardian figure, 38, 39
    stools, 50, 51–52, 52
    throne, 51, 51
    See also Kom kingdom; Laikom
Cameroon Gallery, Museum für Völkerkunde
        (Frankfurt), 120–22, 122
Canaday, John, 65
Cão, Diogo, 144
Caribbean, 241
Catholicism, 128, 146, 149, 152
Cavazzi, Giovanni Antonio, 55
Centre Georges Pompidou, 248
Chef!, 139
chicken coffin, 250
chisendos, 125, 126–27
Chokwe, 57
Christianity, 146–47, 147, 148–49, 152, 212, 223,
        239, 270
    Catholicism, 128, 146, 149, 152
Clinton, Bill, 105
cloth, 96–107
    adinkra, 98, 100, 105–7, 106
    kente, 96, 98, 99–105, 107
    liar's, 99, 100
    something that has not happened before,
        100, 103, 104

unity is strength, 100, 101
    wise old lady, 100, 102
    ndop, 131, 132, 133, 136
clothing
    hat, 131, 134
    hunters' shirts, 63–77, 63, 69, 70, 71, 74, 76
        war shirt, 73, 73
    man's, 131, 134
coffins, 245–50
    chicken, 250
    Mercedes-Benz, 245–51, 245, 249
    shoe, 246
coiffure, shaved, 119, 119
Cole, Herbert, 94
Conakry, 63
Conde, Maryse, 75–76
Congo, Democratic Republic of. *See* Democratic
        Republic of the Congo
Congo Free State, 151
Coquilhat, Camille, 150
Cornet, Joseph, 52
coronation throne, 128, 129, 130
Cosentino, Donald, 198, 208, 209, 210, 279
costumes. *See* masks; masquerades
Côte d'Ivoire, 31, 31, 33, 36, 44, 52, 191, 193, 194, 197
cowry shells, 207
Crowther, Samuel Ajayi, 229
Cuba, 162, 241, 242
Cuttington, 193, 194

daliluw, 70, 71, 74
Dan, 21, 31, 33
    Gle Gbee stilt masquerade, 21, 21
    masks, 179–95, 193
        Man na Gle, 179, 189, 190–191
dance, 17–22, 23, 24
Dansoman, 250
Dapper, Olfert, 150
Dartmouth College, *Royal Art of Cameroon* exhibi-
        tion at, 131
Dawley, Amelia, 212
De Bry, Theodore, 147
deer weight, 82, 83
*De°ant Maids and Stubborn Farmers: Tradition and
        Invention in Mende Story Performance*
        (Cosentino), 209, 279
De Grunne, Bernard, 21
Delamere, Lord, 264
Delta Spirit (Hammons), 163